SAUL BELLOW AND HISTORY

Saul Bellow and History

Judie Newman

St. Martin's Press   New York

ISBN 0–312–69981–6

Library of Congress Cataloging in Publication Data

Newman, Judie.
    Saul Bellow and history.

    Bibliography: p.
    Includes index.
    1. Bellow, Saul—Criticism and interpretation.
2. Bellow, Saul—Knowledge—History.   3. History in literature.   4.
History—Philosophy.   I. Title.
PS3503.E4488Z795   1983   813′.52   83–8708
ISBN 0–312–69981–6

For Ian and Christopher Revie

Contents

Acknowledgements

The author and publishers wish to thank the following publishers for permission to quote from the works of Saul Bellow: A. M. Heath & Co. Ltd on behalf of the author, and Viking Penguin Inc. for extracts from *The Adventures of Augie March* (US copyright 1953, 1981 by Saul Bellow), and *The Last Analysis* (US copyright 1962, 1965, 1972 by Saul Bellow); Martin Secker and Warburg Ltd and Viking Penguin Ltd for extracts from *Humboldt's Gift* (US copyright 1973, 1974, 1975 by Saul Bellow), and from *To Jerusalem and Back: A Personal Account* (US copyright 1976 by Saul Bellow); Weidenfeld and Nicolson Ltd and Viking Penguin Inc. for extracts from *Henderson the Rain King* (US copyright 1950, 1959, 1974 by Saul Bellow), from *Herzog* (US copyright 1961, 1963, 1964 by Saul Bellow), and from *Mr Sammler's Planet* (US copyright 1969, 1970 by Saul Bellow).

Preface

In the preparation of this study I have been assisted by the comments of Dr Tony Tanner, of King's College, Cambridge, who supervised the research from which it springs. I should also like to express my thanks to Professor Andrew Hook, of the University of Glasgow, who first awakened my interest in Bellow. I am grateful for financial assistance from the Carnegie Trust which funded my initial research, and from the University of Newcastle-upon-Tyne Staff Travel Fund which enabled me to undertake research in other libraries. I should like to express my thanks to the staff of the Library of the University of Newcastle-upon-Tyne, in particular the Library Loans Department, for speedy and efficient assistance in obtaining bibliographical material, and to Grace Young, Doris Palgrave, Kathleen O'Rawe and Barbara Kugler for secretarial assistance. I acknowledge a general debt to colleagues and students at the University of Newcastle-upon-Tyne who helped me to define my ideas, and in particular to Dr Linda Anderson for invaluable advice and encouragement. For their assistance and encouragement I should like to thank Cash and Alice Newman, Ivy Revie, Liz Statham, Yvonne Jerrold and K.W. Ross. Above all I am indebted to the persons to whom this book is dedicated for their unfailing support.

J.A.N.

1 Introduction

For Nietzsche the historical sense in our time forms a sixth sense, pervading the philosophy, art and culture of the modern era.[1] For most readers, however, the notion of a sixth sense operating in the novels of Saul Bellow more readily suggests a sense of transcendent realities, Platonic homeworlds, Steineresque meditations and intimations of immortality. Overwhelmingly the critical consensus presents Bellow as a writer more concerned with the universal than with the particular, with the timeless than with the historical. When Bellow is credited with a sense of history it is generally seen as merely ancillary to his fiction. This analysis, and the resultant false emphasis, can be challenged, and it is the function of the present study to do so. While the transcendental strain in Bellow's fiction is a factor of major importance it is my contention that a sense of history, in its many guises, pervades the novels and governs the dynamics of plot, character and theme.

Criticism of Saul Bellow's writings is now so extensive that booklength bibliographies have been published.[2] From the large body of critical assessment there emerges, however, a surprisingly consistent critical view. Of the major studies, all assume the importance of a transcendental and religious vision in the novels, and stress the psychogical rather than the social, the atemporal rather than the historical. Keith Opdahl defines Bellow's imagination as 'basically metaphysical and religious, passing from the historic fact to the larger universal issue'.[3] In his view Bellow's heroes are engaged in a quest for religious transcendence, in a universe in which evil is assumed to be a spiritual force. In the course of his career Bellow turns increasingly from sociology to psychology, and his heroes reconcile themselves to a passivity which entails 'the surrender of the self to history'.[4] John J. Clayton develops this psychological emphasis, drawing upon psychoanalytic theory. Clayton underlines Bellow's despairing vision of life, and argues that 'Bellow is a psychological novelist before he is a social novelist or moral spokesman.'[5] Both Opdahl

1

and Clayton see an unresolved conflict in Bellow's imagination, in that Bellow is unable to choose between scepticism and belief, and therefore does not make clear what the state of transcendence involves.

Adopting a formalist stance, in a study based upon the assumptions of the New Criticism, M. Gilbert Porter[6] discerns a development in the novels from existentialism to transcendentalism. Robert R. Dutton argues that Bellow depicts man as a subangelic creature, shaped in the image of God, and occupying an intermediate position on a cosmic chain of being. In *Mr Sammler's Planet* he notes the use of cyclical interpretations of history, in particular those of Toynbee and Spengler, but subsumes this sense of history to a transcendental reading. Thus, at the close of the novel the reader is described as

> ready to move with Sammler back to that point in history when we first discarded the better image of man, back to the Thirteenth century when science and religion were in dubious battle, and, through a reinterpretation of religious institutions, strike a more equable balance between the two forces.[7]

Tony Tanner expresses reservations about the literary consequences of Bellow's transcendental vision, deploring the lack of real dialogue in the novels in which lonely flights into metaphysics replace a dramatic dialectic between man and society.[8] As a consequence, Tanner argues, the novels lack plot, dramatic necessity and the impact of a sequence of linked incidents. Brigitte Scheer-Schäzler[9] has levelled a similar charge, lamenting the absence of an effective chain of action.

From a somewhat different perspective, Howard Harper has argued that Bellow's works present two worlds and are centred on two themes, 'of man adrift in a world he never made, and of man's yearning for transcendent power'.[10] Harper therefore develops a reading in which some attention is paid to time, describing *Henderson the Rain King* as 'a looking-glass view of human history'[11] and arguing that Bellow's heroes learn that the full significance of life is to be found in the here and now. Transcendence, when it occurs, is essentially rational in that the human mind is able to transcend the limitations of life by its capacity for reason. Harper characterises the novels as existential and absurdist, involving a search for meaning in a meaningless world. While Irving Malin[12] also describes time as a fundamental theme in Bellow's fiction, he emphasises its sacramental importance and attributes Bellow's interest to the influence of Judaism as a religion of history. Malin, however, pays more attention to myth than to history, in particular the myth of the eternal return. Thus Joseph in *Dangling Man* learns to live with an awareness of myth, ritual and eternity, Asa and Augie reject the past as determinism, and Henderson undertakes a mythic quest in which his role as Sungo lifts him out of time.

In general periodical criticism tends towards a similar detection of mythic parallels and religious themes. Some writers applaud the transcendent trend of the novels, others see it as a major flaw, but it is generally assumed to be of dominant importance. Those writers who welcome this emphasis have variously described the novels as metaphysical quests,[13] as representative statements of a spiritual dilemma,[14] and as celebrating the mystery of life.[15] Abraham Chapman argues that the dichotomies of existence are transcended in the novels by the tempered soul of a protagonist who has endured the trials of the spirit.[16] Bellow's heroes are described as Christ-figures,[17] as contemplative men on whose dilemmas a religious solution is imposed,[18] and as spiritual activists.[19] Metaphysical and spiritual affinities with Blake[20] and Kafka[21] have been delineated. In studies of particular novels the emphasis is firmly upon the religious. *Dangling Man* is examined in relation to mysticism.[22] Augie, Henderson and Herzog are compared to Adamic figures,[23] and Herzog to the Biblical Moses.[24] *Seize the Day* is described in terms of a spiritual struggle between real and pretender souls.[25] *Herzog* is analysed as a modern Paradise Regained,[26] as Edenic,[27] as Puritan allegory,[28] orthodox Christianity,[29] in terms of an Emersonian concept of transcendent humanity,[30] and as expressing Hasidic mysticism.[31] Sammler is seen as a mystic with strong affiliations to Eckhart,[32] as Odin,[33] and as representing the spiritual exhaustion of man.[34] His eschatological vision[35] is emphasised, and Heidegger's term '*Gelassenheit*' (man's submission to the mystery of existence) has been invoked in this connection.[36] *Humboldt's Gift* is analysed in connection with anthroposophy,[37] and described as metaphysical farce.[38]

A smaller group of writers have found the transcendent emphasis to be a flaw in Bellow's art. Jennifer M. Bailey[39] condemns Bellow's unconvincing attempt to mythicise Herzog and canonise Sammler. Maxwell Geismar[40] attacks Bellow's semi-religious philosophy and concept of the hero, both of which tend to negate any historic sense of the Jewish heritage. Theodore Ross[41] objects to a Christianising tendency in the fiction, which fails to dramatise the realities of history. Kingsley Widmer[42] attributes a decline in naturalistic power to the desire for mythic consciousness. John Updike argues that the spiritual preoccupations of *Humboldt's Gift* make the veil of Bellow's fictional phenomena somewhat worn and thin.[43] In his introduction to the most recent collection of critical essays Stanley Trachtenberg laments the 'almost messianic critical reception'[44] to Bellow. He argues however that in his more recent fiction Bellow develops a stronger sense of metaphysical than of social explanations of human behaviour, and that the transcendental impulse at times leads Bellow into passivity and alienation. In Trachtenberg's survey of the trends of criticism history scarcely receives a mention.

There are however some isolated exceptions to the consensus, in periodical criticism. These are few in number but indicate some critical opposition to the atemporal transcendent view. C.J. Bullock, for example, considers that criticism of Bellow has largely failed, as a result of fashions in American criticism. In the forties and fifties criticism of the contemporary novel in America was informed by an Arnoldian moral sense; it was sensitive to the links between man and society but unsympathetic to theoretical elaboration or political ideology. Writers such as Irving Howe, Lionel Trilling and Alfred Kazin therefore fail to come to terms with the historical specificity of contemporary fiction.

A central weakness of this current has been its too ready acceptance of the 'metaphysical' label for the contemporary novel.[45]

In the sixties and seventies critical works concentrate upon the apocalyptic, the psychological and the existentialist as opposed to political matters. Representative critics are David Galloway, Ihab Hassan and Helen Weinberg[46] in their studies of absurdist heroes, radical innocence and the Kafkan mode. Bullock connects this latter current with the dominance of the ideology of modernism, as described by George Lukacs, a view of man as by nature asocial and unhistorical, as opposed to the image of man as social being which dominated great realist literature. In Bullock's analysis, Bellow is a critical realist addressing himself to social problems. In his works the activity of the hero is problematic because he is orientated, not towards a metaphysical realm, but to qualities of human sociality not available in a market-value society. While this is a pertinent argument, directed against metaphysical and atemporal readings of the novels, its overall conclusions are flawed by the inflexibility of a Marxist ideology. While the novels are directed towards an awareness of historical specificity, they are not best apprehended within one rigid conceptual frame.

More modestly, other critics have touched upon the socio-historical nature of Bellow's writing. Sanford Pinsker declares that:

> In Saul Bellow's latest fiction, stage-centre is monopolised by the protagonist-as-historian, rather than by the traditional concerns of the 'historical novel'. By that I mean, history becomes the reflection of an individual sensibility, mirroring that which must be synthesised for the culture's good at the same time as it is transcended for the heart's deepest needs.[47]

Pinsker, however, defines the development of the hero as always towards transcendence. Herzog learns 'to replace polemics with prayer, History with Transcendence',[48] Sammler learns that knowledge needs 'no bulky citations to history'[49] and Citrine's development culminates in a 'gruelling spiritual workout, complete with brisk exercises in a mystical gym'.[50] In this study of Bellow's heroes no attention is paid to the temporal dynamics of the novels.

Only one such analysis exists. Alexandre Maurocordato[51] has analysed the precise time-scheme of *Herzog*, detailing the various techniques of flashback and flashforwards, and rendering this scheme diagrammatically as three concentric circles of immediate, distant and 'lost' past. Maurocordato clarifies the temporal organisation of the novel but does not really indicate what Bellow gained by his obscurity. In his view the adroit manipulation of time is designed to throw light on Herzog's psyche which refuses to look to the future. This denial reflects both a damaged Romanticism, cut off from prophetic faith, and the contradictions of Jewish and Christian attitudes to history. While paying less attention to the sequence of time in the novel, Harold J. Mosher similarly analyses the synthesis of past and present in *Herzog* in terms of these contradictory understandings of history.[52] Gabriel Josipovici[53] claims that *Herzog* may be read as the rejection of two extremes, 'potato love' and 'crisis ethics', each a facet of one attitude to history, the belief that the world can be changed by fiat. In his analysis, Herzog learns that intellectual history is always inadequate. James M. Mellard describes Herzog as mediating a concept of self through metaphors of drama to reach the plane of history, where meanings for life, if not rigid definitions are found. Moses therefore reaches a state of 'existential historicism'[54] sharing with Comte the belief that the field of knowledge must be in actual phenomena, not in metaphysical assaults on the void.

Bellow's other novels have not attracted much emphasis upon the historical sense. James Gindin[55] sees Bellow as avoiding metaphysically directed forms, and rather as shaping his material from an awareness of the density and complexity of historical flux. Tony Tanner emphasises the importance of the process of fictional recall.[56] C.W.E. Bigsby locates Bellow in the liberal tradition rather than the apocalyptic or absurdist.[57] Malcolm Bradbury describes *Humboldt's Gift* as invested with a sense of historical motion.[58] Brian Way argues that the dual aspect of time in *The Adventures of Augie March* provides a sense of the immediate present as history.[59] Robert Alter commends the innovative use of flashback in narrative method as dramatic enactment.[60] There has been, however, no systematic attempt to analyse the sense of history in Bellow's novels, together with the temporal structures within which it is dramatised.

The state of the critical consensus has not changed appreciably in recent years. In 1977 the various contributors to a symposium on 'Saul Bellow and his Work'[61] emphasised above all the transcendent view. In a paper entitled '*Humboldt's Gift*: Transcendence and the Flight from Death' John J. Clayton argued that the novel asks the question – Can man be saved?

> In the World of Distraction, the world in which the ego, the social self, moves, the answer is no. But there is always another world in a Bellow novel: it is a world of love, of search for the light of God and the will of God, a world in which the person is no fool, or is a holy fool, in which the soul (not the ego or personality but something deeper, truer) is worthy of salvation.[62]

In Clayton's view, Bellow's protagonists are in exile from a Platonic homeworld, enmeshed in a shadow world of distraction. Memory is only a psychological symptom, and Citrine's memories are merely 'hysterical memorialisation',[63] an attempt to preserve the core of a childhood world by remaining loyal to the values of the dead. Clayton identifies *Humboldt's Gift* as displaying a more complete yearning for transcendence than any of Bellow's preceding novels, and he reads as one of the meanings of the title 'the intimation of immortality'.[64]

M. Gilbert Porter, describing 'Bellow's Transcendental Vision', stressed as a major dimension of Bellow's thought his debt to the American transcendentalists, in particular to Thoreau, Emerson and Whitman. For him, the Bellovian character knows a connection to supernal life.

> The knowledge is transcendental knowledge, intuitive and instinctual, and its intimations of immortality come straight from the hearts of nature and men in an epistemology that defies logical analysis.[65]

Brigitte Scheer-Schäzler, on the other hand, contended that epistemology is a key narrative device in the novels which undertake an investigation of the origin and nature of knowledge. Like Clayton, Scheer-Schäzler sees two worlds in Bellow's fiction. The concept of knowledge is based upon a dualistic concept of reality, the reality of distraction and the reality of contemplation. It is in the latter that 'the true human enterprise'[66] resides. Scheer-Schäzler notes the retrospective character of the novels to argue that the fascination with the past is a product of the fact that the past may be used as a sourcebook for applied solutions. She concludes, 'Bellow in trying to discover the universal in the particular, echoes the Transcendentalist epistemological quest.'[67]

Close analyses of Bellow's style were also offered. While describing the style as realistic, Keith Opdahl commended 'his use of literal detail to portray a transcendental reality'.[68] In its freshness and clarity Bellow's style is credited with 'creating an aesthetic emotion not unlike that of religious awe'.[69] In his view Bellow writes vividly because of a religious theme, for the transcendent gives great value to his specificity and contributes to the illusion of depth. Edmond Schraepen, in an essay on patterns of imagery in *Herzog* similarly argued that the particular image contributed to a 'cosmic interfusion'[70] of Herzog with the universe, in a transcendental experience. Schraepen notes Herzog's orientation to the past as a compensatory strategy to counter the agitation of his mind. In his introduction to the proceedings of the symposium he acknowledges a need for a closer investigation of Bellow's treatment of myth and history.

At the symposium two contributors raised this question. Earl Rovit, describing the development in Bellow's novels from the figure of the victim to that of the survivor, pointed out that Bellow's handling of time sequences changes significantly after *The Victim*. The narrative structure of the later novels, 'the rambling, episodic, picaresque character of jumbled sequential events'[71] patterns itself loosely on the myth of the eternal wandering, in particular that of the Wandering Jew. Unlike the quest figures of Western tradition, this wanderer does not reach a moment of mystical embrace between himself and his goal. Rather he 'remains in the world of time and mortality, moving inexorably towards his death.'[72] The Wandering Jew is an analogue to the Bellovian hero who is unable to influence history. Bearing the history of the world on his shoulders, 'he can act in the present only as impotent witness.'[73] Rovit points to the importance of the moment. In his view memory is of special moral importance in that

> the Bellow survivor struggles against the blurred diffusion of time by trying to respond to each instant fully and to hold it whole in his mind.[74]

This emphasis on the real world rather than some other realm was continued by Malcolm Bradbury, who argued that Bellow's novels encounter the chaos and contingency of the historical world, remaining within the historical and experimental continuum. While acknowledging that Bellow has always sought transcendental revelations, these affirmations take place amidst time and history. If a metaphysical intent runs through the novels, it is accompanied by a registration of the power of a modern world where individual experience is dwarfed by process and history. Associating Bellow's novels with a Whiggish history, where there is a community of progress between self and society, Bradbury describes them as attentive to history seen as onward, sequential process. Perceptively Bradbury accounts for the ambiguity of the endings of Bellow's novels by emphasising the historical rhythm which pervades them. The endings are provisional, in some ways unsatisfactory, because 'the rhythm involved is ceaseless, continuous, and very much in history'.[75] Bradbury also locates Bellow in an alternative literary tradition, pointing out that mythic interpretations of American literature have tended to ignore the extent to which classic American novelists are as much concerned with history, historiography and historicism as they are with spatiality, pastoral and transcendence.

Concluding the proceedings of the symposium, Tony Tanner began by arguing against the transcendent interpretation:

> To be sure, by adroit and legitimate quotation, one can find 'transcendental type' statements in Bellow's work, but then whom has he not read, whom does he not quote?[76]

By such methods, Tanner claims, Bellow can be made into a Dostoevsky or a Dreiser. In his view, in Bellow's writing,

> the pained, hyperactive, omnivorous, all-remembering habit of perceiving the given world is more powerful and more convincing than the yearning ... to assert the existence of some Transcendental reality.[77]

Tanner, however, also objects to the historical interpretations offered by contributors. For Tanner, Bellow's novels fail to incorporate any analytic sense of the dynamics of history. Transcendent glimpses are offered as a reprieve saving the protagonists from trying to comprehend history. They become either victims, passively suffering history, or survivors evading history, but in no sense do they understand it. Though Tanner sees Bellow as aware of the problems of history, he argues that such problems 'do not functionally enter his fiction'.[78] Moreover the comic impulse in Bellow's novels raises doubts. Tanner wonders whether it is satisfactory for a writer to admit that 'history is all too much for him and attempts to analyse and comprehend what, exactly or inexactly, is "going on", can only be rendered comically or farcically.'[79] Is it acceptable to laugh our way out of history, to be merely a metaphysical comedian under its inexorable sway? Tanner notes that little was said in the symposium about *To Jerusalem and Back*, a work in which Bellow does try to confront and comprehend one of the more intractable problems of contemporary history. But the attempt appears to be flawed. In *To Jerusalem and Back* Bellow refers to 'the transforming additive, the gift of poetry'[80] as a temporary relief from the problems of time and history. Art and history therefore appear to be mutually incompatible, and Bellow's art merely an escape from engagement with history.

It is the function of the present study to develop an alternative reading of Bellow's novels, as works which are responsive to historical specificity, and which also incorporate a subtle understanding of different theories of history. The interaction between theory and specific fact dictates a narrative form in which time is of extreme importance, governing the logic and the ironies of the action. This is a literary study and not an essay in the philosophy of history, though a proper attention will be paid to the historians of culture whose ideas enter the fiction. The list of these is endless, including amongst others, Hegel, Marx, Nietzsche, Ortega, Karl Jaspers, Burckhardt, Freud and Heidegger. Each of these figures has, of course, been variously located on the ideological continuum. In critical expositions there are many Hegels and many Freuds, and they are as susceptible to the abuse of selective quotation as is Bellow himself. There is no space in the present study to engage with these intellectual debates in detail, but merely to indicate the function served by the ideas of particular thinkers in the novels, and to detail which particular aspects of their thought are important to literary understanding. It is my contention that the ideas of historians do not enter Bellow's fiction merely in quotation marks, but are inscribed within a sequence of events, a temporal action, which delineates their applicability. The specific time of a particular novel is set against the universalising theorists of history, the time of the reader against the distanced view of the speculative philosopher. The concern with history therefore reveals both an analytic sense of its dynamics, together with an ability to allow it to function formally in the text.

The importance of paying close attention to the specific modes in which Bellow organises the time of his novels necessitates detailed analysis of individual novels. This study is therefore organised in chapters which each provide a discrete study of an individual novel, in order to reveal how the sense of history is actively embodied in the action. In addition the need for close analysis demands a concentration upon those novels in which history is of major importance. Various critics have remarked upon the change in style which occurs with the publication of *The Adventures of Augie March*[81] to which an extended treatment will be given. *The Adventures of Augie March* displays a distinct modification of Bellow's form, from the tightly controlled, short, spatially ordered forms of *Dangling Man* and *The Victim* to the loose and baggy monsters of the later fiction, which express the contingency of the historical process and offer a larger historical sweep. After *The Adventures of Augie March* Bellow published a long novella, *Seize the Day*, which has been seen as a return to a more formal poetic novel. In interview, however, Bellow has described writing the novella as early as 1951[82] and has recognised that it 'belongs to the victim group',[83] that is, with his two first novels.

Bellow's interest in history has, however, been obvious from the start of his career. Bellow's second published short story, 'The Mexican General'[84] considers the role of the great man in history (Trotsky) together with Marxist historiography and the opposition of nature and history. *Dangling Man*, generally considered an absurdist novel, is set against the background of the Second World War, and *The Victim*, while almost classically compressed, takes as its theme anti-semitism and the guilt of the survivor. In *Seize the Day* Tommy Wilhelm attempts to live for and in the present, a present unthreatened by past or future, but learns that this is also the creed of financial America. His 'day' becomes a day of atonement, subsuming his entire history and reasserting its importance. Short stories such as 'Leaving the Yellow House', 'The Old System', 'The Gonzaga Manuscripts' and 'Mosby's Memoirs'[85] are much concerned with attempts to come to terms with the past, whether personal, familial or cultural. Bellow appears, however, to have abandoned the short story form, for reasons which may be linked to the increasingly complex investigation into history, for which the novel form is more appropriate. This study will therefore concentrate upon the novels, on both formal and thematic grounds.

2 History, Nature and Freedom: *The Adventures of Augie March*

In 'How I Wrote Augie March's Story' Bellow wrote:

> We are called upon to preserve our humanity in circumstances of rapid change and movement. I do not see what else we can do than refuse to be condemned with a time and place. We are not born to be condemned but to live.[1]

In *The Adventures of Augie March* Bellow focuses upon the degree to which man is conditioned by his place in time, and the extent to which he may preserve his humanity amidst the flux of events. Formally and thematically the novel revolves around an extensive exploration of the dictum of Ortega Y Gasset:

> Man has no nature: what he has is history.[2]

Bellow develops this thesis, and its counterarguments, in all its ramifications, questioning the viability of a humanistic faith in unchanging human nature, and at the same time developing a critique of historicist explanations of the individual. Warring concepts of 'nature' and 'history' are the field across which an embattled Augie moves. The novel reveals a close familiarity with Ortega's historicist philosophy, which dictates both the intellectual argument of the novel, and major incidents in its plot. While the novel offers the impression of an episodic narration, in a picaresque mode, its adventures are carefully organised to strike a series of variations on the central opposition of 'nature' and 'history'. As will become evident, the title refers, quite precisely, to Ortega's definition of the modern novel, a definition which Bellow challenges.

13

In the form of the novel Bellow cunningly dramatises its central concern. Two structural patterns govern the novel, each enacting the problematic nature of involvement in time. In the general movement of the novel, Augie March is repeatedly adopted by different characters – Grandma Lausch, Einhorn, Mrs Renling, Thea – who recruit him to their own version of reality. In each episode Augie assumes a different role, following the direction mapped out by his mentors but withdrawing at the last moment from final commitment. In his protean changes of circumstance, Augie therefore embodies an individual refusal to be condemned by the conditioning force of a temporal and spatial environment. As a result, however, the reader is left with a problem. Augie's humanity is ungraspable, his character that of an evasive shape-shifter, undefined but also uncommitted. Whether his course amounts to an assertion of human freedom within time, or merely an evasive lack of commitment remains problematic.

A second formal structure also directs the reader's response to the novel. Augie March begins with the assertion that 'a man's character is his fate'[3] but the phrase is double-edged for Augie is writing his own autobiography, and therefore creating the character of himself. The double form of first-person narration emphasises the ambiguity. Looking forwards from Augie's birth the reader may entertain the view that Augie defines himself only by his actions, assuming and shrugging off roles in a continual process of becoming. Looking backwards, from the standpoint of the older Augie who relates events, the actions are controlled by the character, the essential narrative voice of Augie March, whose boisterous colloquial larkiness is a constant controlling device. Augie may therefore be seen as having an essence, a nuclear self which governs his fate. Alternatively he may appear as an existential being whose actions in time define his 'character'. In order to dramatise the problems of existence within time, Bellow skilfully exploits the perennial formal duplicity of first-person narration, its double time scheme in which two linear journeys double back upon each other: prospective experience, the setting out at the beginning when nothing is known, and retrospective evaluation, the analysis at the end of the journey by a wiser man. The formal implications of the technique emphasise the dynamic tension at the heart of the novel between two views of man: man as the creature and victim of time, and man as a constant humanity. As an autobiography, albeit fictional, the form of the novel explicitly lends itself to the consideration of historical meaning.

Wilhelm Dilthey, philosopher of history, describes autobiography as the highest form of historical enquiry:

> Autobiography is the highest and most instructive form in which the understanding of life confronts us. Here is the outward phenomenal course of a life which forms the basis for understanding what has produced it within a certain environment. The man who understands it is the same as the one who created it ... The person who seeks the connecting threads in the history of his life has already, from different points of view, created a coherence in that life which he is now putting into words ... The power and breadth of our lives and the energy with which we reflect on them are the foundation of historical vision.[4]

By its very nature, of course, autobiography, unlike the novel, is abandoned rather than finished. Conclusions as to the coherence of the life are of necessity provisional. Henry Adams, unable to find a meaning in his own life, refused it also to history.[5] As a novel, however, *The Adventures of Augie March* is of necessity shaped and controlled, and is therefore prejudiced towards the discovery of coherence.

The novel begins with a deliberate attempt to eclipse the reader's awareness of the shaping power of narration. Augie throws off a reference to Heraclitus, philosopher of flux, and announces his intention to tell his story, in Ranke's terms *wie es eigentlich gewesen*, without subordinating the events of his life to any organising structure, as if the facts will flow, unmediated from his pen:

> I am an American, Chicago-born – Chicago, that sombre city – and go at things as I have taught myself, free-style, and will make the record in my own way: first to knock, first admitted;   (p. 7)

There is to be no embellishment of the facts:

> There isn't any way to disguise the nature of the knocks by acoustical work on the door or gloving the knuckles.   (p. 7)

In addition, Augie claims that nothing will be suppressed:

> Everybody knows there is no fineness or accuracy of suppression; if you hold down one thing you hold down the adjoining. (p. 7)

Augie opens his tale with the metaphor of the self as door to experience, inviting the reader to believe that as each event presents itself, so it will be immediately relayed, without any attempt to shape the record in accordance with an artistic framework. What, however, is the first role in which our hero presents himself? It is that of liar. In order to obtain glasses for Mama Augie is despatched to the free dispensary.

> Coached by Grandma Lausch, I went to do the lying. (p. 8)

Augie obtains the glasses by telling a story in which at least one major fact – the existence of the Charities – is suppressed. He learns his lesson assiduously:

> You must say nothing about the Charities, but that sometimes money from my father came and sometimes it didn't, and that Mama took boarders. This was, in a delicate and choosy way, by ignoring and omitting certain large facts, true. It was true enough for them. (p. 8)

Truth therefore becomes relative and doubt is immediately cast on Augie's professed ability to tell things as they were, free-style. The obtaining of free lenses is dependent on a carefully constructed story. The opening anecdote functions as an analogy to the form of Bellow's novel, in which the loose, discursive, free-style narration conceals an artistic framework of extreme subtlety. While this *caveat lector* introduces the question of the nature of truth in narration, the following description of Simon relates it to historical analysis. Paradoxically Augie is sent to the dispensary in preference to Simon whose notions of schoolboy honour prevent him from lying; Simon's 'honour' is conditioned by a biased version of American history:

> The mayor was at that time ordering the schoolboard to get history books that dealt more harshly with the king, and Simon was very hot at Cornwallis. (pp. 8–9)

Simon's refusal to lie is therefore the byproduct of a lack of respect for balanced historical reporting. Augie, however is under the tutelage of Grandma Lausch, 'one of those Machiavellis of small street' (p. 8), who founds her views, like Machiavelli, on the belief that human nature is fixed, and that history teaches by examples, providing object lessons which demonstrate that human nature is always identical. To this end she presents George and Mama as illustrations of her thesis, that human beings must protect themselves by subterfuge, lies and schemes, always attempting

> to wise us up, one more animadversion on the trustful, loving and simple surrounded by the cunning-hearted and tough, a fighting nature of birds and worms, and a desperate mankind without feelings. (p. 15)

Within her household Grandma demonstrates a Machiavellian grasp of power politics, a sovereign full of guile, strategy and command, converting the Marches into her subjects. Variously described as like Timur, jesuitical, an autocrat, a member of the elite intelligentsia, and a pouncy old hawk of a Bolshevik, Grandma presents the face of historical power in its many guises, suggesting that amidst its historical variations it depends upon the same, suspect human nature. Augie, however, finds that historical identity also governs his childhood. As a Jew in a Polish neighbourhood, his friendships are mostly 'cut short by older loyalties' (p. 18). His particular time and place expose him to historical antagonisms.

> Sometimes we were chased, stoned, bitten, and beaten up for Christ-killers, all of us, even Georgie, articled, whether we liked it or not, to this mysterious trade. (p. 17)

When Augie's friend, Stashu, appears in the gang which beats him up, Grandma sees in the incident confirmation of her view that human affection merely ensnares the individual. In 'The Writer As Moralist' Bellow drew attention to the duplicity of American life in the thirties. As a child in Chicago, he recalls, he was daily taught to moralise, to assimilate sententious and affirmative formulae from Longfellow, Emerson and Whitman.

> But while this was happening, the Chicago papers reported gangland killings almost daily. Dion O'Bannion was shot in his flowershop, Hymie Weiss died violently on the steps of a

church, the Capone headquarters was shot up by machine guns
... To survive such events, the moral teachings of literature had
to be very strong ... 'Give all to love' they read in Emerson. But
in City Hall there were other ideas on giving and we had to
learn (if we could) how to reconcile high principles with low
facts.[6]

From the beginning of the novel, in the juxtapositon of loving
Mama, of George who sings of love, of Simon's ideals and
Grandma's schemes, Bellow insists on the disjunction between
high ideals and low facts. Love forces Mama into servitude and
exposes Augie to betrayal by his friends. Simon's code of honour,
as taught in the schools, is irrelevant to the family's situation.
Augie finds himself torn between contradictory imperatives –
American honour, Machiavellian *realpolitik*, loving simplicity,
and the need for complex constructions. In this first chapter the
major themes of the novel are introduced. Is history governed by
men of honour and aspiration? Or by lower phenomena – greed,
prejudice and deceit? Can the individual stand aside, or is he
conditioned by his historical situation? Can history be objectively
presented? Or is all history interpretive, narrated subjectively?
Can object lessons be learned from history? Is human nature a
constant? Or is there a sense in which the self consists only in its
history? The novel develops in answer to these questions, all of
which revolve around the fundamental opposition of nature and
history, exploring Ortega's dictum in the sphere of historical
existence (Chicago) in the world of nature (Mexico) and finally in
a European world of artistic constructions. The Chicago adventures offer a detailed historical time scheme, relating the events of
Augie's life to the discernible facts of the Depression. The Mexican adventures move out of time, at least initially, into a realm of
plumed serpents and nature deities. And the closing pages of the
novel engage directly with Ortega's view of history as narration,
with man as the existential creator of himself.

Events in Chicago suggest, first and foremost, that Augie is
conditioned by a time and place, at the mercy of historical forces.
Augie is immersed in a richly textured historical world, in which
the events of his life appear to be closely related to historical facts.
Events are reported in some detail from Augie's adolescence
onwards. 'After the age of twelve' (p. 19), Augie works in the
summers for the first time, employed by the Coblins. Augie gets to

know Coblin Senior 'about the time when O'Bannion was knock-ed off' (p. 29), which event occurred on 10 November 1924. Coblin then follows the Chicago gang wars with interest (1924–6). Augie occupies Howard's room, as Howard has run away to join the Marine Corps and is now in Nicaragua, fighting Sandino. The Marine Corps were in Nicaragua until 1933, fight-ing Sandino who first took up arms in 1926. Augie therefore appears to work first for the Coblins in summer 1926. After the summer Augie returns to school on 'a red fall morning' (p. 37), and in the following year Simon graduates. Meanwhile the ex-panding consumer buying of the twenties is illustrated by the Coblins, 'Coblin and he were hipped on superabundance. . . . There was always much money in sight' (p. 30), as are the risks of the period. 'Everybody was playing the stock market, led by Insull' (p. 34). For a time Augie works in Woolworth's, and on a newstand, and sells razor blades in 'November' (p. 51) with Jimmy Klein. At Christmas, already a high-school sophomore, he is a Santa Claus's helper at Deever's. In the following year Grandma Lausch falls in the snow on 'an election day' (p. 66) presumably the defeat of Al Smith by Hoover on 6 November 1928.

George is committed to an institution at the 'late start of spring' (p. 68), and Winnie dies in May of that year, 1929. As a high school junior Augie now goes to work for Einhorn, 'not long before the great crash, during the Hoover administration' (p. 72). The Crash occurred on 24 October 1929, so that we may assume that Augie first works for Einhorn in summer 1929. Augie then telescopes several summers, describing the Einhorn household in typical form:

> Let it be hot – for I'm reporting on summers, during vacations, when I spent full time with him.   (p. 82)

> Suppose we're at lunchtime.   (p. 87)

The trip Augie takes with Nails Nagel occurs 'at the time of the great jailbreak at Joliet' (p. 102), which was on 25 May 1931. On the trolley to the pier Augie reads the paper, the *Examiner*, and notes the shooting of one of the Aiello brothers. A similar shooting is reported in the *Chicago Herald Examiner* of 25 May 1931.[7] In Augie's absence there is a fire at Einhorn's, and in the 'Indian

Summer' (p. 114) of that year, Grandma Lausch is removed to a Home. In Autumn proper the Commissioner dies.

> The Commissioner died before the general bust, and wasn't very long in his grave when the suicides by skyscraper leaps began to take place (p. 125)

After his death, Augie mentions the 'slowness of the undeveloping winter' (p. 131), when he ran with Jimmy Klein. Prior to this, 'towards the last high-school terms' (p. 132) he saw little of Jimmy as Tommy Klein had lost his job at City Hall 'when the Republicans were pushed out by Cermak' (p. 132), which was in 1931. After the Commissioner's death, which we may tentatively locate as Autumn 1931, Einhorn is wiped out financially, largely because 'Thousands of his dough were lost in Insull's watered and pyramided utilities' (p. 125). Insull's investment companies went into receivership in April 1932 and finally collapsed on 20 September of that year. In April, now presumably 1933, Augie commits a robbery with Bulba and Gorman, and shortly afterwards graduates. For a short time Augie attends college and works in a shoe store.

At New Year Simon disappears with Molly Simms, whom he then fires. 'Within a few weeks' (p. 152) of her replacement, Augie drops out of college and comes under the wing of Mrs Renling, who tells him that she 'voted for Cox ... for Al Smith ... for Roosevelt' (p. 154). Roosevelt was elected in November 1932. The time is therefore at least early 1933, and given the preceding seasonal time references, more probably 1934. In July Augie goes to St Joe to spend the summer, returning to Chicago in the 'first and best autumn' (p. 181). During the winter he works as a paint salesman. 'At the tail end of winter' (p. 188), he meets Gorman and sets off with him for Canada when 'it was beginning April' (p. 190). Returning from Lackawanna Augie falls in with a group of Bonus marchers, 'an organization of the unemployed, many veterans, wearing Legion caps' (p. 192). There were several such marches in Spring 1933, 1934 and 1935. On his return to Chicago, however, Augie realises that it is the first night of Passover, and mentions 'the favourite purple of Chicago April evening' (p. 209). This specifically dates events to 18 April 1935. While in 1933 Passover was on 11 April, this is too early, given Mrs Renling's comments on Roosevelt and the summer spent at St Joe. It cannot be 1934 for in that year the first night of Passover was on 31 March. Augie now learns of Simon's disappearance and hears from him only 'some months later' (p. 220). At their meeting Augie comments 'it was summer' (p. 229). 'By the end of summer' (p.247) Simon is secretly married and 'in spring he leased a yard' (p. 263). After this, 'one summer afternoon' (p. 275) Simon blows up because Mama is assembling Roosevelt campaign buttons. Roosevelt was re-elected on 3 November 1936. Then, 'when the cold weather came' (p. 277) Simon's fortunes prosper and he marries in public. Augie divides his time between the coal business and Mimi. In December, still of this year, Simon beats up Guzynski. Mimi's abortion appointment is made for 'the end of Christmas week' (p. 315) and she is hospitalised on 31 December. Augie wakes up on New Year's Day at the Coblins. After a spell on the W.P.A. Augie becomes involved in the C.I.O. drives. 'This was soon after the first sitdown strikes' (p. 336). The first of these, in Cleveland, began on 28 December 1936. Augie also mentions the strikes in the automobile and rubber industries, (1936–7). Augie's affair with Sophie Geratis begins in mid-April or May, for she is 'going to be married in June, six weeks time' (p. 348). Thea appears on the scene on a 'May night' (p. 354) and Augie abandons his labour activities just before the Decoration Day Massacre, of 30 May 1937, when Grammick is clubbed on the head in front of Republic Steel. Augie leaves Mexico before Trotsky is assassinated and returns to Chicago.

Within this detailed time scheme there is of course considerable flexibility, political regimes, strikes, gang wars and labour agitation covering periods of time rather than specific dates. Events are narrated in a discursive style telescoping some events and describing typical rather than unique events. Seasonal references to Indian summer, Chicago April, flowery spring and slow winter are unobtrusively integrated in the text, almost as throwaway remarks. None the less a coherent time scheme is observed, and the fictional adventures juxtaposed with historical facts. What is particularly striking is the extent to which these historical events are left behind in 1937 with the war and the forties skimmed over. Once Augie has departed for Mexico the context is almost entirely barren of historical detail. In Chicago, then, Augie is within history in the simplest sense of the term. Were the reader to espouse a single-track conception of history, Augie's life to this point would illustrate the conditioning force of economic laws and market trends, and the domination of the 'low facts' of life over any idealising constructions.

Events however refuse to confine themselves to one frame of historical explanation. Augie is not merely involved in the events of the American twenties and thirties. Through a host of minor characters a wider historical dimension opens up. Augie begins his life on a certain level of accumulated past, inheriting a repertory of different views of history from those around him. While his adventures locate him in relation to empirical historical facts, he is also enmeshed in the attempts of those around him to square these events with pre-existent explanations. Augie finds himself in a richly varied immigrant society in which each character has his own personal history and explanation of events. The society which surrounds him is presented primarily as an assemblage of different histories, conforming to Ortega's perception that 'society is, primarily, the past'.[8] For Ortega the American notion of man as Adam beginning life afresh without the burden of the past is quite erroneous, for man is a creature of history not of nature.

> It can be said that the tiger of today is neither more nor less a tiger than was that of a thousand years ago: it is being a tiger for the first time, it is always a first tiger ... Man is not a first man, an eternal Adam: he is formally a second man, a third man.[9]

It is for this reason that the early pages of the novel offer little action but a succession of personal histories as the reader is introduced to Grandma Lausch, the Russian exile, Kreindl the Austro-Hungarian conscript, Anticol, the survivor of a pogrom, and the Jewish Coblins and Einhorns. As Augie admits, suggesting that his time and place condition him,

> All the influences were lined up waiting for me. I was born, and there they were to form me, which is why I tell you more of them than of myself.   (p. 52)

In the different views of the characters, views formed by their own histories, history is established as interpretive, as not merely the facts of experience but the way in which those facts are understood. While the characters share a common time and place, the events of the Depression in Chicago, they interpret these events in radically different ways. A tension therefore exists between two senses of the word 'history', a tension succinctly described by Karl Jaspers.

> History is at one and the same time happening and conscious-
> ness of this happening, history and knowledge of history.[10]

Augie begins his working days in the Coblin household, a house which embodies this tension. Anna Coblin exists in a medieval world, outside the conditions of her own place and time.

> Anna was terribly religious and had her own ideas of time and
> place, so that Heaven and eternity were not too far.   (p. 25)

When Howard departs for Nicaragua Anna has no idea of the factors involved, dosen't know who Sandino is or where Nicaragua lies. She subordinates a contemporary event of which she has no real comprehension to a sacramental view of history, casting herself as a Biblical martyr, 'in the suffering mothers' band led by Eve and Hannah' (p. 25). A grotesque disproportion exists between the model, Biblical martyrdom, and its re-enactment, the grotesque Anna Coblin, with her warts, bumps, moles and blebs, her immense body and grandiose cursing. Anna uses sacramental history for the purpose of self-aggrandisement. Her besetting practice, even in the midst of wailing and self-flagellating martyrdom, is to observe herself in mirrors. In con-trast to Anna, Coblin moves in the twentieth century, his atten-tion entirely on present events. A newspaper seller, he takes pride in keeping up to date with gang wars, stock quotations and sports results. While Anna lives in an atmosphere of archaic peasant filth, Coblin eats American style breakfasts of cornflakes, dines on Boston beans and frequents the burlesque houses of the Loop. Though coevals, he and Anna might as well be living in quite distinct historical epochs.

> She was, you might say, in a desert, pastoral condition of
> development and not up to the fancy stage of Belshazzar's Feast
> of barbaric later days.   (p. 29)

Coblin lives quite a separate existence from Anna, governed by his own individual ego. He 'had his own motives and he had established his own right of way' (p. 28). The disjunction between past and present is emphasised by the third adult in the household, Anna's brother Five Properties. In the past Five Properties has been a participant in European history, driving wagons of Russian and German corpses to burial on Polish farms. Now however, he has become the stock greenhorn of the Yiddish theatre, divorcing himself from the past.

> Five Properties cared absolutely nothing about the absent or the dead and freely sagd so. Hell with them. He had worn their boots and caps while the stiffs were bouncing in his wagon.
>
> (p. 27)

As a result he reduces his ethical code to 'one simple moral . . . you have no one to blame but yourself' (p. 27). For all their differing views of their place in time – atrophy of the past, atrophy of the present – the Coblins share a common hypertrophy of the self, a common egotism, demonstrating to Augie that man's nature determines his actions more than his place in time, which he may distort to fit his own egotistical needs. Although Anna claims to view events *sub specie aeternitatis*, directing Augie in her religious teaching to the 'great eternal things' (p. 35) her account of the Creation and the Fall reduces the Bible to a tale of sex and violence. In her concentration on the punishment of Lot's wife, the lewdness of his daughters, Isaac sporting with Rebecca and the rape of Dinah, she brings these events down to the level of the yellow press which Coblin peddles. When Augie reads the Iliad at the Coblins' he reads only 'how the fair Briseis was dragged around from tent to tent and Achilles racked up his spear and hung away his mail' (p. 33). The epic world of heroism is reduced to its lowest facts – the prostitution of woman and the decline of the hero. Bible, Iliad and gutter press enforce the vision of man as an unchanging quantity, pursuing his own egotistical course in spite of his historical situation.

Events in the March household develop the sense of contradictory historical attitudes. On the one hand Grandma Lausch subscribes to a belief in democratic freedom, the premise being that history offers each individual the chance to attain nobility. Examples are drawn from democratic and republican contexts to justify this belief. 'What did Danton lose his head for, or why was there a Napoleon, if it wasn't to make a nobility of us all' (pp. 36–7). The foundation of Grandma's creed is the Horatio

Alger myth, characterised by Bellow in 'The Writer as Moralist' as 'the message that worldly asceticism leads to worldly success'.[11] Grandma therefore trains Augie and Simon in clean habits, duty and restraint, encouraging them to perfect themselves by their own efforts. Simon is induced to take a job at a news-stand, within hailing distance of financiers and captains of industry, as the latter board the 'Twentieth Century' train. Confident in the Alger myth of 'the stroke or inspiration that brought you to the notice of eminent men' (p. 43) Grandma pushes Simon into the main-stream of American capitalism. Augie, at a smaller stand, away from the main thoroughfare, loses money and is fired. It does not occur to him to recoup his losses in the customer's change. Honest Augie is roundly condemned by Grandma, however, while dis-honest Simon gains her favour. When Grandma warns Augie of the terrible fate which awaits him if he does not pull up his economic socks, she reveals her true values, converting Anna's religious account of damnation into a vision of economic doom:

> work certificates, stockyards, shovel labour, penitentiary rock-piles, bread and water, and life-long ignorance and degrada-tion. (p. 52)

When Augie is offered a second chance to prove himself, at Christmas, he acts on the real imperatives of his society: that to make money is to make good and that honour has no place in the mainstream of American finance. Dressed as elves he and Jimmy successfully swindle Deever's store. When the swindle is detected however, Grandma adopts a Calvinistic code making Augie feel that his crime is evidence of the 'disfigurement of my soul' (p. 55).

Augie's two experiences reveal to him the contradiction in Grandma's views. On the one hand, she claims that history offers examples of the individual's freedom to better himself. On the other she interprets Augie's actions as evidence of his determined nature. Augie refuses to divide the world in this fashion into Calvinistic sheep and goats.

> I lacked the true sense of being a criminal, the sense that I was on the wrong side of the universal wide line with the worse or weaker part of human-kind. (p. 53)

Grandma's belief in the eligibility of each human being to be noble, to elect his own path in life, founders on an alternative sense of 'election', as governed by a force beyond the individual. It is this contradiction in her beliefs which seals her own fate. Grandma commits George to an institution in the name of inexorable necessity. Augie argues that George 'hadn't done wrong yet' (p. 62) but Grandma will not wait for him to do so. For her he has 'reached his development of a man' (p. 61) and his nature is such as to cause him inevitably to do wrong. Using the future as a threat, she is happy to act 'in behalf of this inexorability' (p. 62). If events are inexorable, however, and man's nature fixed, there is no need for the perfecting guidance of Grandma Lausch. Her benevolent despotism can serve no useful function. As Augie and Simon escape from her control, she accepts that

> what counted was natural endowment, and on that score she formed the opinion bitterly that we were not born with talents. (p. 70)

By accepting that human nature conditions events, not historical development, Grandma initiates her own decline in power. The clash between Calvinist election ethics and the free election of democracy is rendered imagistically in Grandma's fall on election day. On a day which marks the individual's free control over his actions in history, Grandma falls. Once Augie and Simon have seen her weak and fallen, her power is lost. Grandma saw Augie's failure as evidence of his determined nature, Augie and Simon draw the same lesson from her weakness. When she re-emerges from her room, Augie feels 'a change in the main established order' (p. 66) and sets himself free of her tutelage. Grandma cannot hope to exercise temporal power on the basis of atemporal determinism.

Augie's next tutor, William Einhorn, presents an altogether more optimistic creed, that of the ever-open possibility of man overcoming his nature to become 'great'. Augie describes Einhorn as 'the first superior man I knew' (p. 71) and locates him in the line of great men in history:

> What would Caesar suffer in this case? What would Machiavelli advise or Ulysses do? What would Einhorn think? (p. 71)

Einhorn is introduced with a meditation on history in which

Augie rejects the view that man is in decline from some former golden age. Einhorn is great:

> Unless you want to say that we're at the dwarf end of all times and mere children whose only share in grandeur is like a boy's share in fairy-tale kings, beings of a different kind from times better and stronger than ours. But if we're comparing men and men, not men and children or men and demigods ... then I have the right to praise Einhorn.   (p. 71)

Despite Einhorn's crippled state he refuses to allow his nature to confine him. To this end he relentlessly culls from history all the examples he can find to prove his point. He is particularly interested in the history of cripples:

> the dumbness of the Spartans, the fact that Oedipus was lame, that gods were often maimed, that Moses had faltering speech, and Dmitri the Sorcerer a withered arm, Caesar and Mahomet epilepsy, Lord Nelson a pinned sleeve.   (p. 85)

From his immense stock of historical examples, his files on the American Legion, the Republican party, archaeology, and gang wars Einhorn can prove any point to his own satisfaction. He is involved in a mass of swindles but excuses himself on the ground that the great man stands independent of normal morality, merrily quoting Henry V, 'We are the makers of manners, Kate, and the liberty that follows our places stops the mouth of all find-faults' (p. 79). After the Crash he is quick to switch to an alternative frame of explanation – economic history – cutting off his tenants' heat on the grounds that 'I'll stick by economic laws' (p. 126). Einhorn is especially keen on classical examples, identifying himself at different points with Hephaestus, Seneca, Aristotle and Pythagoras, and finally settling on Socrates for himself and Alcibiades for Augie. His selection is, of course, entirely risible. One of his pet projects is an edition of the plays of Shakespeare indexed for businessmen under such headings as Slack Business, Bad Weather, Difficult Customers, Stuck with Big Inventory of Last Year's Models. Bellow's satire is unerringly aimed at the attempt to select from the available historical data only such facts as fit the bill. Einhorn uses history as a stock of examples from which he can make personal capital. In this he illustrates Ortega's characterisation of the modern philologue, the man who lives by past models. Ortega, discussing the reverence of the Graeco-Roman for the past, writes:

> He searches out in the past a model for the present situation, and accoutred with this he plunges into the waves of actuality protected and disguised by the diving dress of the past ... But this does not imply being insensible to time. It simply means an incomplete 'chronism', atrophy of the future, hypertrophy of the past ... This mania for catching hold of everything in the present with the forceps of a past model has been handed on from the man of antiquity to the modern philologue.[12]

Einhorn's hypertrophy of the past is amply demonstrated in the multitude and variety of his historical models. History however outmanoeuvres him, and in his description of the effect of the Crash on Einhorn the later Augie turns Einhorn's own weapons against him.

> I'm thinking of the old tale of Croesus, with Einhorn in the unhappy part.... The Crash was Einhorn's Cyrus and the bank failures his pyre, the poolroom his exile from Lydia and the hoodlums Cambyses, whose menace he managed, somehow, to get round.
>   (p. 125)

The very arbitrariness of the comparison mocks Einhorn's own views. There is no real parallel between Einhorn and Croesus, except in so far as each lost an empire on a turn of fortune's wheel. Augie emphasises that the great figures of the past share the same character faults as those of the present. Solon is a condescending tourist, the Queen a revengeful monster, Cambyses a lunatic. There is no suggestion that Einhorn is a falling-off from some great model, rather that the past offers no useful lessons. The death of the Commissioner underlines the extent to which the past offers no benefits. One of Einhorn's ideas is that man inexorably advances. He therefore writes his father's obituary in terms of this belief, identifying his father as a great man in the forefront of a progressive civilisation:

> The return of the hearse from the newly covered grave leaves a man to pass through the last changes of nature who found

Chicago a swamp and left it a great city. He came after the Great Fire, said to be caused by Mrs. O'Leary's cow, in flight from the conscription of the Hapsburg tyrant, and in his life as a builder proved that great places do not have to be founded on the bones of slaves. (p. 123)

No sooner is the Commissioner dead than his life-history is inflated and glorified. History as fabrication is what we might expect from Einhorn, who has won competitions by concocting fictional 'most embarrassing moments' and imaginary experiences. The later Augie comments at this point on Mrs Karas (who snubbed the young Augie but later claims warm friendship with him). When they meet years later she completely falsifies their relationship, disconcerting Augie who is 'stumped by such major will to do over the past ... to adorn the past with imaginary flowers' (pp. 121–2). Once Einhorn's grandiose obituary is written, he rifles his father's desk for his inheritance. In the obituary Einhorn described the lesson of his father's life as demonstrating that 'achievements are compatible with decency' (p. 123). Ironically his claim proves true. His father leaves behind him only a series of memoranda in which his debtors appear under nicknames, and there are no I.O.U.s. Einhorn finds himself 'subject to the honour of lots of men he hadn't always treated well' (p. 124). The records yield nothing largely because the Commissioner dealt in personal obligations, in terms of decency between associates. Einhorn inherits only an ironic demonstration of his own earlier statement that we are given nothing by the past.

We never learn anything, never in the world, and in spite of all the history books written. They're just the way we plead or argue with ourselves about it. (p. 124)

The past singularly fails to equip Einhorn to deal with the sudden changes of the present, the Crash and the Depression. History outdistances Einhorn despite his study of it. Retrospectively he may be able to impose selective patterns on events – history as the history of cripples, of great men, of progress, of economic laws – but retrospective analysis is of little assistance in the present which escapes from the models of the past. History does not advance in the ordered fashion which would permit prediction of events.

The events of the plot, at this point, contribute to the impression that life is predominantly rapid change and movement, and
cast a sardonic light on the notion of history as purposive advance.
Two episodes – the trip with Nails Nagel, and Augie's visit to the
brothel – raise the question of the individual's ability to direct his
own actions amidst the rapid changes of time. Dingbat, Einhorn's
brother, is distinguished by his energy, an energy he is never able
to direct constructively. As a fighter Dingbat never wins.

> He went on springing and boxing, rushing out from the pool-
> room on a fresh challenge to spin around on his tango shoes and
> throw his tense, weightless punches.   (p. 74)

Dingbat considers Nails, his pet prizefighter, as an object lesson in
the virtues of self-discipline, taking him as his text at boys' clubs to
argue the merits of ascetic training. The three set off for the boxing
match, confident in Nails's energies, as if 'sailing to a victory'
(p. 104). Once aboard the steamer however Nails loses all control.
Motion disagrees with him and the noble animal succumbs to *mal
de mer*. Sapped by the motion of the lake, Nails cannot generate
sufficient fresh momentum to win the fight. After the Crash this
failure of momentum becomes general. Augie comments on the
overall slowing down of pace as the laborious task of reconstruc-
tion begins. 'Things had low action these mortified times'
(p. 128). Those who appeared to be moving towards their goals
are checked, their motion dissipated in the flux of events. The
notion that history is the record of the advance of civilisation
yields to retrogressive motion, in which a series of sickening ups
and downs replaces any progressive advance. Simon is 'on soggy
ground and forced to cut down the speed he had been making'
(p. 130). The Depression 'had halted Einhorn too' (p. 140).
Einhorn's parlour is disfigured by fire. The civilisation of the
March household declines to the point at which Grandma can no
longer summon up enough energy to domesticate the new puppy.
Confident that she is 'going to a better place' (p. 112) Grandma
finds herself committed to the inertia of a Home for the Infirm. All
around people are forced to change direction, normal generation-
al expectations are reversed, sons giving up college to support
fathers, and plans of advance thrown into reverse. History displays only a series of contradictory movements, elevating and
deposing in a chaos of sudden change.

Augie's visit to the brothel, however, has somewhat different implications, suggesting that, even in the unfamiliar circumstances of changing events the individual maintains some ability to direct his course. Rather than emphasising the instinctive ease of natural sexual activity, the visit to the brothel is characterised by difficulty of action. The emphasis falls on the awkward access of the house, its steep stairs up which Augie carries Einhorn, and the problems Einhorn's paralysis poses for the sexual act. With the whore, however, Einhorn remains in control, purposeful, managing and giving directions. Augie adopts his attitude, behaving in these unfamiliar circumstances

> as if I knew exactly what I was doing and from an idea that at a critical time it was best and most decent to have my own momentum.   (p. 145)

Within the contingency of events the individual retains some degree of control. Indeed, this contingency in itself contributes to his freedom. Einhorn sees Augie's involvement in a robbery as the product of the pressures of the critical time of the Depression, arguing that it is the result of the influence of the poolroom, and reading the sociological riot act over him. Augie, however, counters this determinism by his awareness of the variety of pressures upon him. In the poolroom he meets criminals and hoodlums, but also physicists, philosophers and political thinkers. As a result 'I touched all sides, and nobody knew where I belonged' (p. 134). Because he is pulled in so many different directions Augie is able to slip the noose. His life is not plotted for him, precisely because so many different factors affect him. Augie's tutors represent different views of the determinism of history – history as governed by economic laws, by Great Men, by a providential plan, as progress or as decline. Amidst so many determinisms Augie escapes definition. Up to this point in his adventures the issue of Augie's freedom in history remains open.

Augie prefaces the next chapter of his memoirs with a cautious disclaimer: 'From here a new course was set – by us, for us: I'm not going to try to unravel all the causes' (p. 147). In Augie's stay with the Renlings Bellow dramatises the opposition between nature and history within the framework of American myths exploring a nexus of historical interpretations which centre on the clash between the Puritan belief in innate depravity and the

Transcendental faith in America as new Eden. A subsequent development of the Puritan view consists in its economic application – the belief that wordly goods are an indication of divine election, a belief which in Weber's thesis determines the connection between Protestantism and Capitalism. Subsidiary to the Transcendental vision is the American belief in rugged individualism, the frontier myth that in a new Eden man may prosper by his own efforts. In the former view man is defined by his nature, in the latter defines himself in his history.

Augie's new occupation, selling in a saddle shop under a Western timber, training as a rider, suggests the frontier myth. Renling is cast in the mould of the Westerner, is keen on fights, feats of stamina, fast cars and barbecues. A strong silent type Renling is associated with the days of continent opening, building the North Shore viaduct

> the year the Panama Canal was opened. Thought the job would knock me out in the stomach muscles. Buck and a quarter was pretty good dough in those days.   (p. 157)

His terse, clipped speech echoes with Western slang. Augie is to be 'schooled' and 'broken in' (p. 153). Mrs Renling is described as riding fence on her face (p. 161). She describes Willa as 'a little Indian' (p. 158) who is trying to get Augie 'roped' (p. 159). Mrs Renling spirits Augie away to Benton Harbour, a town described as occupying a pastoral environment, set back in time to a Pre-Industrial America. The 'territory round about . . . was mostly fruit country farmed by Germans, the men like farmers anywhere, but the older women in bonnets, going barefoot in long dresses' (p. 159).

This is a land of fruit, milk and honey, in which 'the peach branches shone with seams of gum, leaves milky' (p. 159). The vision is of plenty in a pastoral setting, with echoes of an earlier America. Its ahistorical status is emphasised: part of the land is farmed by the House of David Israelities, a sect of pious vegetarians who 'spoke of Shiloh and Armageddon as familiarly as of eggs and harnesses' (p. 160). Though Augie notes that the leaves are in fact milky with insecticide, and that the sect are millionaires with a miniature railway and two jazz bands he yields to the appeal of his new life, soaking up its rich atmosphere 'where you are not a subject matter but sit in your own nature, tasting original tastes as good as the first man' (p. 160). As Adam at one with nature, Augie turns to love as a confirmation of his view of the world as blessed, and presents himself to Esther as if favoured by God: 'as if God had not left out a single one of His gifts' (p. 163), in a sly variation on Weber's thesis.

Other mythical views than the Adamic occur however. With Mrs Renling the voice of the Calvinist is heard in the land. At breakfast she indulges in damnation chats, calling on

> her whole force of frights, apocalypse death riders, church-porch devils who grabbed naked sinners from behind ... infanticides, plagues, and incests.   (p. 162)

Bellow ironically frames the warring American myths within a larger mythical context. Mrs Renling 'praised the male in all things as if she was working for Athena' (p. 168). The sacred bird of Athena, goddess of skills and warfare, is the owl, and Mr Renling is described as 'a nightbird ... a crude, big, brown-barred shape' (p. 180). It is Mrs Renling who points out the innate depravity of Miss Zeeland, daughter of one of the founding families of America, who threw her child from a window to its death. The appearance of New World progress merely conceals the same violent events as the past. Augie rejects any mythological idea of new and innocent beginners, comparing Miss Zeeland to Medea:

> It wasn't Medea, a good, safe long time ago, chasing her pitiful kids, but a woman I saw in the dining-room, wearing feathers.   (p. 162)

Augie's pursuit of Venus, in the shape of Esther Fenchel, draws its comedy from the deflation of mythical innocence. Honourably pursuing a pure and perfect love, Augie offers himself to Esther like a courtly lover. Her rejection, couched in less than courtly terms, is based on the belief that 'you service the lady you're with' (p. 170). Aghast, Augie drops the Grail with a clang, feeling 'as if I had been carrying something with special sacred devotedness and it had spilled and scalded me' (p. 170). Recovering from his faint he sees Miss Zeeland in the doorway, 'in her evening feathers ... visionary, oriental with her rich hair swept up in a kind of tower ... she glided or fanned away' (p. 168). Miss Zeeland's 'unbroken roll' of body, and her serpentine and bird like motion – 'glided' 'fanned' – suggest that living in a state of nature is not altogether Edenic. Athena's other sacred animal is the serpent. Nature appears behind the myth. The escape from history into myth is unsuccessful, for the goddesses Augie serves are not innocent ones. The Fenchel sisters see him, not as innocent Adam, but as gigolo to the corrupt old world. Augie is forced to discard his Adamic notions and to remember

> where I came from, parentage, and other history, things I had never much thought of as difficulties, being democratic in temperament, available to everybody and assuming about others what I assumed about myself.   (p. 173)

This Whitmanesque faith in romantic possibility, in social mobility, casting off the weight of the past, has been tested and found wanting. Augie realises that he cannot slough off his past and therefore rejects Mrs Renling's offer of adoption because 'I wasn't a bulrush-hidden infant by any means. I had family enough to suit me and history to be loyal to' (p. 179). The history and family to which Augie is loyal do not however prove themselves as certain as Augie would like. Augie's trip to Canada with Joe Gorman follows Gorman's comment on his indigent state – 'These days they take care of their relatives first. And what have you got in the way of relatives?' (p. 188). When Augie visits Grandma Lausch he finds that she has forgotten George's name and that her memory of the March family is unreliable. While she is a central fact in Augie's history he realises that he is quite peripheral to hers. 'How small a part of her life compared with the whole span she had spent with us' (p. 184). Grandma Lausch's life, like all human history, is not a systematic advance, building on what went before, but, in Augie's description an old and varicose channel, with its own byways and dead ends. Augie therefore sets off for Canada in the belief that he is uncommitted by his past and can act independently. Invited to smuggle immigrants by Gorman, he rationalises his decision to accept, believing that at any point on the road he can withdraw. Unknown to him, however, his decision is final. Once en route he is committed in spite of himself, for Gorman's car is stolen. The measured decision he plans to take has been pre-empted by Gorman's preceding crime. The ordered stasis and ahistorical paradise of Benton Harbour yield to a world of chaotic motion in which hellish overtones predominate, and the individual is defined by past events. Gorman is Satanic, red-faced and lurid. The car is 'hot' and has 'hell-energy' (p. 190). The journey takes Augie through a sulphurous industrial landscape to a place which 'had a demon' (p. 191). Augie's motion is generalised by the presence on the roads of hobos and Bonus marchers, a 'wanderer population without any special Jerusalem or Kiev in mind' (p. 195). Amidst these victims of history Augie observes a scene of human waste:

> an industrial sub-town – battlefield, cemetery, garbage crater, ... Hooverville crate camps, plague and war fires like the boiling pinnacle of all sackings and Napoleonic Moscow burnings. (pp. 199–200)

To Augie however this entropic dissipation of energy is almost a relief; he surrenders to the sense of his own insignificance, dwarfed by the vast spaces through which he travels and the speed of his motion. Events, however correct his isolated and purposeless freedom. Alone on the highway Augie is dangerously suspect and joins the marchers to find safety in numbers. Next day, however, he leaves them, it being easier to get lifts alone. Huddled in the box car he withdraws from the overtures of the man beside him, only to be forced to cling to Stoney for warmth. Travelling with Stoney and Wolfy, however, exposes him to the attention of the police who see him as one of a gang. In the police station Augie observes the deaf mutes, arrested for fighting. Even these isolates from the world have to learn, in the cop's words, that 'they aren't alone by themselves in the world and can't be carryin' on as if they was' (p. 202). Augie leaves Chicago to try his luck alone, unsupported by family, only to find that he cannot maintain individual solitariness and that history catches up with him. Wolfy is arrested because Jimmy, the great memory man, remembers his history, his police record. Augie narrowly escapes guilt by association, almost condemned by Wolfy's history. The adventure with Gorman suggests that the individual is the plaything of large historical forces, that he is placed and identified in the record, and that his freedom is threatened by the preceding actions of others. Augie cannot wipe clean the slate, to move at his own pace under his own direction. He exists amidst the mysterious pull of different histories, in a world of chaotic and contingent change.

Back in Chicago, Augie finds fresh changes have occurred. Simon is goaled, the family home broken up, and Grandma dead. Paradoxically Augie returns at Passover to find the Jews celebrating the beginning of their own exodus. Traditionally the Passover ritual celebrates the covenant established between Jehovah and his people to bring them salvation in history. Augie's is a parodic Passover, however. Einhorn's candles are lit, not in ritual observance, but because the electricity has failed. His door is left open, not for Elijah, but for Blavatsky the handyman. Augie's own response to Passover is quite at odds with any suggestion of a divinely ordained pattern completing itself in history. Augie describes Passover from the opposition side, as

> the Angel of Death going through all doors not marked with blood to take away the life of the Egyptian first-born   (p. 209)

The chapter emphasises the lack of solidarity among historical victims. While Jews rejoice, Egyptians are slain. While Five Properties celebrates his engagement to Cissy, Simon, the disappointed suitor, languishes in gaol. History becomes Toynbee's process of rout-rally-rout, the disadvantages of the one group forming the advantage of the other in a relentless see-saw world in which only force counts. Einhorn informs Augie of Simon's betrayal (Simon kept the money destined for Augie) and urges him to rejoice in Simon's misfortune, and turn it to his own advantage. Lacking any belief in a providential purpose to history Einhorn puts his faith in force, claiming that

> as there were no more effective prescriptions in old ways, as we were in dreamed-out or finished visions, that therefore, in the naked form of the human jelly, one should choose or seize with force.   (p. 214)

Simon acts on this imperative, seeing in the defeat of his plans clinching evidence in favour of force. He concurs with Einhorn's opinion that striving for the best merely lays one open to the perfidy of the world. 'While they're looking for the best there is . . . everything else gets lost' (p. 233). As a child Simon's sights were set high, but now he decides that human nature is limited. 'First comes all the selfish and jealous stuff, that you don't care what happens to anybody else as long as you get yours' (p. 230). His

ideal lost he settles for a rich marriage to Charlotte Magnus.
Augie, however, sees in the ups and downs of history evidence for
the grandeur of man, concentrating on the rallies not the routs.
Reading the history books which he has stolen he observes:

> Everybody knows this triumphant life can only be periodic. So
> there's a schism about it, some saying only this triumphant life
> is real and others that only the daily facts are. For me there was
> no debate, and I made speed into the former.   (p. 227)

Augie does not retaliate against Simon but retains his own ideals,
ideals founded on a larger historic vision of humanity. Einhorn's
lesson falls on deaf ears largely because Augie is mourning the
death of Grandma Lausch, and is enveloped in unselfish sorrow
for the inevitable suffering of humanity. Where Simon adopts a
low vision of human nature, Augie sees reverse evidence in human
history, which emphasises that the human condition is shared.
While history may not be governed by a providential plan, may
indeed appear as mere directionless movement, man is not alone
within it but a part of humanity.

How far Augie is able to preserve that humanity depends upon
the question of his freedom. Augie prefaces his next sequence of
adventures, his involvement with the Magnus family, with an
analytical comment:

> Now there's a dark Westminster of a time when a multitude of
> objects cannot be clear; they're too dense and there's an island
> rain, North Sea lightlessness, the vein of the Thames. That
> darkness in which resolutions have to be made.   (p. 235)

As Augie's previous experiences have demonstrated, the individual makes his decisions in darkness, without being able to see
and understand all the factors involved in any action. Augie does
not ascribe this obscurity of events to any inherent inaccessibility
of first causes, but rather to the multiplicity of circumstances, the
density of circumambient events, and the inability of the individual to co-ordinate the available data into a coherent theory of
causation. In his subsequent remarks Augie describes this darkness as the human condition, a general mystery in which decisions
have to be taken. At the same time Augie suggests the positive
aspect of this darkness:

With the dark, the solvent is in this way offered until the time
when one thing is determined and the offers, mercies, and
opportunities are finished. (p. 235)

This somewhat hermetic utterance introduces the reader to the
principal concern of the Magnus plot: the question of man's
freedom in history. The lack of knowledge of the multitude of
factors which act upon the individual carries with it the implication, on the one hand, that man is the plaything of incomprehensible forces. Yet, because the individual does not know all the
factors involved in any decision he therefore feels free to act.
Darkness is 'solvent', allowing free resolutions to be made. If the
individual did enjoy a global comprehension of all the factors
pressing upon him he would act rationally, but not freely. Because
the individual exists in time, he forms a part of events and cannot
dissociate himself from them to form a total impression. Time
therefore both contributes to, and limits, his freedom. Man,
however, seeks to represent his history as a succession of free
choices, rationally taken. The events which follow this disquisition of Augie's concentrate upon the degree of freedom enjoyed by
the characters, in particular Simon and Mimi, who understand
their freedom in quite contradictory senses.

Simon operates within an acceptance of fixed limits, and his
career exemplifies his decision to abandon ideals and accept a
settlement in his marriage to Charlotte. Augie comments that all
men are limited by time, by old age and death, and that therefore
there is some logic in Simon's position.

You don't actually have full choice ... Most people make do
with what they have, and labour in their given visible world,
and this has its own stubborn merit. Not only did Simon make
what he had do, but he went the limit. (p. 250)

Augie is astonished by Simon's rapid progress, his ability to reach
his goals and carry out his plans to the letter. Simon appears to be
able to direct the course of his own life, setting its pace. While
ostensibly only engaged, he is in fact married to Charlotte.
Conventional time is outwardly respected but in reality Simon
has stolen a march on time, settling for imperfect but immediate
satisfaction rather than postponing the fulfilment of his desires for
some future moment. In Simon the Magnuses welcome a man

who can 'keep up their speed' (p. 261). In the coalyard however Augie glimpses the underside of Simon's life, an area of summer stagnation. Simon's movement is paradoxical: it has the appearance of freedom, but is in reality mapped out by the Magnuses. Simon appears to impose his will on contingent and multiple events, exhorting Augie 'not to dissolve in bewilderment of choices but to make myself hard, like himself, and learn how to stay with the necessary' (p. 280). From his Louis XIV bed in the governor's suite of a luxury hotel Simon paints a future of political office, ambassadorships and power, forcing Augie to agree that 'one is only ostensibly born to remain in specified limits' (p. 281). Charlotte's entrance, however, ironically recalls the limiting initial condition on which Simon's aggrandisement must always stumble. 'The best that Simon could do brought him back to her' (p. 282). Because Simon is committed to the rational exercise of his own choice, imposing his will on the multiplicity of events, on the basis of a clear-cut appraisal of the 'necessary', he lacks any true freedom. His life is fixed and settled. Paradoxically Simon longs for an accident to interrupt his course, to remove events from his control. Augie notes Simon's reckless driving, his propensity for deeper and deeper dives at the beach, and the 'consents to death' (p. 253) in his voice. Simon's life is dominated by a deathwish, for the way in which he understands his freedom amounts to a slavery to reason. In a sense, in discounting the contingency in which he lives, Simon has killed time, imposing himself upon events. It is appropriate therefore that his activities should be of a time-killing nature, his life a vacuum which he fills with low entertainment, erotic floorshows, repeated barbershop visits, and womanising. In accepting the limits of human nature, Simon can only cater to the needs of physicality. The Magnuses also go to the limits of human nature. Their Brobdignagian massive physicality, immense breadth and heavy bodies are fundamentally animalistic. Uncle Charlie, with his 'white hide' face is described as 'rearing' over the clan, an assembly of 'neighing' women, 'heavy-pelted aunts' and a grandmother who wears a necklace like grizzly teeth. Charlie's blunt obscenities freely admit the physical nature of man. His daughter, Lucy, is not shy to make 'declaration of honest sensuality under the scrutiny of the whole clan' (p. 258). In their lives the Magnuses illustrate the consequences of the belief that man is defined by his nature, and can exercise his freedom only within certain pre-

existent limits, rather than perfecting himself in time. Time hangs
heavy on their hands and they welcome any form of entertainment. To Augie their salon

> lacked white stockings and fans to resemble the Directorate –
> I'm thinking of commoners suddenly in the palaces of power.
> But the Magnuses seemed less to know what to do.   (p. 257)

Ostensibly freed by material progress and republican liberty the
Magnuses feel a power vacuum and promptly enlist Simon as the
Napoleon their bourgeois republic requires:

> He went both deep and far into the place of star and sovereign.
> They had patriarchs and matriarchs but they had no prince
> before him.   (p. 253)

Simon finds in his own power only emptiness; Augie compares his
dissolute pleasures to those of Caracalla and Commodus before
the senate. While Simon sees himself as a great man, seeing
clearly in the murk of events, he sees a different self-image in
Mama's sightless eyes. Simon discovers Mama at the Blind
Home, assembling Roosevelt buttons, and reacts out of all proportion to the imagined slight. The Blind Home, furnished like a
'public forum' (p. 274) exemplifies 'leisure gone bad' (p. 274).
Mama is willing to assemble buttons because of her enforced
idleness, because 'It's good for her to have something to keep her
occupied' (p. 276). Simon sees in Mama an image of his own
vacuous existence. He complains that Mama is being exploited
for political ends, yet owes his own advancement to a similar
exploitation of family, in the Magnuses. Augie describes the
malaise of the Home as a result of lack of freedom – 'the sick evil of
not even knowing why anything should ail you since you're
resigned to accept all conditions' (p. 275). Total power amounts
to total slavery: there is no real distinction between the dark
emptiness in which Mama lives and the rational clarity of Simon's
life. The servitude which Mama owes to her simple nature is akin
to the slavery to his nature which Simon has accepted.

   Where Simon has made speed into the bourgeoisie and a settled
existence, Mimi Villars lives amidst the transients of a rooming
house, and frequents Marxists and libertarians. Devotee of free
love, scorning marriage and family as the domestic institutions of

capitalism, Mimi believes in individual freedom. For Mimi the self is not already formed at birth but creates itself in time. In her view:

> all that you inherited from the mixing peoples of the past and the chance of parents' encountering like Texas cattle was your earthy material, which it was your own job to make into admirable flesh. (p. 249)

Mimi's decision to have an abortion reflects this belief in man as existential creator of self, a mere nothing at birth. Mimi's brother-in-law Sylvester has similar views. He presents himself as the master of events, trying to impress Augie with his command over Marxian statistics, plenary dates and factional history. Sylvester however has been stoned by his wife for his lack of immediate dynamism, for being in Mimi's terms 'mere uncompleted mud' (p. 249). Augie recognises that Sylvester's delight in history is in fact Utopian. 'What he had really was the long-distance dreaming gaze of the eyes into the future' (p. 249). Frazer, his fellow Marxist, shares this longsight hypertrophy of the future. He knows nothing of Mimi's pregnancy, nor does he want to know.

> It was part of Frazer's style not to know about such things. There was always something superior to what was happening in the immediate view. (p. 302)

In the long term Frazer justifies Augie's thievery as the expropriation of the expropriators. In the short term he lives off Augie's credit. Kayo Obermark, Augie's fellow lodger, also holds that the complications of the present are irrelevant, and that the 'greatest purity was outside human relations' (p. 304). Long distance views, however, are of little assistance in the complications of the immediate time. Mimi's pregnancy poses its problems in the here-and-now. The pressures of time and immediate contingency are focused in the pregnancy – a contingent event, unplanned, about which a swift decision has to be reached. The accident of circumstances, and the short term contingency in which the individual actually operates, is strongly emphasised in the plot. Mimi describes her pregnancy by Frazer as accidental. 'If I wouldn't marry him before, why should I now because of an accident?' (p. 296). In the plot accidents multiply. When Mimi

takes Augie to a drugstore to discuss abortion methods a dis-
oriented dog rushes over and urinates on her leg, a demonstration
to Augie of 'that lack of respect in occurrences for the difficulties
that there already are!' (p. 297). Already shaken by a visit to the
Morgue, and late for a date with Lucy, Augie has a car accident in
the snow. Later, when he is late because he has been caught
stealing books, he telephones Lucy to discover that she has no ear
for his problems, because she has bent the fender of her car in
another accident. While Augie is trying to pursue one goal, to gain
Mimi admission to hospital, he panics and swings at an orderly,
and on top of his major problem has to deal with a policeman who
wants a full explanation of his conduct. Rushing from the hospital
to Lucy he demolishes the bushes in front of her house. Dismissed
by Mr Magnus he has yet another mishap, this time a flat tyre,
and has to alter course to spend the night at the Coblins. This
catalogue of accidents reinforces the impression of the dark
contingency of human life, in which the individual cannot arrest
the flow of events to deal with one problem at a time, but is forced
to contend with fresh mishaps at every point. The positioning of
events in late December is also significant. The days are dark and
short and the streets icy. When he is caught out by Weintraub
Augie feels 'general darkness and fear, like the unlighted gathered
cloud that hung outside' (p. 320). Watching over Mimi in the
afternoon Augie has to gauge time 'by the hour and not by
darkness, which was the same that day at six as it had been at
three' (p. 322). Augie's actions occur in darkness, and he has an
uncertain hold on his course.

As Mimi's pregnancy advances she feels the pressure of time
more and more urgently, unable to recuperate from her operation
for fear that it will soon be too late for an abortion. Augie's course
also speeds up as he rushes from Simon to Lucy to Mimi, never
quite catching up with himself. Simon reproaches Augie for his
double life:

> I think you're going a little too fast, aren't you, trying to keep up
> with two dames? . . . If one of them didn't haul your ashes you
> might make faster time with the other. (p. 308)

Unlike Simon, Augie is not able to be single-minded amidst the
multiplicity of circumstances, and the events of the plot, accidents, swervings off course, near arrest by the policeman and by
Jimmy Klein, emphasise his inability to direct his own actions.

Mimi, however, sticks to her objective, telling Augie that 'you can't let your life be decided for you by any old thing that comes up' (p. 319). For Mimi her pregnancy is accidental and therefore reversible. The parallel between it and the accidents that dog Augie's course is made explicit in Mr Magnus's double entendre when he dismisses Augie:

> Something was said about the damage to her car.... Her father said of course it would be fixed. As long as nothing else was broken, this being his delicacy about the hymen.   (p. 329)

Human life, however, is not so easily 'fixed'. Mimi tells Augie that by his illegitimate birth he is himself an accident, and she argues that, given the choice, most people would choose not to be born at all. Augie disagrees:

> I can't complain about having been born ... if you ask me whether obliviousness would have been better for me, then I'd be a liar if I answered 'yes' or even 'maybe', because the facts are against it.   (p. 298)

This particular choice is not open to men. Though Augie's birth may be an accident it is now a fact and must be reckoned with. Once an event, in no way necessary in itself, has taken place it becomes part of the chain of necessity. The individual cannot live as if everything is undefined and reversible, as if he could re-negotiate his existence from scratch. Once an event has occurred the clock cannot be turned back. Choices are made on the basis of preceding accidents which now condition decisions. When Augie sees Mimi in hospital he is unsure 'whether she had outwitted a fate or met it' (p. 330). Mimi acts on behalf of individual freedom. But the problem of freedom is compounded by the shared nature of existence. Despite her belief in free love, the difficulties of Mimi's affair with Frazer have previously forced her to employ tactics of coercion, which quite contradict her beliefs. While she lives in rebellion against social mores, stealing from shops, she none the less shoots a would-be stick-up man in the thigh. Though she cherishes her freedom she denies it to her child. From Mimi, Augie learns that 'everyone sees to it his fate is shared' (p. 247), that the individual is never alone with his freedom but exercises it over others. Human beings cannot escape each other: in the labour ward Augie sees a mother and child, both screaming and bloody, who appear to confirm the slavery of human existence. They are 'like enemies forced to have each other, like figures of a war' (p. 331). In the hospital Mimi is melancholy, despite having gained her ends. She illustrates Kayo's belief that 'everyone has bitterness in his chosen thing' (p. 305). For Kayo, individuals in their actions offer evidence of the bitterness which is always a part of choice. Man is not born endowed with pure freedom, but is always fatally compelled to exercise choice. He cannot choose not to choose, and amidst the accidents of his life each choice is accompanied by the bitter realisation that a choice had to be made. In her particular choice Mimi appears to have exercised her freedom, but it is also her general fate to choose, one way or the other.

The depth and complexity of Bellow's enquiry into the opposition of nature and history is demonstrated in the logic of these events. Simon accepts human nature as fixed and condemns Augie for abetting an abortion. On the basis of a belief in human nature as formed and distinct at birth, abortion is indefensible. The parallel between Mimi's child and George March is also instructive. Mimi fears that her own child may be born similarly handicapped. When Kelly Weintraub tries to discredit Simon by revealing the existence of his idiot brother, Simon freely acknowledges George. The moral balance appears to slide towards Simon, who accepts human nature with all its limitations. Yet when Weintraub catches Augie at the abortionist's Simon rejects Augie on the grounds that 'You must really be like Ma' (p. 323), that his nature is fixed in the feckless mould of his mother. Simon therefore appears inhumane.

If, however, the opposing view is taken: that man is a mere nothing at birth and creates himself in history, Mimi's abortion is less heinous. Yet Mimi depends on Augie for the abortion, and there is the parallel between the child and accidental Augie. If the clock could have been turned back Mimi would have consigned Augie to oblivion. Her freedom therefore depends on the lack of freedom of Mama. Augie therefore falls between two stools. He sees freedom in the contingency of events but does all in his power to annul Mimi's 'accident'. He interrupts the course of nature, only to be condemned by Simon for being fixed in his own. While he attempts to preserve his humanity, caring for Mimi, he finds himself condemned by a time and place, guilty by association.

Augie's following adventures as a labour organiser confirm the complexity of human action, which cannot be easily dichotomised into morally right and wrong, good and evil, natural and historical. On the face of it his job as a union organiser suggests active participation in history in the cause of social freedom and justice, a direct reversal of his strike-breaking activities with Simon. Augie finds himself in the same slum rooms which he had previously entered to hire coal-hikers for Simon, but comments 'no use assuming that I had reversed all and was now entering these flop-house doors from the side of light, formerly that of darkness' (p. 342). While ostensibly working for human progress, by political action to change the course of history, Augie discovers that human nature remains a fixed quantity. In the sudden rush to join the unions he sees not the free decisions of rational beings but a biological urge.

> People were rushing to join up, and it was a haste that
> practically belong to nature, like a change of hives.   (p. 337)

People are drawn to Augie as if by instinct.

> I'd have been found had I been in a steel vault by the feeblest
> signal of possible redress, or as faint a trace as makes the night
> moth scamper ten miles through clueless fields.   (p. 338)

Augie is besieged by all the varieties of humanity but sees in the horde of hash-house workers, old Wobblies, Indians, and Bohunk women, only an unchanged human nature:

> If this collection of people has nothing in common with what
> would have brought up the back of a Xerxes' army or a
> Constantine's, new things have been formed; but what struck
> me in them was a feeling of antiquity.   (p. 338)

The historical situation may have changed from the wars of the Greeks to the conflicts of American labour, but human beings have not. The battle between capital and labour is by no means clear cut. Augie is caught in a case of dual-unionism, as the A.F.L. and C.I.O. war over the allegiance of the workers. When the workers unburden themselves to him he feels that 'true and false light was distributed just about as usual' (p. 340) and when he attempts to organise the maids at the Northumberland hotel he is forced to repress their battle eagerness with legalistic jargon as he explains the correct procedures in their case. The new order merely re-enacts the hypocrisies of the old.

When Augie deserts the labour movement to run to Thea's arms, his motives are not distinct from the union members'. Political actions have been described as natural urges and Augie no longer believes in historical change, but in the constant of human nature. His political activities are enmeshed with his sexual urges. He undertakes to sign up the women, responding to the shapely persuasion of Sophie Geratis, their delegate. When they fail to understand his explanations he seizes the political pretext and

> asked Sophie to come out with me and I would make the position clear. The corridor being empty for the moment, we kissed at once.   (p. 348)

Sophie tells him that he can explain the political position later and promptly goes home with him. The position remains ambiguous. Has Augie been moved towards Sophie out of the excitement of political action? Or is he led to the political struggle by sexual motives? When Thea intervenes between Sophie and Augie, Sophie uses politics to contact him again, as the strike breaks out at the Northumberland. Augie plunges into the hot-house atmosphere of assembled women, dominated by Sophie, 'on top of one of the hogsheads, with her gams wide apart in their black stockings' (p. 359). Augie is glad of the 'nooky protection' of the women, and runs from the Union slugger to Thea, acknowledging the real motive behind his actions. 'I jumped into a taxi and drove to Thea's which had been my real objective of days' (p. 362).

Willed participation in historical change is undermined by unchanging human nature. During his activity Augie visits Einhorn and discovers Arthur's child. For Einhorn this is more evidence of sensuality at work beneath the high ideals of his poet son. No hope now remains that Arthur will save the family fortunes, for his nature has overwhelmed his ideals. After Thea's first visit Augie sleeps and has

> nightmares ... of the jackals trying to get over the walls of Harar, Abyssinia to eat the plague dead – from a book Arthur had left lying around, about one of his favourite poets.   (p. 355)

The book is Enid Starkie's *Arthur Rimbaud in Abyssinia* in which reference is made to the hyenas of the Harar famine of 1891. Augie's physical symptoms at this point are modelled on those of Rimbaud in his last illness, fever, nausea and a swollen knee joint, as a result of which, in Enid Starkie's description

> the circulation of the blood now seemed to be impeded and pain used to rack every nerve from his ankle to his hip.[13]

Rimbaud dragged himself to the office where he lay unable to rise. Augie feels puffy and swollen, and his veins

> seemed slowed up with lead. ... I dragged myself to the office ... I felt the toil of all my processes, down to the arteries of the feet ... and I prayed I wouldn't have to get up.   (p. 355)

Augie is suffering, of course, not from physical disease, but from Thea's visit, engendering a hypersensitive state of dizziness, pleasure-pain and engorgement. The reference to Rimbaud underlines the disjunction between high ideals and the sensual limitation to which they are subject. The belief that man progresses by acting within history is checked by the paralysis of human nature which is always one. As Augie reclines in his office, events around him increase their speed but he can no longer keep up:

> In my harassed inability to keep up, it was like a double-quick-time stamping or dancing; angry grim waltz in which the clutched partners were out to wear one another down.   (p. 355)

Human beings move, history whirls them along; but they go nowhere and are merely drawn into a dance of death. While men may believe that they make history from idealistic motives as poets or legislators of mankind, they are in fact moved by their human and physical nature, to which final motivation belongs. As he runs to Thea Augie withdraws from participation in history, refusing to attempt to impose his will on events:

> I couldn't feel the importance of the cause much, or that it would benefit anyone for me to fight on in it. ... I was with Thea. It wasn't even in my power to be elsewhere.   (p. 363)

When Augie departs with Thea for Mexico he leaves behind him the world of dateable historical events to enter a realm of nature gods, a world which appears curiously time-free. From the beginning Thea and Augie deliberately cast off the past. Thea brushes aside Augie's account of his union job because 'The reality was now' (p. 364). Living always temporarily, out of boxes and suitcases, squandering money on trifles which are immediately lost, Thea never saves money for a rainy day, but spends carelessly what she has, letting the future take care of itself, vague about her past, and dismissing Augie's as unimportant. Augie responds to Thea from a desire to escape the conditions of Chicago. Events have amply demonstrated the lack of freedom he enjoys there and he therefore decides to escape. 'Why hunt for still more ways to lose liberty?' (p. 370). In love with Thea, Augie lives in a suspended perfect moment feeling that he sees the world with a new freshness, an American sense of wonder:

> Some things I have an ability to see without feeling much previous history, almost like birds or dogs that have no human condition but are always living in the same age.   (p. 382)

Timelessness and nature are yoked together in Augie's mind; in Mexico Bellow explores one possible escape from history, an escape characterised by Karl Jaspers as follows:

> We overstep history by addressing ourselves to nature. Face to face with the ocean, in the mountains, in the tempest . . . we may experience a feeling of liberation. A homecoming into unconscious life, a still deeper homecoming into the clarity of the inanimate elements can sweep us along into stillness, into exultation, into painless unity. But all this is a deception . . . If we really find sanctuary there we have run away from men and from ourselves.[14]

Augie's adventures in Mexico make much of the clarity of inanimate nature. Mexico is a world almost without seasonal variations, a world of essences in which Augie contacts nature in the shape of Thea's eagle. In love with Thea Augie experiences painless unity, almost as if he had found his Platonic other half. 'It seemed as if an exchange or transfer had happened of us both into still another person who hadn't existed before' (p. 364). Making love in the great outdoors Augie feels at one with nature, his eyes resting on clouds, birds and trees, feeling 'released' (p. 386). The complications and rapid change of Chicago appear to have been left behind.

Augie's eagle training brings to the forefront the role of nature. As eagle-trainer, Augie is associated with the noblest image of natural being, the king of birds, soaring above the limitations of lesser animals. In the eagle Augie sees a proud free nature which dominates from on high, and has been worshipped through the ages as a transcendent being. When Augie describes Caligula he mentions Lermontov's poem 'The Eagle', the eagle of money, the eagle of Jupiter and Caesar, Colonel Julian the Black Eagle of Harlem, and of course the eagle knights of the Aztecs. The implication is that in changing historical circumstances the eagle imposes worship, that despite the contingency of history nature remains constant and to be worshipped. In Augie's adventures with Caligula, however, Bellow forcibly reminds the reader that 'nature' is a term with a history of its own, that it too changes. When Augie first introduces the subject of the eagle, he draws attention to the real eagle-trainers of recent times:

> She had gotten the idea for this hunt from reading articles by Dan and Jule Mannix, who actually had gone to Taxco some years before with a trained bald eagle and used the bird to catch iguanas. (p. 373)

The facts of the Mannixes' trip[15] obviously form Bellow's source, not only for details of how to train an eagle, its food and habits, but also in such points as the Mannixes' horse, also a veteran of various wars, the children who greet the eagle with cries of 'Es un aguila', the age of the eagle, also a haggard, the couple's subsidiary snake-catching, and the fact that the Mannix eagle also met with an iguana that fought back, ending its hunting career. Jule Mannix's comment on first seeing their eagle was,

> I wonder if she's got any hunting instinct ... Lots of times an eagle that's been caged up loses all her spirit. It would be rough if we took this bird right down to Mexico and then found that she wouldn't hunt.[16]

This is of course precisely what does happen with Caligula, who refuses to conform to Thea's idea of natural instinct. After Caligula's first failure, Augie defends him to Moulton, 'How's one eagle different from another? They're all more or less the same' (p. 417). Thea insists that Caligula is 'supposed to have instincts' (p. 406) and can't believe that he is a coward. 'She believed fierce nature shouldn't be like that' (p. 406). When he fails a second time she disowns him because 'it was hard to take this from wild nature, that there should be humanity mixed with it' (p. 414). Yet Thea is of course responsible for the eagle's cowardice: she has domesticated him and he therefore no longer acts the part expected. If nature is a constant, it can be so only because it is entirely independent of man. If nature can be trained, changed to fit man's assumptions, it is no longer a constant and cannot support the beliefs man constructs upon it. Before Augie falls from Bizcocho he feels triumph in his ability to hunt with a living animal, 'a living creature you had known how to teach because you'd inferred that all intelligences ... were essentially the same' (p. 420). But a second creature is present here. Bizcocho, old and exhausted by the role he has played in history, in wars and revolutions, stumbles and lets Augie down. As he lies on the ground Augie wryly comments that 'It takes some of us a long time to find out what the price is of being in nature' (p. 421). Nature is not a fixed quantity, an essence, but as open to change and decay as man, and as much a part of history as he is. The point has been made by Ortega, who argues that 'nature' is a concept which has undergone radical change from its initial meaning as the law of phenomena, and concludes:

What then, down the long evolution has remained constant in nature? Nature is a transitory interpretation that man has given to what he finds around him in life.[17]

As for nature as an escape into unconscious life, Caligula disproves his mentor's ideas. Thea's training of the eagle relies on the hooding of its eyes, an image, in the novel, of lack of consciousness. When Augie feels Caligula's ferocious gaze he wonders why

awful despotism belonged to the eyes? Why, Cain was cursed between them so he would never be unaware of his look in the view of other men. .... Chiefs and tyrants of the public give no relief from self-consciousness. Vanity is the same thing in

private, and in any kind of oppression you are a subject and
can't forget yourself.   (p. 391)

Once Caligula shares their quarters Augie's and Thea's perfect
union is interrupted; Augie finds that his presence interferes with
their love-making and that he is almost a castrating force. Inter-
estingly Bellow has changed the sex of the Mannix eagle: Caligula
is emphatically male. When Augie first sees him he feels 'a
streaming on my legs as if I had wet myself' (p. 386) and when he
is alone in the toilet with the eagle he feels vivid terror. 'I won't
attempt to play down my fear when I had to take him into the
toilet for the first time. I held him as far off as I had the strength to
do' (p. 391). Nature unmans Augie, making him less than human
rather than allowing him to achieve a state of perfect unity in
unconscious life. Unconsciousness, when it comes, comes parodically from a kick of Bizcocho's foot.

Once the experiment with Caligula has failed Augie finds
himself once again in a realm of chance. The former image of
nature as constant and free is replaced by that of nature as falsity,
as survival by any means. Augie becomes a master poker-player,
excelling at bluff, concealing himself behind a face of innocence,
just as 'nature made us live and do as worms and beetles do, to
escape the ichneumon fly and swindle other enemies by mimicry'
(p. 429). Snake-nature replaces eagle-nature and Augie's early
hopes collapse. In his convalescence Augie reads a book of
Utopian writers, More, Campanella, Saint Simon, but comments
'In those utopias set up by hopes and art, how could you overlook
the part of nature' (p. 419). Similarly Augie's perfect love founders on the rocks of his dissembling nature and his self-
consciousness. Augie responds to Stella's appeal for help out of his
own need for a flattering self-image. Thea attacks him for this
desire to look good in the eyes of others. 'By a little flattery anyone
can get what he wants from you' (p. 450). Augie's escape with
Stella is described in terms of the eagle's soaring flight. 'We rose
above the town', 'flying up the mountain' (p. 450). On the
unfamiliar road, however Augie takes a false turn and ends up on
the edge of a precipice. Looking down he is unsure whether he can
see human lights or the stars of the southern heaven, and he
comments 'even to say "southern heaven" is to try to familiarize
terrific convulsions of fire in the million light-year distances'
(p. 452). In attempting to rise above the ordinary complication of

life the individual risks a fall into the less than human. Isolated in
a world which is unfamiliar to him, man tries to familiarise it, to
make it conform to his own views. Regretfully Augie realises that
all human constructions are mere fabrications to conceal the alien
strangeness of the world of nature. 'Everyone tries to create a
world he can live in, and what he can't use he often can't see. But
the real world is already created' (p. 440).

To invent a world is also to falsify, and this invention extends
also to love. When Augie accuses Thea of being 'fantastic' in her
ideas she argues that familiar ways are ways of deception. 'I only
know these strange ways of doing something. Instead of sticking
to the ordinary way and doing something false' (p. 459). She is
horrified to learn that Augie finds her bizarre. As love depends
upon the need for one's self-image to be flattered and confirmed,
so it depends upon a suspension of disbelief in the invented world
of the lover. It is merely one more organising fiction, an attempt to
co-opt another to one's own fabrication, 'each in his own way
trying to recruit other people to play a supporting role and sustain
him in his make-believe' (p. 465). The tale enacts Ortega's belief
that each man is a novelist, creating a self to meet the circumstances of the world, modifying that self as circumstances alter,
having an existence rather than an essence. Ortega writes:

> Man is impossible without imagination, without the capacity to
> invent for himself a conception of life, to 'ideate' the character
> he is going to be. Whether he be original or a plagiarist, man is
> the novelist of himself.[18]

Increasingly the Mexican adventures draw attention to this
capacity of man. Augie is surrounded by writers. When he meets
Sylvester he rehearses various stories to account for his presence
in Mexico. Thea rejects Augie as a liar and teller of stories. Augie
attempts to tell his life-story to Iggie who shows little sympathy.
When Augie tells it all over again to the Cossack, the latter merely
counters with his own story and that of an uncle, forcing Augie to
recognise that 'he too had a life' (p. 476). Man is not alone amidst
inanimate things but lives among other people, and as novelist of
himself must meet with other fabricators. Life becomes reducible
to a series of fictions – love, nature, history, the self – all false.
Despairingly Augie comments 'That's the struggle of humanity,
to recruit others to your version of what's real. Then even the

flowers and the moss on the stones become the moss and flowers of a version' (p. 466).

Augie's growing cynicism is reflected in his encounter with Trotsky. The last historical personage to appear in the novel, Trotsky illustrates and sums up the lesson Augie has learned. When he first sees Trotsky, the man described by Lenin after their first meeting as an eagle[19] Augie feels a sense 'of navigation by the great stars, of the highest considerations, of being fit to speak the most important human words and universal terms' (p. 435). Impressed by Trotsky's persistence at the 'highest things' Augie begs Sylvester to introduce him. When he is later offered a secret mission for Trotsky, after the trip with Stella, Augie has misgivings. He is attracted to the role of rescuer but has reservations as a result of his escapade with Stella.

> Naturally I wanted to be of help, and rescue and peril attracted me. But I wasn't up to it at all, going up and down the mountains of Mexico through the bazaar of red nature and dizzy with deaths and noises.... Was I so flattered by the chance to be with this giant historical personality. (p. 482)

He and Stella have also gone up and down the mountains as a result of Stella's flattery, speeding dangerously and finally saying farewell in a Mexican bazaar surrounded by bloody carcasses. Augie has already soared, eagle-like, and fallen. He is therefore wary of throwing in his lot once more with history, for the dangers of both history and nature have been amply demonstrated in the small sphere of his own life. Belief in high ideals and soaring aspiration leads inexorably to a fall. In Trotsky Augie sees only the power of death:

> Out in Russia was his enemy ... he'd kill him. Death discredits. Survival is the whole success. The voice of the dead goes away. There isn't any memory. The power that's established fills the earth and destiny is whatever survives. (p. 482)

Both 'history' and 'nature' are equally subject to change and decay. In the historical world of Chicago Augie learned only the immutability of human nature. Paradoxically, in Mexico, a world of essences, he learns the converse: that nature is itself a human fabrication. All certainties collapse, and Augie is faced with the possibility that there are no truths upon which he can rely, only transitory interpretations. Nature is a transitory concept, changing in accordance with the historical situation of man. History is interpretive, and in narrating the story of his life the individual distorts events in order to fabricate a pleasing self-image. From historicism to relativism is an easy transition. If man is only historical, an existence rather than an essence, all truths become entirely relative to his own position in time, and all his activities mere organising fictions.

After Mexico the discernible facts of history are left behind, and Augie becomes increasingly enmeshed in a series of fictions. The reader becomes aware of the shaping activity of writing, rather than reading the novel as an unmediated record of experience. At the beginning Augie eclipses this awareness in the reader, arguing that he will not suppress or shape, that his memories will flood out unobstructed by any attempt to arrange them in an artistic form. After Mexico, however, history gives way to story and the value-free autobiographical genre is replaced by parable, exemplum and fable, by stories which are narrated entirely to carry forward the narrator's point of view. Events are narrated at second hand, as Augie becomes increasingly the audience to the stories of others. The Cossack tells the tale of his uncle to illustrate the horrors of life. Clem describes the children smelling imaginary flowers to argue that all experience is subjective. Basteshaw tells of his aunt's sleeping sickness, of the death of his cousin Lee, of the German goldsmith whose works were melted down for bullion. Mintouchian treats Augie to a series of cautionary tales on the general theme of marriage. The entire ship's company of the Sam McManus pour out anecdotes, poems and personal histories to Augie, though with one exception only a line or so of these tales is given in the text. Each story is related in skeletal form, with no concessions to realism, setting or character, governed only by fabulative design. As Augie discovers the extent to which other people create their own versions of the world, fabrications to which they attempt to recruit him, so his opposition grows and the stories grow more and more obviously fictive. Implicitly, therefore, the status of the novel as enquiry into truth is questioned. In the final adventures of Augie March the action centres on the opposition of nature and history but approaches it from a consideration of man's interpretive and ideological propensities. Ortega's philosophy is again the point of departure, but is now subjected to a rigorous evaluation, and the general attention paid to human inventions leads inexorably to the question of novelistic form.

In Chicago Augie moves amidst ideas, versions and inventions. He is employed by Robey, an amateur historian who is writing a 'history of human happiness from the standpoint of the rich' (p. 507). Robey is beset by ideas and overburdened by interpretive schemes. Too many perspectives on the past are open to him, and his project is a mish-mash of different historical interpretations which fail to cohere into any meaningful synthesis. Beginning from an interest in Great Men, Robey deviates into an analysis of the failures of the bourgeoisie, assigns Augie to read Weber, Tawney and Marx, drops that scheme in favour of a pamphlet condemning philanthropic millionaires, diverts Augie towards Renaissance humanism, and introduces Christ, Aristotle and the French Revolution along the way. His enquiries merely confuse him.

'It's too much for me. I need help.... I discovered much too m-much' (p. 508) he stammers. Augie firmly rejects this burdensome activity, arguing that 'I never could have got through all those Greeks and Fathers and histories of Rome and the Eastern Empire and whatnot in years' (pp. 512–13). As Augie tells Arthur, 'My personal preference was for useful thoughts. I mean thoughts that answered questions that moved you' (p. 505). At this point Augie is identified explicitly with Ortega, for one of the planks of Ortega's ratio-vitalistic philosophy is the contention that man must beware of all rationalistic tendencies to overpopulate the world with abstract ideas and principles. Ortega maintains that ideas must not be deprived of their vital basis, which is that they are evolved to answer the needs of the individual. For Ortega man is not born to illustrate the principles of history, nor to dedicate himself to intellectual pursuits, but rather to use thought to solve his immediate problems. 'We do not live to think but we think in order that we may succeed in surviving.'[20] Around him, twentieth-century man finds a host of conflicting ideas, interpretations and thoughts, a capitalism of culture which leads to its own devaluation and Crash. For Ortega the solution to this cultural overload lies in renouncing the belief that reason is paramount, and rather in regarding ideas as the tools of man, practical aids to life. Man inherits from the past both ideas and material goods, but must, in Ortega's view, beware of enslavement by either. Robey's project begins from a consideration of the role of material plenty in human history and is financed by Robey's own millionaire inheritance. Ortega comments on material plenty as follows:

> There might be a deceptive tendency to believe that a life born into a world of plenty should be better, more really a life, than one which consists in a struggle against scarcity.[21]

Such is not the case, however, for

> The aristocrat inherits ... conditions of life which he has not created and which therefore are not produced in organic union with his personal individual existence ... He has to live as an heir, that is to say, he has to wear the trappings of another existence ... He is condemned to represent the other man.[21]

Secondhand ideas, inherited from the past, and the products of these ideas in the shape of material things, may overwhelm the individual. Robey's concern with gay prosperity does not prevent him from offering Augie mouldy ham; or from quibbling over his wage. He postures as a Renaissance humanist but is discovered in his long robe spraying roaches with bloodlust and fury. His assumed guise of Elizabethan courtier exposes him to the ridicule of cheap whores. His concern with 'practical examples of the highest happiness' (p. 510) has little effect on his own misery. Inherited ideas are of little assistance to Robey.

The dominance of things, the technological products of ideas, is further illustrated in events in Chicago. When Augie returns to his home town, friends and family demand that he settle down, choose a path in life, and assume an occupation. Augie resists. He is, he maintains, a man, with a fate rather than a function. In conversation with Clem, he refuses to accept the limited role offered by each of his mentors. Augie ascribes their desire to pigeonhole him to the specialisation of labour. 'In the world of today your individual man has to be willing to illustrate a more and more narrow and restricted point of existence. And I am not a specialist (p. 503). Augie feels the sinister domination of material things over man, and his disquietude expresses itself in the odd dreams he has. In the first Augie finds in his house three grand pianos. 'This seemed downright sinister' (p. 502). In his dream he pretends that it is quite normal to possess three pianos and therefore feels like 'a terrible faker'. Things appear to be taking over, forcing men into false roles. In the second dream, Augie dreams that his children have been born, one a bug, the other a calf, and that his wife has hidden them behind a piano. When Augie looks behind the piano he finds only Mama. Earlier Augie had visited Mama and had been struck by the material luxury of her surroundings, and by the way in which she was oppressed by the need 'to live up to what Simon and Charlotte were doing for her' (p. 487). At Simon's house, he found Mrs Magnus hiding in the dark, banished by Simon for her refusal to dress up to his station in life. The dreams conflate these two experiences to suggest the extent to which the human being has become peripheral to the material advance of society, that things govern man and deform him. Augie makes this point to Kayo:

> In the world of nature you can trust, but in the world of artifacts you must beware. . . . We live under shadow, with acts of faith in functioning of inventions . . . Things done by man which over-shadow us. (p. 519)

As personal relations have become merely the adoption of the one into the story of the other, as history has become purely interpretive, so ideas and their byproducts dominate man. In each pared-down fable in this part of the novel characters are chosen merely to illustrate a point of view, an idea – just as Mama and Mrs Magnus must illustrate Simon's wealth.

Renée, Simon's mistress, is described as a similar illustration. Not so much a person, more a work of art, Renée has carefully constructed herself by artifice. Augie is struck by her golden 'tone' make-up, her lips 'drawn' to a point, her padded out hair and the gold colour 'sprinkled' and 'rubbed' onto her surface. Thus endowed, Renée assumes a place in the long line of 'femmes galantes', from the priestesses of Attis to the courtesans of later years. For Augie, however, this is only an assumed role. Renée 'didn't bear this gold freight with the fullest confidence. . . . This was what Renée was supposed to be, and in my opinion she wasn't entirely' (pp. 533–4). Renée is burdened by a historical weight, illustrating a role which she imitates from history. Indeed, she is above all else an imitator, constantly checking Charlotte's activities to demand the same clothes, doctor, car and holidays as

Charlotte. Far from being liberated from care by Renée Simon finds himself forced into continual thought. 'What poisoned his life... was the slavery of constant thought and arrangement-making' (pp. 538–9). While Renée checks up on Charlotte, Simon checks up on Renée, and Charlotte is obsessed with Simon. Augie describes her as 'somebody wrestling a bear for dear life, and with forehead lost against the grizzly pelt, figuring anyway what to do next Sunday, whom to invite for dinner and how to fix the table' (p. 538). Allegiance to ideas continues beyond their practical application. In thought man can lose himself, pursuing a train of ideas which may be completely irrelevant to his real situation, acting a role inherited from the past which no longer serves a purpose in the present.

Augie, however, attempts to escape this relentless pressure of ideas. It is at this point in the novel that he expounds his vision of the 'axial lines' according to which man has his existence. Superficially the vision appears to suggest a mystic intuition of transcendent realities. Arguably, however, it is better understood in relation to Ortega's overriding conception of man as a historical being, dwelling in the contingency of the historical process, rather than being the illustration of a divine principle. In the first place Augie explains his feeling for the axial lines as a rejection of the dominance of ideas, and as a re-establishment of the primacy of the individual self. Augie accepts that he has to solve his problems in time, and that he cannot first master all explanations in order to think out a complete programme for life. The practical application of ideas is paramount:

> Since I've been working for Robey I have reached the conclusion that I couldn't utilize even ten per cent of what I already knew.... Anything that just adds information that you can't use is plain dangerous. Anyway, there's too much of everything of this kind, that's come home to me, too much history and culture to keep track of.   (p. 525)

Time is man's element and he has to work within it, not prepare interminably for such action by contemplating its past works, or escape altogether into the transcendent. When Clem asks Augie, 'What are you trying to prove?' (p. 526), Augie answers 'not a thing'. He is not out to illustrate a point but to live his life. Augie explicitly rejects the idea, in his comment, 'I don't want to be representative or exemplary or head of my generation or any model of manhood' (p. 526). Augie does not entirely reject thought, but establishes his right to use it to his own purposes. In his view history is not the working out of ideas with man in their train, whether those ideas are divine providence, Hegel's cunning of reason or economic laws. Man may appear to be the victim of history, but with all his limitations the individual possesses a unique self, with its own priorities. In describing Augie's intuition as involving 'axial lines' Bellow refers to Ortega. Ortega describes the hierarchy of man's activities and interests as follows:

> These actions and interests may be represented by a series of concentric circles whose radii measure the dynamic distances from the axis of human life where the supreme desires are operating.[22]

For Ortega this 'axis of enthusiasm' is the backbone of the individual, who stands at the centre of life and dominates his activities by his ideas, rather than being their servant. This dominance is individual, not the power of some World Historical Individual living as the embodiment of an idea. Augie stresses the finite and limited quality of the individual.

> At any time life can come together again and man be regenerated, and doesn't have to be a god or public servant like Osiris who gets torn apart annually for the sake of the common prosperity, but the man himself, finite and taped as he is, can still come where the axial lines are.   (p. 524)

The individual is not a god, not an illustration of, or sacrifice to, divine principles but an independent entity with its own existence.

Ironically, Augie's determination to escape the schemes of others and remain true to himself is immediately tested. War breaks out and Augie unceremoniously abandons his projects to plunge into action. This is not a limiting comment on the vision of the axial lines, but underlines the individual's inescapably historical existence. Screaming his hatred of the enemy, speechifying to his friends, Augie is completely beside himself. Writing about the war, Ortega drew attention to the precariousness of the individual, holding on only with the greatest difficulty to his own concerns:

Almost all the world is in tumult, is beside itself, and when man is beside himself he loses his most essential attribute: the possibility of meditating or withdrawing into himself.[23]

For Ortega the self is not a fixed entity but a process of becoming, a risky enterprise, in which at any point man may regress:

Each of us is always in peril of not being the unique and untransferable self which he is. The majority of men perpetually betray this self which is waiting to be; and to tell the whole truth our personal individuality is a personage which is never completely realised, a stimulating Utopia, a secret legend, which each of us guards in the bottom of his heart. It is thoroughly comprehensible that Pindar resumed his heroic ethics in the well-known imperative 'Become what you are'.[24]

Augie adopts Pindar's phrase in his conversation with Mintouchian, but he adds a moral rider.

I have always tried to become what I am. But it's a frightening thing. Because what if what I am by nature isn't good enough?
                                                                    (p. 559)

Where Ortega makes his assumptions on a metaphysical, non-ethical ground, Bellow shifts the analysis onto the moral.

How far Bellow ultimately rejects the amoral, fabricating aspect of Ortega's vision of man as change and movement, as a self which is independent of moral imperatives is made clear in Augie's shipwreck with Basteshaw. Ortega argues that life is uncertainty, danger and change, and that ideas are evolved in direct reaction to the immediate challenge of man's circumstances. He develops this point by a repeated metaphor, shipwreck:

Life is, in itself and forever, shipwreck. To be shipwrecked is not to drown. The poor human being, feeling himself sinking into the abyss, moves his arms to keep afloat. This movement of the arms which is his reaction against his own destruction is culture – a swimming stroke. When culture is no more than this it fulfils its function and the human being rises above its own abyss. But ten centuries of cultural continuity brings with it, among many advantages, the great disadvantage, that man believes himself safe, loses the feeling of shipwreck and his culture proceeds to burden itself with parasitic and lymphatic matter ... Consciousness of shipwreck, being the truth of life, constitutes salvation. Hence I no longer believe in any ideas except the ideas of shipwrecked men.[25]

Cunningly Bellow dramatises Ortega's metaphor in order to question his fundamental assumptions. In Ortega's view the individual is committed only to the duty to follow his own vital imperatives, his own course of life. Bellow presents two individuals, each shipwrecked, and centres the action on their debate over which course to set. Basteshaw believes that he is setting course for the Canaries, there to be interned for the duration of the war, acting on his own vital imperative, the need to continue his experiments with protoplasm. Augie argues that 'I already have a course of life' (p. 587) and makes strenuous efforts to be rescued by other ships. Basteshaw's ideas as a shipwrecked man are based on a false certainty: he has misread the charts and his calculations would condemn them both to a slow death in the African sea, as they drift beyond the Canaries. Basteshaw's experiments with protoplasm are designed to change nature and therefore the course of history. By his experiments he intends to make, in his own words, 'a historic contribution to the happiness of mankind. ... Injustice will go, and slavery, bloodshed, cruelty. They will belong to the past' (p. 586). Augie, however rejects the belief that nature can be altered, and a new course set for humanity. Horrified to discover that some of Basteshaw's culture is now floating free he exclaims 'Damn you guys, you don't care how you fiddle with nature!' (p. 582). While Basteshaw insists that his new biological culture will benefit humanity Augie contends that 'No one will be a poet or saint because you fool with him ... I've had trouble enough becoming what I already am, by nature' (p. 587). The logic of events supports Augie in his view of man as unchanging nature, equipped with a moral sense which he can exercise to his own betterment, rather than merely an intellect. As saviour of humanity Basteshaw's first action is to bludgeon Augie over the head with an oar. While he sees his research as essential to human survival he comes close to killing both Augie and himself. Basteshaw's idea as a shipwrecked man is vested in culture, but a culture of living cells which may evolve with horrendous results.

The protoplasm offers a living image of man-as-history, creating himself anew, a nothing developing in time, and also an image of a culture reacting to immediate circumstances without moral sense or past. Basteshaw believes that he can withdraw from the immediate struggles of time (the war) to solve all history's problems. Time and tide wait for no man however, and Basteshaw's boat is carrying him to extinction.

Augie, on the other hand argues from a belief that human nature is a constant and that man therefore shares with others a common humanity. He is horrified by Basteshaw's treatment of his father, and his cousin Lee, whose love for him Basteshaw ascribes to the action of the increased temperatures of pulmonary phthisis on the erogenous zones. Despite his dislike, Augie determines to make every effort to coexist with Basteshaw, asserting the oneness of human nature. 'It's enough like yours, this soul, as one lion is pretty nearly all the lions' (p. 583). When Basteshaw succumbs to a fever, Augie cares for him, rather than murdering him, as he is tempted to do. In doing this he refers to a historical precedent. 'I sat up with him all night. Like Henry Ware of the Kentucky border and the great chief of the Ohio, Timmendiquas. He might have stabbed Timmendiquas but he let him go' (p. 590). Augie and Henry Ware are comparable beings despite their different historical existences because they share a common human nature. The question of man-as-nature, or man-as-history has therefore turned its full epistemological circle. Man is historical, existing in the flux and change of time. Yet all historical narrative rests on one postulate: the eternal identity of human nature. It is impossible to comprehend men's actions at all unless it is assumed in the beginning that their moral and physical beings have been at all times what they are today. If nature has a history, history itself has a nature, human nature, which allows man to comprehend it. Culture must evolve in answer to historical problems. Yet culture must begin from a basis of human nature; it cannot be generated in a void. The shipwreck therefore represents Bellow's final evaluation of the Ortegan idea, accepting man's historical status while refusing to discount the moral imperatives which are a part of his nature.

The relevance of culture to man's situation in time also conditions Bellow's view of the novel, and forms the basis of his literary manifesto. In the boat Basteshaw describes a book by Ghiberti which told of a German goldsmith whose works were melted down for bullion. To Basteshaw this illustrates the continual flux of history. 'That's what they mean by the ruins of time' (p. 578). After the war Augie finds himself in Florence and, remembering Basteshaw's story, goes to visit Ghiberti's doors at the Baptistery. These doors are not selected at random by Bellow, but deliberately chosen to extend the questioning of the Ortegan idea into the realm of literary form. In *Notes on the Novel* Ortega introduces the doors as an analogy to the formal, timefree aesthetic in art which he is defending. Contrasting 'an art of figures' to 'an art of adventures' Ortega argues that 'in our time the novel of high style must turn from the latter to the former',[26] a movement which is, of course, entirely negated in the picaresque *Adventures* of Augie March. Ortega argues that form is all. 'The material it is made of does not hallow a statue. A work of art lives on its form not on its material.'[27] – a view which has been somewhat discredited by being placed in the mouth of the sinister Basteshaw, describing the goldsmith. For Ortega, the historical and material quality of art must be reduced to a minimum, so that the novelist can work entirely within his own imagination. It is this necessity which, in his opinion, complicates the writing of historical novels, which involve the clash of two horizons, the historically correct, and the imaginary, a clash which he describes as follows:

> The aspiration that the imagined cosmos shall at the same time be historically correct leads to a perpetual clash between two different horizons ... Any attempt to merge the two worlds only leads to their mutual annihilation.[28]

In Bellow's novel however, historical and imaginary events are juxtaposed to the detriment of neither, producing a novel which is a full enquiry into the complexity of their interaction. Ortega concludes his argument in favour of a tightly organised formal novel of figures, governed by the artist's own imaginary constructions, and he concludes:

> Let all novelists look at the doors of the Florentine baptistery wrought by Lorenzo Ghiberti! In a series of small squares they show the whole Creation ... The sculptor was concerned with nothing but to model all those forms one after another.... Similarly a novelist must be inspired above all by a wonderful enthusiasm to tell a tale and to invent men and women and

conversations and passions ... In simpler words a novelist while he writes his novel must care more about his imaginary world than about any other possible world.[29]

This is not how Augie reacts to the Baptistery doors however, which to him are not artistic forms but a record of human history, recounting 'the entire history of humankind' (p. 595). Bellow rejects the notion that the novel must concentrate entirely on the imaginary and the ahistorical. If all men are novelists of themselves, all art is amoral construction and fabrication, man's only hope is to maintain an awareness of shared human nature at the centre of the enterprise. Otherwise the novel loses its moral power, and the individual becomes entirely solipsistic in a world in which he may only figure as the illustration of a preconceived role. Bellow's novel describes the relentless tendency of man to construct himself, from himself, by thought, but argues that the results are dehumanising. He espouses then, a novel of adventures, a novel in which the historical and the imaginary exist side by side, a novel which is free-wheeling, loosely organised, and tied to time. If culture saves, it does so by retaining its relevance to human beings, and this implies a historical dimension. Art cannot begin again, afresh, as Basteshaw's vital culture does, generating new forms. Such forms without humanity would be meaningless and sinister. Art demands a temporal dimension.

The form of Bellow's novel therefore answers Ortega's objections, by keeping more than one horizon always in view, by not being over-formed, nor merely picaresque. The manner in which Bellow narrates Augie's adventures, freestyle, moving between historical events and imaginary characters, therefore enacts its purpose. Bellow contends that the novel must remain true to life, which involves construction and narration, thought and culture, but which is lived by human beings who are of paramount importance. While the novel is studded with ideas, with fictions and philosophic discourses, the action of the novel establishes the primacy of the human being, grappling with the changes of time. In time the individual must act. In narrating his actions however he must guard against the illusion that his history is governed by a rationale, a scheme. From formal, timefree art Bellow returns the novel to a renewed concern with the profoundest problems of humanity.

At the axis of both history and nature stands the individual self.

When Augie visits the Baptistery he is accosted by an old lady, bearing visible witness to the ravages of time. The season is wintry, horses are shivering from the wind, people huddled in doorways. The old lady is a victim of history, a Piedmontese aristocrat reduced by the war to penury, but also a victim of the natural process of ageing. The terms of the description emphasise the inevitable decline of human vitality through time, a process human beings share with animal nature. Her face is 'covered by mange spots ... The fur of her coat was used up and the bald hide broken and crust-like' (p. 596). When Augie rejects her advances the old lady cries angrily 'This is happening to *me!*' (p. 597). Brusque as Augie's rejection then is, he later concedes that the old lady 'was right too, and there always is a me it happens to' (p. 597). The phrase is significant. In 'The Writer as Moralist' Bellow lamented the passing of an older form of novel, dependent upon a fuller conception of self.

> There was a carefree time in the history of the novel when the writer had nothing to do but to tell us what had happened. Experience in itself then pleased us, the description of experience was self-justifying. But nothing so simple now seems acceptable. It is the self, the person to whom things happen, who is perhaps not acceptable to the difficult and fastidious modern consciousness.[30]

In her anger the old lady is incensed that she is no longer special, a person with a famous name and an individual identity, but lumped in with the other people who keep approaching Augie. 'I am not other people' she cries (p. 597). Augie responds to her rebellion in the following terms:

> Death is going to take the boundaries away from us, that we should no more be persons. That's what death is about. When that is what life also wants to be about, how can you feel except rebellious. (p. 597)

For Bellow the idea that the individual is only a cipher, a mere happening, a nothing which lacks definition is untenable. In the juxtaposition of the old lady and the figures of the doors, Bellow insists that human beings are not merely the creatures of history who can be artfully inscribed as timefree illustrations of its processes, but individuals with an innate sense of self, subject to nature, but in rebellion also against it. In his ironic rhetoric Augie adopts the viewpoint of the universal historian as he observes the old lady.

> O destroying laws! What was the matter, hadn't this thing taken long enough . . . ? What was the matter that she was still as if in the first pain of a great fall. (p. 597)

To the individual, however, the long vista of history, with its universalising implications, provides little comfort. The observation of history in the making, the deduction of laws therefrom, does not make the facts of life and death any easier to bear. Man must therefore eschew the tendency to take away the boundaries from the self, to see the self as formless and existential, for in doing so he collaborates with death.

In the final scene of the novel this sovereign self reasserts its own right to exist. Augie sets out for Bruges passing through a landscape which suggests the inexorable triumph of alien nature over man's historical efforts. The fields he crosses are those of the Hundred Years War where English corpses lay, where 'wolves and crows had cleaned up' (p. 616). The 'wolf-grey' sea breaks on the coast beside the ruins of Dunkirk, 'like eternity opening up right beside destructions of the modern world' (p. 617). When his car breaks down, however, in the last accident of the novel, Augie and Jacqueline, his maid, set off singing and laughing across the desolate landscape. Faced with Jacqueline's irrepressible vitality Augie is no longer certain that nature has the last laugh on man.

> What's so laughable, that a Jacqueline, for instance, as hard used as that by rough forces, will still refuse to lead a disappointed life? Or is the laugh at nature – including eternity – that it thinks it can win over us and the power of hope? . . . But that probably is the joke, on one or the other, and laughing is an enigma that includes both. (p. 617)

The opposition of nature and history is an epistemological circle, an insoluble enigma, but at its axis stands the sovereign human self. Augie determines to be a 'Columbus of those near-at-hand' (p. 617), a discoverer of the humanity around him. Near at hand to Augie stands Jacqueline, an image of his own former self. Like

Augie Jacqueline has an 'adventurous spirit' (p. 615), is vital and comic, has suffered blows but is not without hope. Like the former Augie she sees in her lover 'some great ideal' (p. 615) and dreams of visiting Mexico. As Augie emerges into the present of the novel's closure he is in the company of another self, strongly akin to his own. The enigma of nature and history is therefore subordinate to the self at its axis, a self which shares its essential nature with all human beings. Augie closes his account with a reference to another historical figure – Columbus. 'Columbus too thought he was a flop, probably, when they sent him back in chains. Which didn't prove there was no America' (p. 617). In his own individual experience in time the individual may see only defeat and failure. But the longer vistas of human history reveal otherwise. As he sets off across the *terra incognita* which surrounds him Augie rests his case on the common experience of all human beings. Rather than being determined by time, Augie realises that time is not a limiting condition on man's existence, but the revelation of a shared humanity.

The Adventures of Augie March is a sprawling episodic novel, in which the logic of events is by no means clearcut. As this analysis demonstrates, however, its weltering multiplicity is conditioned by its central preoccupations. Encyclopaedic in scope, it engages fully, for the first time in Bellow's writings, with the problem of history and its relation to individual experience, a problem which is to be the principal concern of all Bellow's major novels. The form of the novel enacts its fundamental thesis, that the individual exists within a changing historical world but can, none the less, retain humanity. In the double quality of the first person narration, in the eclectic range of ideas, in the succession of different tales and varied worlds, in the provisional nature of its closure, the novel appears unformed, a loose and baggy monster in which no authoritative point of view dominates. Within this fundamentally modernist mode, however, the human individual remains central. In refusing to sacrifice the historical dimension to the dictates of form, Bellow creates an image of the human individual as no mere victim or illustration of the forces of time. While the novel engages with the question of the importance of inherited culture in human society, ideas are inscribed within an action which, in its temporal ironies, modifies and questions them. The risks which Bellow takes with the form of the novel are amply justified by the wider horizons opened up at its close.

3 *Henderson the Rain King*:
A Dance to the Music
of Time

Several problems face the reader of *Henderson the Rain King*: the clash between Bellow's avowed intention, as expressed in 'Deep Readers of the World, Beware!',[1] to go beyond symbolism in the novel, and the highly symbolic realisation in *Henderson the Rain King*: the related problem of integrating the parodic elements present into a serious novel of quest:[2] and finally the degree of change in the hero. Announcing at the outset that 'the world which I thought so mighty an oppressor has removed its wrath from me'[3] Henderson suggests a degree of transformation which has appeared to many readers to be somewhat unsupported by the events of the text. The note of affirmation as Henderson runs over the ice at the novel's close (p. 318) seems unearned, almost an evasion. Though making allowance for the problems of closure posed by the romance form, the comic tone, and the first person narrator J.J. Clayton, for one, is forcible in his objections to this lack of dramatisation.

> Bellow is still unable to bring off the change because he cannot dramatise it. We see desire to change, symbols of change; we are told that change has occurred. But we do not see the change ... Henderson affirms. Bellow affirms. Perhaps, however, Philip Toynbee is right that 'this is the book of a sad man who "decided" to be affirmative'. At any rate the affirmation is too cheaply won.[4]

Other critics have been equally uneasy on this point.[5]
    The problem is related to the overall problem of attitudes to time in the novel. The assumption underlying the criticisms outlined above presupposes a linear, chronological development

69

of the hero extending into a future beyond the novel. The progress of this particular hero, however, relates to an intuition of the degree of repetition and recurrence inherent in life. Henderson's African adventures allow him an excursion into atemporal realities, divorced from human time and material society. Henderson's problem is precisely his desire for an absolute change, a total transcendence of the present. He has to learn that, while some change is possible, it can occur only within time, within an acceptance of a role which is in some ways essentially repetitive. In the novel, everyday conceptions of time are challenged, and change becomes a theme rather than an accepted premise, a theme leading to a speculation on time, salvation and immortality. In many respects *Henderson the Rain King* appears to be the least 'historical' of Bellow's novels, an excursion into fantasy and into transcendental concerns. The mythic or romance setting is, however, a pretext to the exploration of the bases of the historical sense. The prologue, in America (pp. 7–41), to Henderson's African adventures, grounds the novel in psychological and cultural attitudes to time. In cultural terms the African experiences are designed to juxtapose an American progressive vision of time to an Old World view of time as cyclic recurrence. In psychological terms the African adventures dramatise the warring theories of Freud and Reich, the former holding that society is founded upon repression, begins from a primal crime, and that therefore nature and culture are always in opposition, the latter arguing that freedom from repression would lead to an idyllic society, where nature and culture would be as one, and that therefore progress in time is possible. In religious terms Freudian psychology may be seen as a psychological version of the idea of inherited sin, of the Fall; Reichian therapy may be understood as the psychological equivalent of the American transcendental belief in the possibility of instinctual innocence.

At the beginning of the novel the narrator emphasises the difficulty of dealing with time. Henderson is seen grappling with the problem of organising his memories, unable to cope with their simultaneity in the present.

A disorderly rush begins – my parents, my habits, my money, my music lessons, my drunkenness, my prejudices, my brutality, my teeth, my face, my soul! . . . And they pile into me from all sides. It turns into chaos.   (p. 7)

The alternative to Chaos is Chronos of course; yet Henderson studiously continues to undermine any easy acceptance of the structures within which he is forced to construct his tale. Wandering from one event to another, uncertain where to begin his story, he places a certain distance between himself and events, expressive of his alienated stance and of its roots in temporal uncertainty. 'To go by the ages of the kids, we were married for about 20 years' (p. 8). 'Frances and I were divorced. This happened after VE Day. Or was it so soon? No, it must have been in 1948' (p. 8). Henderson's rambling narration and senseless actions have an underlying logic however. When Lily describes him as 'unkillable' the way in which he reacts is significant:

> And I go to Lily and shake her hand, too, as if she were merely another lady guest, a stranger like the rest. And I say, 'How do you do?' I imagine the ladies are telling themselves, 'He doesn't know her. In his mind he's still married to the first. Isn't that awful?' This imaginary fidelity thrills them. But they are all wrong. As Lily knows, it was done on purpose.   (p. 9)

Henderson takes the statement of his immortality literally as though he were living in an eternal present, in which the past does not exist and everyone is always a stranger. This alienation, in part a personal psychological disturbance, is also that of a culture alienated from its origins, living in the expectation of immediate salvation in a new world. The first four chapters of the novel form an extended meditation on the question of an inherited past – a past which Henderson is trying to erase. This is a problem of both individual psyche and public culture. One would not of course, wish to devalue the rich comedy inherent in the use of madness, incongruity and non sequiturs in the opening chapters. It is, however, comic in a serious way. The melodramatic end to the first chapter, with the promise of extended explanations, 'I'll tell you why' (p. 11) preceding a chapter break, is undercut when the explanation, 'Because her father had committed suicide in that same way' (p. 11) is brief, pat, veers at once into irrelevant dental history, swerves back into invective against Lily's father and ends blankly, 'Personally I never knew the old guy' (p. 12). At every step development is checked, rerouted, the forward advance blocked. The text slips and swerves in circles, akin to the movements Lily and Henderson make in the car on the ice. It does,

however have two governing concerns, passion and death, which
are masked by the superficial lack of development, much as they
are in Henderson's psyche.

In 'Deep Readers of the World, Beware!', published one week
before *Henderson the Rain King* appeared, Bellow dwelt on the
problem of symbolism in the novel and diagnosed beneath critical
symbol-hunting a fundamental cowardice, an unwillingness to
face up to essential issues. According to Bellow the symbol hunter
is 'doing no more than most civilised people do when confronted
with passion and death. They contrive somehow to avoid them.'[6]
Before despatching Henderson into the symbolic landscape of
Africa, therefore, Bellow underlines the degree to which he is an
avoider of these two subjects. Henderson fears mortality and
therefore refuses to acknowledge time passing, or (within the
family time scheme) to acknowledge the parental generation, the
past, or his children, the visible future. By ignoring the claims of
passion he attempts to avoid any connection with the generations
and therefore with time. The series of passionate encounters
between Lily and Henderson is continually being interrupted by
images of death: Lily's suicidal father (p. 14), Frances as a gaping
toothless deathshead (p. 16), Henderson's mother whispering
'Passassassez' (Pass on) from a church door, Lily's own corruption (p. 20). Until Henderson accepts mortality he is condemned
to the same death in life as that of the pallid octopus which so
terrifies him (p. 22).

In the second chapter the psychological theme is set into a
larger cultural context. Henderson's flight from passion and
death had already involved him in the desecration of religious and
cultural monuments, when his problems with Lily led to his
drunkenness in all the great French cathedrals. At Monte Cas-
sino, scene of the destruction by US troops of an irreplaceable
European treasure, Henderson decides to breed pigs in his
father's house with its 'handsome old farm buildings, the carriage
house with its panelled stalls ... and the fine old barn with the
belvedere, ... a beautiful piece of architecture' (p. 23), allowing
the pigs to root out statues from Florence and Salzburg. The
choice of pigs is itself motivated by a conscious desire to violate his
friend Goldstein's religious taboo, and at the same time symbolises Henderson's ambivalence towards the past. Henderson rejects both the European past, and that of his WASP ancestors (in
whose portrait gallery he refuses to take his place), and even his

own parents. Henderson therefore typifies the American belief in the ability to wipe out the past and begin again in a new world, where salvation from inherited guilt is a product of salvation from inherited tradition and customs. Such a belief is impossible in psychological terms, however. Bellow implies a deep-rooted schizophrenia in American society. In the African experiences an exploration of different views of the individual's relation to time offers a solution.

Moreover Henderson's military character links his avoidance to a common cultural phenomenon by means of the parody of the Hemingway code. Bellow's own views on the subject are well known. Indeed his first novel begins with an explicit rejection of the 'hard-boiled' hero. Henderson's journey to Africa to find truth, and escape women, the .375 Magnum he buys because he reads safari articles by 'a fellow from Michigan who had one', the disruption of the all-male trip by Charlie's wife, Henderson's heroics in the war, in Italy, his thigh wound, the references to fathers and sons blowing out their brains, the parodic big game hunt of the tenant's cat, and the general elements of Braggadoccio brawling, all constitute a thoroughgoing parody. Rejecting this type of hero Joseph, of *Dangling Man*, wrote:

> Do you have feelings? There are correct and incorrect ways of indicating them. Do you have an inner life? It is nobody's business but your own. Do you have emotions? Strangle them.[7]

Henderson's society does not allow him the expression of his emotions, or his inner longings. As a remedy he takes up the violin, described, in terms which connect the themes of love and death, as a woman in a coffin. 'Inside that little sarcophagus, with its narrow scrolled neck and incurved waist and the hair of the bow undone and loose all around it' (p. 27). At the same time he sees the violin as a link to his dead father and therefore the past. Since he also does his courting of Lily in between lessons the musical expression is clearly psychotherapeutic. This is the first appearance of a musical theme which runs through the novel. Haponyi's method of teaching, beginning not with scales but phrases, 'keeping time with the voice within' (p. 33), its only command 'not to kill vid de bow' points away from the two repressive forces operating on Henderson, the alienation from time, and the aggressive Hemingway code. Henderson cannot

free himself from his cultural conditioning entirely – he sees the
lessons in terms of 'discipline' (p. 32) – but the music does reveal
the emotional hunger within him.

In the fourth chapter of this prologue to Africa the image of the
child dominates, both in Henderson's daughter Ricey and the
foundling she brings home. The child appears at the winter
solstice (p. 34). Henderson however does his best to ignore its
presence, drowning its cries with pistol shots and violin music.
Lily comments on his actions,

> 'Can you hear it?'
> 'I can't hear a thing, you know I'm a little deaf, . . .'
> 'Then how can you hear the violin?'   (p. 36)

Henderson's attempts to renew relationship with his father are in
opposition to the future as symbolised by the children. While
Henderson will not accept his own position as husband and
father, how can he make contact with his own dead father? While
this Christmas child is ignored, how can he hope to find some sort
of afterlife, whether for him or his father? Henderson refuses to
countenance the suggestion that Ricey may be a mother. He
clings to a noble conception in which innocence is unsullied,
children have no mother or a virgin mother, and bear no relation
to sin or death. This refusal to accept passion and death implies a
rejection of any regeneration. The foundling is both a Christian
symbol, and by its association with the winter solstice, suggests
the cyclic nature of human life. Henderson fears this repetition
without progress. The winter scene now takes on a desolation
explicitly reminiscent of Eliot's Wasteland, as Henderson de-
claims, 'There is a curse on this land. There is something bad
going on. Something is wrong. There is a curse on this land!'
(p. 39). When Miss Lenox dies Henderson realises that

> You too will die of this pestilence. Death will annihilate you and
> nothing will remain, and there will be nothing left but junk.
> Because nothing *will have been* and so nothing *will be* left. While
> something still *is* – now! For the sake of all, get out. [My
> emphasis]   (p. 40)

While there is no past there can be no future. Henderson is

established as a serious quester after real values, victim of a representative American malaise, setting out to bring back a healing boon to society.

This extended analysis of the prologue to the novel proper resolves the apparent contradictions inherent in the juxtaposition of the novel with Bellow's essay on symbolism in the novel. Before Henderson sets out for Africa, Bellow is careful to show the 'meanings' which he is to explore there, cyclic and Judaeo-Christian modes of time, passion and death, rebirth and regeneration, as deeply embedded in a psychological reality. Henderson insists several times that the African adventure is akin to a dream (p. 24, p. 160) but it is a dream firmly connected to social and psychological reality. The major themes of Henderson's unrest – the conflict between the Messianic dream in America and its cyclic realisation – find structural expression in the juxtaposition of Arnewi and Wariri. The African experiences work as a refraction and exaggeration of elements which are only hinted at, or alluded to, in the prologue. The tenant's cat and Miss Lenox's cat become avenging lions; the misery inflicted on Ricey conjures up a weeping African maiden; the literary allusions to romance and ritual become two full-blown episodes. Minor guilts are punished by massive retributions in the 'dream' which distorts scale and proportion in terms of absolute degrees of guilt and innocence. The past avenges itself in no uncertain terms. Aware of his own violence and amorality Henderson is transported to a land where these are the norm. He rejects a coloured child to find himself surrounded by Africans who hold him in their power. He desecrates his ancestors and the code of his society, only to become part of a society in which reverence for ancestors and observance of taboo almost prove fatal to him. Particular parallels and echoes abound. Frances's gaping grin, Lily's father knocking out her teeth, suggest the skulls of the Wariri and Henderson's broken bridgework. Lily and Henderson consummate their affair in a storm suggestive of the storm following the lifting of Mummah. In the African experiences the emphasis shifts from passion to death, though the passional theme continues as an undercurrent, recalled by Henderson's periodic excursions into memory, and by the figures of Willatale, Mtalba and Atti. (Mtalba's courting of a reluctant Henderson recalls Lily's. Both women are massive redheads, though Mtalba is a grotesque version, of course.)

Although the fantasy framework permits metaphysical excursions into questions of time, death, immortality, good and evil, it is firmly rooted in the realities of the prologue.

Henderson's journey into Africa forms a spatial equivalent for chronological progression as he travels from the very beginnings of history towards the present. The experiences with the Arnewi suggest above all an escape from time, whether into prehistory or into art. In the first section of the African journey (pp. 43–105) Henderson's journey into Africa is presented as a journey into prehistory. From the air Africa looks like 'the ancient bed of mankind' (p. 43). In evolutionary terms the world is fresh, hardly cooled from its origins in the solar 'big bang'. Flying over it Henderson feels like

> an airborne seed. From the cracks in the earth the rivers pinched back at the sun. They shone out like smelters' puddles, and then they took a crust and were covered over. As for the vegetable kingdom, it hardly existed from the air; it looked to me no more than an inch in height.   (p. 43)

Once arrived he enthuses over its newness:

> we saw no human footprints. Nor were there many plants; for that matter there was not much of anything here; it was all simplified and splendid, and I felt I was entering the past – the real past, no history or junk like that. The pre-human past.
>   (p. 46)

On the mountain slopes clouds are 'being born' and the cooling rocks give off vapour. At night Henderson feels coextensive with the universe, which is beating gently, moving rhythmically in a divine harmony, a harmony of the spheres, outside time:

> then there were the calm stars, turning around and singing, and the birds of the night with heavy bodies fanning by. . . . When I laid my ear to the ground I thought I could hear hoofs. It was like lying on the skin of a drum . . . and I lost count of the days.   (p. 46)

Music and rhythmic movement interrupt the flow of time. On reaching the Arnewi village Henderson sees it as static, a picture of gold, silence and radiance. 'Hell, it looks like the original place. It must be older than the city of Ur' (p. 47) he comments, and is carried away by the vision of Messianic possibilities to the extent of re-enacting the Burning Bush for the benefit of the assembled populace. Salvation from time and mortality seems to be at hand, until Itelo, politely regretful, shatters the illusion, 'you thought first footstep? Something new? I am very sorry. We are discovered' (p. 53). The footprint image, repeated more than once, recalls Bellow's own source for much of the incidental detail of the African trip, Burton's *First Footprints in East Africa*.[8] Henderson has to realise that he is 'no explorer' (p. 53) and that the past pervades the present. The inherent contradictions in his attitude are made explicit. He comments, 'the antiquity of the place had struck me so, I was sure I had got into someplace new' (p. 53). Nevertheless the timeless aspects of the place recur. When Itelo invites Henderson to meet his aunts he declares that 'we will go to see the queen, my aunt, Willatale, and afterward or maybe the same time the other one, Mtalba' (p. 55). The aesthetic elements of the place are insisted upon. The people 'would have satisfied the standards of Michelangelo himself' (p. 55). Around Itelo's eyes there is 'a glitter which made me think of gold leaf' (p. 54). Aesthetic beauty is a product of the stilling of time: 'the air was still and as if it were knotted to the zenith and stuck there, parched and blue, a masterpiece of midday beauty' (p. 57).

This golden age of man is not, however, all perfection. Into the primal innocence there obtrudes a Freudian opposition of nature and culture. The Arnewi are unable to water their cattle because of a social taboo against the frogs in their cistern. The timeless artificial quality of the Arnewi has its counterpart in the atmosphere of hopelessness, the paralysed inertia of the people and the stagnant cistern water. Given the associations of frogs with the primal slime it is significant that they should be the taboo animal. They are described in terms which suggest the life in time, and the regeneration inherent in it. They are 'at all stages of development, with full tails like giant sperm' (p. 58). Though grotesque, conforming to no aesthetic canons, the frogs are an image of the inevitable change and vitality of life. Henderson's comments on them have a resonance of which he is unaware. 'Of all the creatures in the vicinity, bar none, it seemed to me they had it best' (p. 58). Compared to the static Arnewi their lot is preferable. Although Henderson comments in astonishment 'You call this a curse?' he fails to realise that he has been seeing life as a curse, which condemns man to change and mortality. In typical American fashion Henderson pins his faith on the annihilation of custom, the breaking of the taboo, and a Messianic new beginning. 'The last plague of frogs I ever heard about was in Egypt' (p. 59). The romance elements of the episode, curse, weeping maiden, stranger knight, are subsumed in a materialistic faith. Posing as a saviour, Henderson preaches against taboo:

> 'Do you know why the Jews were defeated by the Romans? Because they wouldn't fight back on Saturday. And that's how it is with your water situation. Should you preserve yourself, or the cows, or preserve the custom? I would say, yourself. Live,' I said, 'to make another custom'. (p. 60)

The Arnewi remain, however, bovine as their cattle, their laws precluding any change. 'When stranger guest comes we always make acquaintance by wrestle. Invariable' (p. 62). Winning and losing are not part of the game for them. The wrestling is only a ritual formality. Where there is no change there can be only one emotional state, therefore 'bitterness' and 'happiness' are interchangeable terms.[9] Even sexual differences are eroded in this atemporality. Willatale is described as both male and female, mother and father. As a Mother Earth she suggests the eternal. 'There was the calm pulsation of her heart participating in the introduction. This was as regular as the rotation of the earth' (p. 69), and when he touches her Henderson draws 'an endless breath into my lungs' (p. 69). Everything in the queen suggests stability and benevolence except for her one defective eye which suggests that the viewing of all things in one plane, spatial or temporal, imposes certain limitations. When Henderson speaks of his troubles she is impassive. Like Atti, foreshadowed by the queen's lion skin, and her licking of Henderson's face, the queen is less than human, almost a force of nature. Her creed of 'Grun-tu-molani' (p. 81) comes close to an animal grunt. The conversation with Willatale almost founders on the question of origins. Henderson falls silent, recapitulating the past in terms similar to the opening of the novel. 'A crowd of facts came upon me with accompanying pressure in the chest. Who – who was I?' (p. 74). The oracular nature of Willatale's utterances – Sendsations, Frenezy, Suffah – is a product of their being unmarked by tense, understandable as statements diagnosing his present or past state, or as future predictions. He briskly translates the experience into aesthetic terms (p. 76) in a further strategy of avoidance. Willatale's phrase, 'World is strange to a child. You not a child, sir?' (p. 81) is double edged. On the one hand it suggests the American capacity for 'wonder', for childlike innocence. Less optimistically it suggests that Henderson is alienated, refuses to grow up and take his place in the world, so that it is always strange to him. Henderson outlines the latter view:

> The world may be strange to a child, but he does not fear it the way a man fears. He marvels at it. But the grown man mainly dreads it. And why? Because of death. (p. 81)

His spirited rendition of the Messiah suggests that he espouses the belief in innocence largely in reaction to a more deeply rooted fear.

Mtalba's night visit to Henderson, a parody version of the tempting of the knight by the beautiful maiden, underlines the tempting quality of the aesthetic attitude, in the flight from real passional involvement into the atemporal. In the dance which Mtalba executes duration is expanded. The verb forms give a habitual rather than a punctual frame of reference. 'Sometimes she wore a half veil ... and occasionally as she jingled ... she would saunter, she would teeter,' (p. 93). The ambiguity of 'would' gives the dance possible extension from the past into the future. Even the stars are no longer small points of light occupying a clearly defined place, but 'great white blotches of fire [which] burned at irregular points around the horizon' (p. 93). Henderson disguises his fear of Mtalba beneath a glorification of the experience in aesthetic terms:

> This was enchantment. This was poetry ... And what I had felt when I first laid eyes on the thatched roofs while descending the bed of the river, that they were so ancient, amounted to this same thing – poetry, enchantment. Somehow I am a sucker for beauty and can trust only it, but I keep passing through and out of it again. It never has enough duration. (p. 94)

The dance at this point forms an image of Henderson's attraction to the continuous rhythm, the idea of eternity as endless extension. Henderson's following epiphany however is not religious but aesthetic, Wordsworthian, as he recalls his perceptions as a small child. Though he describes this sensation in terms of reaching the fringe of Nirvana, he translates the experience into linear, temporal terms, seeing it as a prevision, and 'go-ahead sign', rather than an intimation of the timeless.

From the epiphany Henderson returns to the homemade bomb, and its technological problems, centring on 'the whole question of timing' (p. 97). Before constructing it he explicitly rejects the urge to escape from reality:

> There is that poem about the nightingale singing that human-kind cannot stand too much reality. But how much unreality can it stand?
> (pp. 99–100)

Needless to say Henderson does not complete the quotation:

> Time past and time future
> What might have been and what has been
> Point to one end, which is always present.[10]

Though in literal terms Henderson gets the timing right (the bomb explodes) in fact it is his attitude to time which is responsible for the overall failure. Wedded to an ideal of technological progress which is the secular equivalent of the American idealistic faith, Henderson pins all on 'operation cistern'. 'This is the day and this is the hour' (p. 101) he comments, keen to deliver once and for all on his promise of salvation. After contemplating the 'patriarchal-looking wick' Henderson shuts his eyes and waits for the spirit to move him. The ambivalence of the supposed salvation is revealed in his opening interjection 'Damned if my soul didn't rise with the water' (p. 102). For the American reader a second ironic parallel is given by the oblique parallel with Twain's Connecticut Yankee, Hank Morgan, whose similar attempts to renew the Well of Holiness, with technological pyrotechnics, in a world distant from him in time, also eventually end in disaster. The final horrific image of the Arnewi is that of a culture at war with nature – 'the cows of course obeying nature and the natives begging them and weeping' (p. 103), akin to Henderson's own America with its Freudian repressions. In Arnewiland two attempts at secular transcendence are defeated: the romantic-aesthetic and the progressive-technological, obverse and reverse of one devalued coin. The problem of human change cannot be resolved either by ignoring it or by its elevation to a supreme material value. Nature and culture remain locked in conflict, with Henderson as the battleground.

The contradictions of the Arnewi, locked in a Freudian opposition of nature and culture, despite the timeless innocence of their surroundings, are reversed in Waririland. The Wariri occupy a fallen, temporal world, yet their king is an exponent of Reich. The journey to the second tribe is introduced in terms which emphasise the landscape of a fallen time-bound world. To some extent there is an implied evolutionary progression from Arnewi primitivity to a greater degree of social organisation, more vegetation, and greater rock erosion. Romilayu gets distinctly older (in realistic terms an effect of dust) his face 'utterly in wrinkles' his hair 'filled with grey powder' (p. 111). The world of the Wariri is not timeless, but steeped in time and irremediably fallen. This is suggested in several key images. Romilayu describes the Wariri as 'chillen darkness', and the travellers arrive in the 'last of the light' (p. 112) as the evening star, Lucifer, rises. The Arnewi were clearly the children of light, their village bathed in gold and their palms pale 'As if, you know, they had played catch with the light and some of it had come off' (p. 51). The guide with the twisted stick who directs the two travellers reminds Henderson of the man on the road to Dothan who 'knew the brothers were going to throw Joseph into the pit' (p. 109). Joseph, the dreamer, the exile in Egypt, is an analogue for Henderson. Around them rocks are strewn as though they had rolled straight down from heaven (p. 110). Within the rocks are caves, ideal places for siestas 'provided no snakes came' (p. 110). Even the sun is in decline 'trumpeting downward' (p. 110). Even without Romilayu's sudden fall the implications of the last trump, the fall of man and that of Lucifer, are overwhelming. The fire-power of the Wariri is part of a traditional linkage of fire, devils and technology. Within this fallen world Henderson moves through two spheres of influence – the Wariri religion and the Reichian psychotherapy undergone in Atti's den.[11] Dahfu encapsulates both creeds, and his character dramatises their contradictions. The Wariri religion of cyclic recurrence is a variant form of the belief that life is a curse, in which man is doomed to a pointless repetition of passion and violence. Dahfu himself describes it in terms of a primal crime. 'In the beginning of time there was a hand raised which struck'

(p. 200). Wariri kings inherit only by the murder of their father, and then live in constant terror lest they be denounced by their women for lack of virility, leading to instant death. Henderson's own fears are magnified here, in Freudian terms. To this the Reichian therapy is opposed. Dahfu counsels Henderson to express his fears, to act them out and therefore to overcome them, and thus be liberated from his repressions. For Reich total freedom from repression would lead to social progress. In the words of Philip Rieff,

> Reich never bothered to argue against the probability that sex suppression functioned to hold societies together against the pressures of nature. It was a dogma to him that nature and culture could not be in tension. . . . In its nature worship Reich's writing has an old-fashioned edifying cast. He never confronts the horrible possibility, which obsesses all of modern art, that the reality behind the appearance may be even more unpleasant than the appearance.[12]

Though in terms of the individual psyche Reichian therapy appears to work for Henderson, Bellow places the individual regeneration in a cultural context which leads to a less optimistic conclusion. Dahfu uses Atti as a symbol of the terrors besetting Henderson. The reality is a real lion. The lion hunt in the hopo leads Henderson to recognise precisely the possibility outlined by Rieff – that nature may be even more terrifying than we think, that Melville may be closer to the truth than Emerson. Henderson's terror of Atti pales once he sees the real lion and learns the unpleasant reality of his symbolic role as rain king.

Before Henderson meets Dahfu, however, there is a hiatus in the novel, a Kafkaesque period waiting for the Unknown Examiner. At this point Henderson breaks his bridge and embarks on a long Remembrance of Teeth Past,[13] comic in its superficial incongruity. The memory is not just light relief however, but extends into that area of Henderson's life which has been largely left behind in Africa, physical passion. He and Lily, we remember, had dental problems in common. The first dentist of the reminiscence, Mlle Montecuccoli is an exotic female who 'forgot herself' in her work, smothering the patient with her huge bust, while from her heart-shaped face her black eyes stared, 'fearfully roused' (p. 114). There are Reichian overtones to her instructions

– 'Grincez les dents! Fachez-vous!' – foreshadowing the anger therapy Henderson is to undergo in order to overcome his fear of passion and death. Mademoiselle Montecuccoli is also inserted into a historical framework:

> A General Montecuccoli was the last opponent of the great Marshal Turenne. Enemies used to attend each other's funerals in the old days, and Montecuccoli went to Turenne's and beat his breast and sobbed.   (p. 114)

Henderson responds to the belief that love and forgiveness are superior to expressions of wrath, foreshadowing the eventual resolution of the novel. For the moment however he is still locked in avoidance. The image of Bertha, the maid who pretended to be delirious and, rolling in the bed with fever, bit Henderson's hand, suggests his continued fear of sex as dangerous. His memory of the second dental treatment, in New York with Klaus Spohr, is interrupted by a remembered conversation with his son Edward, also in love with an exotic foreign maiden, Maria Felucca, who fills Henderson with apprehension. 'If I leave him with this girl she will eat him in three bites' (p. 119). Finally he remembers Clara Spohr, a twin image of love and death, 'Time and nature had blown the whistle on her and she was badly ravaged' (p. 119). In her youth Clara had spent time in exotic Samoa 'and had experienced passionate love on the beaches, on the rafts, in the flowers. It was like Churchill's blood, sweat and tears, swearing to fight on the beaches and so on' (p. 120). She and Henderson kiss in her overheated lobby full of Samoan souvenirs 'as if the next moment we were going to be separated by the stroke of death' (p. 121). For Henderson the satisfaction of physical appetite without repression still suggests death. The exotic African world is established as a sphere in which the two themes are explored. Henderson now recognises his errors in relation to his children, in particular in the memory of Edward. Edward, the child, a link between past and future, is remembered in a ghastly atemporal limbo:

> The water was ghostly, lazy, slow, stupefying, ... A womb of white. Pallor; smoke; vacancy; dull gold; vastness; dimness; fulgor; ghostly flashing. 'Edward, where are we?' I said. 'We are at the edge of the earth. ... This looks like a hell of a place to meet.   (pp. 116–17)

Without any firm temporal belief the world lacks any but a subjective support. Facing a mirror Henderson questions

> 'Well?' 'And when?' ... 'Your own soul is killing you.' And 'Its you who makes the world what it is. Reality is you.'　　　(p. 116)

Unable to locate himself in a meaningful temporal scheme, unable to contribute to the American dream of progress – Henderson regrets that he and Edward are not 'like that man Slocum who builds the great dams' (p. 116) – Henderson feels that his existence is pointless, a comic circus of passion and death. These gloomy reflections are confirmed for him when the examiner, also with mutilated teeth, poses the question of his origins. No advance has been made since Willatale asked the same question.

> It was like the question asked by Tennyson about the flower in the crannied wall. That is, to answer it might involve the history of the universe.　　　(p. 124)

When however he is presented with the corpse of the rain king whom he is to replace he realises to what extent he does wish for life. The episode balances the dental reminiscences from which it borrows imagery. Henderson's terror is akin to 'an injection of novocaine' (p. 127). He has a blanket tied, bib fashion beneath his chin and as he lifts the man he suffers 'pangs in the glands of my mouth' and makes 'huge muscles in my jaw and shut my teeth' (p. 132). As he struggles to lift the corpse, intimations of a timeless world penetrate him. 'What did this velvet night have to do with clocks?' (p. 125). Yet Henderson raises the corpse 'not because the time was ripe, but because I couldn't bear waiting' (p. 131). In practical action he begins to overcome his fear of death, and to sense its exaggerated former importance to him. When, on the next day, Henderson sees corpses again, the new way of seeing is still with him.

> Through a peculiarity of the light they were small, like dolls. The atmosphere sometimes will act as a reducing and not only as a magnifying glass.　　　(p. 140)

Death, though still terrifying, is not the magnified horror it was.

By the time Henderson reaches Dahfu he has moved far from his original assumptions. The faith in progress is behind him. 'Becoming was beginning to come out of my ears. Enough! Enough! Time to have become. Time to be' (p. 150). Yet what is the nature of this being? Henderson ponders. Man may occupy a place in time, but is this grounds for optimism? 'In the history of the world many souls have been, are, and will be, and with a little reflection this is marvellous and not depressing' (p. 152). The whole problem hinges on that of time. Does it conceal a meaningful pattern – and, if so, is that pattern benevolent?

> Now take a phrase like 'Father forgive them; they know not what they do.' This may be interpreted as a promise that in time we would be delivered from blindness and understand. On the other hand it may be interpreted as a promise that with time we will understand our own enormities and crimes and that sounds to me like a threat. (p. 152)

In mystic terms, time may be considered as a pattern whose order will only become apparent when completed. It is therefore concealed from the human being. What Henderson does not know is the design which Dahfu has upon him! While Dahfu supposedly teaches a Reichian ethic in which a new beginning is possible, free from taint or repression, he actually hands on a social and ancestral role, that of rain king, which can only be seen as a curse. The mystic idea that time completes itself in a meaningful design in eternity is here exposed to the ironies of Henderson's actual situation.

Henderson however returns to his vision of atemporal bliss, in art. Again the image of the dance recurs as a means of interrupting the flux of time, but the emphasis has shifted from passion to death. Henderson watches Dahfu engage in a skull-tossing game, characterised by its silent grace. Death is accepted by Dahfu whose own skull will eventually fly through the air too. The skulls are whirled in circles and flung in arcs from one to another, in an image of the cyclic religion of which the king is a representative. Henderson, however, sees this ordered ritual as entirely symbolic, as art.

Chaos doesn't run the whole show.... this is not a sick and

hasty ride, helpless, through a dream into oblivion. No sir! It can be arrested by a thing or two. By art, for instance. The speed is checked, the time is redivided.　　　　　　　　(p. 165)

From the dance Henderson passes to the lifting of Mummah, an episode pervaded with intimations of mystic transcendence, with clear echoes of Eliot in the image of the dance and the still point. Setting aside the memory of past defeats Henderson wrestles with the absolute, determined to 'work the right stitch into the design of my destiny before it was too late' (p. 174), submitting to a divinely ordained pattern. As he lifts Mummah the world recedes.

The yells of the Wariri, even the deep drums, came very lightly to my hearing. They occurred on a small, infinitely reduced scale, way out on the circumference of a great circle.　　(p. 180)

The suggestion is of the image of the wheel, common to mystic writers, in which material life is the moving circumference around the still centre of God. After lifting Mummah Henderson feels anointed with sweat, all fears banished. He sees life, not in terms of linear time, but as part of a larger circle from the centre of which emanate pulsations. The stone beneath his feet is 'A world of its own or more than a single world, world within world, in a dreaming series' (p. 185). Henderson now himself repeats the image of the skull game, 'dancing on burnt and cut feet over the hot stones' (p. 186) passing beneath the swinging heads of the dead men on the gallows, with streamers of vine and grass flying from him, circling the town to the chant of the Amazons. Henderson's supposed transcendent triumph is however a Pyrrhic victory. Romilayu recoils from him in fear, and the king's comment, 'You have lost the wager' (p. 190) says it all. Henderson's epiphanic moment is inscribed in a context which has sinister implications.

Henderson's Reichian exercises are enclosed in similar ironies. On the one hand they are valuable in that they teach Henderson that he must act in time. Within the lion's den Henderson is shown learning to 'dance' – to submit to his limitations and express himself within them. In the first encounter with Atti it is Dahfu who dances:

In moving from me his step resembled the bounds he had made

in the arena yesterday throwing the skulls. Yes, as he had done
yesterday he danced and jumped. (p. 209)

Atti's tail swipes back and forth 'regular as a metronome' (p. 211),
making 'a big arc on the stone'. Henderson remains paralysed,
afraid that this is 'judgement hour' for him, unable to appreciate
the grace and beauty of the dancers. When Dahfu offers his
version of progress to Henderson, in his delight that 'so many
small spans should have made so glorious one large thing' (p. 217)
Henderson, as we might expect, rejects it. His own loss of faith in
progress has left him unwilling to ascribe human beings any
purposive role in time. He replies to Dahfu with a parable of the
flowers in the desert, flowers which only bloom every forty or fifty
years according to the rainfall. 'Soaking in water won't do it. It
has to be the rain coming through the soil. It has to wash over
them for a certain number of days' (p. 219). Man cannot fathom
the workings of time in nature; nor can he speed up the process.
Given Reichian books to study, Henderson now realises that his
problem is essentially with time and history. 'When I started to
read something about France I realised I didn't know anything
about Rome, which came first, and then Greece, and then Egypt,
going backward all the time to the primitive abyss' (p. 228).
Formerly, he had concentrated on books which emphasise the
victory over pain and death in the present, *The Romance of Surgery*
and *The Triumph over Pain*. Henderson's reflections are interrupted, however, by another image of mortality, the shrunken
skull borne by old Yasra, which is enough to topple his precarious
equilibrium.

Rushing to Dahfu at daybreak, Henderson interrupts another
dance, the dance of the wives. Again this is a dance of love and
death. The fiddler, 'all bone, with knees that bent outward and a
long shiny head, tier upon tier of wrinkles. A few white weblike
hairs were carried in the air behind him' (p. 237), coalesces the
images of the skull throwing, the violin that Henderson played
and the shrunken head. The principal danseuse, Mupi, glorifies in
pain, grinding out hot coals on her thigh. Dahfu loses patience
with Henderson's inability to withstand fear and come to terms
with the limitations imposed on man, and forces him into the den,
where he must stop avoiding, and learn to dance to the music of
time. Atti forces 'the present moment' upon him (p. 243). Henderson has to imitate her, run in time with her, leaping in unison. His

fear leaps with him. 'I was convinced that as I was in motion I was fair game' (p. 246). As the therapy continues Henderson expresses not only a depth of repressed emotions, but also his spiritual hunger, the words Help, De Profundis, Lord Have Mercy emerging of their own accord, their long vowels prolonged into an infinite echo. The dances of Dahfu and his tribe do not answer these appeals, although they do establish the inescapable nature of time and the need to accept it. Henderson recognises that a positive change has occurred here, in an exchange with Dahfu:

> 'You really mean that she might change me.' 'Excellent. Precisely. Change. You fled what you were. You did not believe you had to perish.'   (p. 243)

Henderson now feels ready to return to America and writes to Lily to tell her so. In the letter he claims to have abandoned his dreams of glory, no longer wishing to be an explorer like Burton or Speke, but rather desiring to return to ordinary life. He tells Lily, 'I've matured twenty years in twenty days' (p. 263) and acknowledges that he no longer wants 'to raise my spirit from the earth, to leave the body of this death. I was very stubborn. I wanted to raise myself into another world' (pp. 265–6). The letter, which alternates between a banal written text concerned with ordinary details such as steak knives, the sale of pigs, and false teeth, and italicised memories, underlines in its form the contradictions of Henderson's existence. Again Henderson dwells on strangeness, both as the gift of wonder, and the punishment of alienation, concluding now as not before that he must accept the inherent contradictions of life, and live with others. Lily herself maintained that she 'couldn't live for sun, moon, and stars alone' (p. 265) and she never entirely made sense to Henderson. Just as he has to accept Lily with all her contradictions, so he has to accept life. 'We are funny creatures. We don't see the stars as they are, so why do we love them? They are not small gold objects but endless fire' (p. 267). Henderson concludes the letter with an awareness of the importance of living with other people:

> 'I had a voice that said, I want! I want? I? It should have told me she wants, he wants, they want. And moreover, it's love that makes reality reality.'   (p. 267)

Ironically, of course, Henderson is in no position to return to America. Henderson tells Lily, 'You conned me. Is this how love acts?' (p. 265) but is unaware that he has also been deceived by Dahfu. Dahfu's real allegiance is to a less pleasant creed. The conversation between him and Henderson centres on the idea of blows. Dahfu distinguishes evil as the law of the universe. 'Man is a creature who cannot stand still under blows. Now take the horse – he never needs a revenge. Nor the ox. But man is a creature of revenges' (p. 200). Dahfu links this theme to three versions of the myth of the primal crime, parricide, fratricide and son-murder, the Oedipus, Abel-Cain, and Abraham-Isaac situations. 'Brother raises a hand against brother, and son against father ... and the father also against son' (p. 200). This vision of the world as originating in, and perpetuating evil revolts Henderson who argues for the possibility of moral action. 'There are some guys who can return good for evil' (p. 200). Dahfu agrees that 'a brave man will try to make the evil stop with him. He shall keep the blow' (p. 201). In the event however Dahfu does no such thing, passing on the blow to Henderson his unwitting, and unwilling successor.

In the final African episode in the hopo the degree to which Henderson goes beyond Dahfu's teaching becomes apparent. Reaching maturity at last Henderson sees that human nature and animal nature are not at all the same thing. He no longer desires to return to some supposed innocent state of splendour in the grass.

> What could an animal do for me? In the last analysis? Really? A beast of prey? Even supposing that an animal enjoys a natural blessing? (p. 268)

Reichian psychology now takes second place. Dahfu is now the questioner:

> What are the generations for, please explain to me? Only to repeat fear and desire without a change? This cannot be what the thing is for, over and over and over. (p. 277)

The distinction between natural history and human history hinges on the question of motivation, the belief that any good man will try to 'break the cycle'. In Collingwood's analysis,

Nature has no history. Only human beings have history. The historian is concerned with the motives and thoughts of those people who have played a part in the events constituting history. Questions of motives do not arise about sticks, stones or brute beasts.[14]

Henderson goes further than the impasse Dahfu is in. By conquering fear and desire, passion and death, Henderson does not free himself from them, but learns to live with them. Because he is aware of motivation in time, he realises that he is distinct from the natural cycle of endless repetition. The surroundings of the lion hunt take on a resonance which combines a vivid awareness of the life force with a delighted sensitivity to the temporal process. It is as though processes of change had been speeded up to the point at which they are visible to the naked eye, as if the whole rhythm of life has become audible to the human ear. Rhythm pervades the episode, from the jolting and swaying of the hammock to the music of bugles and drums, accompanied by the 'Tremble of insects as they played their instruments underneath the stems' (p. 274). The raft sways, while around it 'flocks of birds went straight up, like masses of notes' (p. 284) echoing the movement of the cicadas whose sounds rise 'in vertical spirals, like columns of thinnest shining wire' (p. 284). The whole universe seems to speak to Henderson, totally animate, shivering in visible heat, humming with life and motion. The flux of the elements is visible. The light is 'hard enough then to leave bruises' (p. 285) so that Henderson feels 'that I had found, in midair, a changing point between matter and light' (p. 281). The universe is fluid, changing, the platform a raft, the grass shivering like water. The atmosphere breaks down into its constituent elements, 'The blue of the atmosphere seemed to condense, as when you light a few sticks in the woods and about these black sticks the blue begins to wrinkle' (p. 285). For a moment Henderson hovers between reality and vision. This radiant moving landscape, conveying the constant change inherent in life forms a contrast to the radiance of the static Arnewi; it is a 'second blessing' which is dynamic, kinaesthetic. From a timeless golden age Henderson moves towards a musical form of which time is a necessary element. It is at this point that he is represented as waking from the dream.

For the count of about 20 heartbeats I only partly knew where I

was or what was happening.... Then, at the very doors of
consciousness, there was a snarl.   (p. 286)

The sight of the real lion finally dispels any Reichian views of
nature. 'This was all mankind needed, to be conditioned into the
image of a ferocious animal like the one below' (p. 287). Beneath
him small animals are 'writhing' and 'coiling' in the presence of
the lion. One blow from it is enough to shake the fragile super-
structure, destroying Dahfu in a chaos of falling stones. Henderson's earlier comment, 'Time for a word of truth. Time for
something notable to be heard. Otherwise, accelerating like a
stone, you fall from life to death. Exactly like a stone,' (p. 277)
proves prophetic. Dahfu's final action is also a dance of death, 'the
overhead pole was *bucking* and *dancing*' (p. 289). 'His legs were
wide apart in the centre of the pole, which *bowed* deeply and *swung*
and *swayed* under the energetic movement of his legs, and the rope
and pulley and the block made cries as if *resined*' (p. 290). [My
emphasis]. Mere vitalism is not enough, whether passive as in the
Arnewi, or active as in the Wariri. As he dies Dahfu reveals the
deadly legacy to Henderson, and therefore his own lack of nobility.
    While the action of the novel reveals the flaws in the Reichian
view, the logic of the plot does not imply that Henderson must
merely recoil into its obverse. Henderson does absorb the blow.
His love for Dahfu allows him to convert his legacy into positive
action in time. He eschews revenge on the Bunam, escapes from
his role as rain king, and therefore breaks the cycle. On coming
round in the tomb Henderson's first thoughts are of time, in which
he now finds consolation.

Maybe time was invented so that misery might have an end. So
that it shouldn't last forever? There may be something in this.
And bliss, just the opposite, is eternal? That is no time in bliss.
All the clocks were thrown out of heaven.   (p. 293)

For man, change and mortality are consolations. Nobility is part
of life. 'The eternal is bonded onto us. It calls out for its share'
(p. 297). Man's desire for nobility may be defeated but the
existence of the impulse testifies to the possibility of eventual
transcendence. To escape from the tomb Henderson uses the
techniques learnt from Dahfu, making cries of fear and weakness,

screaming that he is dying, but not in a Reichian spirit. Back in Baventai he is able to face the cyclic recurrence in nature with new confidence.

> You can't get away from rhythm . . . The left hand shakes with the right hand, the inhale follows the exhale, the systole talks back to the diastole, the hands play pattycake, and the feet dance with each other. And the seasons. And the stars, and all of that. And the tides, and all that junk. You've got to live at peace with it.　　　　　　　　　　　　　　　　　(p. 307)

Over and above the cyclic there lies the promise of future salvation. 'Is it promised? Between the beginning and the end, is it promised?' he asks Romilayu, (p. 306) only to answer his own question in the affirmative.

Henderson's journey back to civilisation follows the historical path of Western civilisation – Egypt to Athens, to Rome, then Paris, London and finally Newfoundland, the image of America. He does not return entirely to his original belief in new beginnings however, but integrates two ways of approaching time and culture: the Old World cyclic view and the American progressive and prophetic view, each of them represented by a symbolic emblem, the lion cub and the orphan child. On the plane Henderson sees in the air hostess an image of the blessedness of cyclic renewal reconciled now to passion.

> Every 20 years or so the earth renews itself in young maidens. . . . She was all sweet corn and milk. Blessings on her hips. Blessings on her thighs.　　　　　　　　　　　　　　　　　(p. 311)

He tells her that in Africa he 'lost count of time' and finding that it is now Thanksgiving and too late for his planned enrolment, reconciles himself to patient waiting. 'At least something can be done... While we wait for the day' (p. 312). Although he serenades her with the Messiah, a musical expression of the hope for eternal transcendence of the cyclic, he is no longer totally impatient with the past, recognises that 'something of benefit' can be found in it, and even admires his family house. Finally he even faces up to the main reason for his estrangement from his father, the latter's grief over his brother's death. Personal and cultural

problems are resolved together. The child has a double significance. Though he is described as still trailing his cloud of glory,
Henderson is aware that his own 'got dingy, mere tatters of grey
fog' (p. 317). Though the child's eyes are 'new to life altogether'
they are also described as having 'ancient power' (p. 317). In
Henderson's words, 'you could never convince me that this was
for the first time' (p. 317). The memory of the bear with whom
Henderson used to ride the rollercoaster is an image of age-old
misery, beginning again and again. His fur is 'time-abused'
(p. 316), and in his old age he is dressed as a child. He and
Henderson formerly clutched each other in despair, despite the
image of brotherhood they presented. Moreover, if we compare
Smolak to a poem by Bellow's friend, Delmore Schwartz, *The
Heavy Bear who goes with me*,[15] the image is reinforced. In Schwartz's
poem the bear represents the body, and by extension, the heavi-
ness of temporal existence. Schwartz's bear is also a bundle of
fears and appetites, unable to experience a purer way of being,
spiritually, or in relation to the woman he loves. Yet the bear has
been left behind now, in Henderson's past, only a part of his final
worldview. The final image is one of joy. Henderson's last movement is a cyclic dance around the plane, in the arctic stillness,
celebrating not the frozen moment but the motion of time,
'Leaping, leaping, pounding and tingling over the pure white
lining of the grey Arctic silence' (p. 318). Stillness and dance are
both intermingled here, in an interpenetration of the divine frozen
moment with the cyclic dance of human life. Henderson has
reached the position outlined by Eliot in *Burnt Norton*,

> Except for the point, the still point,
> There would be no dance, and there is only the dance.
> I can only say, *there* we have been: but I cannot say where,
> And I cannot say, how long, for that is to place it in time.

With the solution of his personal dilemma comes the resolution of
a wider American schizophrenia, and an escape from its trauma:

> The inner freedom from the practical desire,
> The release from action and suffering, release from the inner
> And the outer compulsion, yet surrounded
> By a grace of sense, a white light still and moving,

Erhebung without motion, concentration
Without elimination, both a new world
And the old made explicit[16]

In the image of the dance and the still point Bellow creates a
bridge between two cultures, two temporal and religious schemes,
the old and the new worlds.[17] The novel moves from the initial
refutation of time to a loving acceptance, the awareness that (to
close the quotation)

The enchainment of past and future
Woven in the weakness of the changing body,
Protects mankind from heaven and damnation
Which flesh cannot endure.

While *Henderson the Rain King* does not discount the possibility
of eventual transcendence of time, the action of the novel directs
its ironies against any possibility of epiphanic transcendence.
While Henderson enjoys glimpses of an atemporal reality in
Africa, these transcendent moments are firmly subordinated to
the importance of a moral life in time. From the Arnewi Henderson recognises the deficiencies of a timeless aesthetic, and admits
that the attempt to sever all connection with inherited cultural
attitudes may end in disaster. From Dahfu's therapy Henderson
learns to live with himself in time, but in contrast to the Wariri
cyclic religion he rejects the vision of temporal recurrence as a
curse. Henderson therefore learns to accept a degree of recurrence
as a blessing, accepts his role as a father, and maintains an
awareness of the possibility of acting morally in time. While some
repetition is inescapable, the good man is capable of interrupting
the cycle and absorbing the blows of history. To this end, Bellow's
novel is careful to avoid converting such fundamental concerns as
passion and death into assimilable symbol.

4 *Herzog*: History as Neurosis

'If I am out of my mind, it's all right with me, thought Moses Herzog.'[1]

Uncompromisingly Herzog's story opens with the statement of his own neurosis, introducing a novel in which the sanity of the central character is seriously in doubt. Yet Herzog is also a historian with several articles, a book, and a doctoral thesis to his credit. In its central character the novel directs the reader's attention to the status of history, and in particular to the Freudian view of history.

More than one critic has drawn attention to the ahistorical quality of Freud's thought. Norman O. Brown points out that

> To see how man separated from nature and separated out the instincts, is to see history as neurosis; and also to see history as neurosis, pressing restlessly and unconsciously towards the abolition of history and the attainment of a state of rest which is also a reunification with nature ... Repression, and the repetition-compulsion generate historical time.[2]

Philip Rieff has also described the meaning of history in Freud's thought as neurosis.

> History, the memory of existence in time, is the flaw. Neurosis is the failure to escape the past, the burdens of history.[3]

In Rieff's view, Freud attaches a negative value to history. The end of psychoanalysis is to emancipate the patient from the burden of his history. Neurosis is understood as an abnormal clinging to the past, a fixation upon it. The timelessness of the *id* with its eternally unchanged concerns, is the goal of psychoanalysis, which moves always back from society towards the individual. All culture is founded upon repression (in Freud's essential fiction of the primal crime) and therefore culture is also neurosis. Individual health, rather than the perfection of society, is the psychological measure. Freudian psychology therefore offers an escape from history. In Rieff's succint phrase,

> If, for Marx, the past is pregnant with the future, with the proletariat as the midwife of history, for Freud the future is pregnant with the past, with the psychoanalyst as the abortionist of history.[4]

Rieff argues that the modern popularity of Freudian psychotherapy depends upon the attractive possibility which it offers to modern man of avoiding the public reference. In response to the harshness and ubiquity of public life the modern individual seeks out those doctrines which are the intellectual modalities of the most private interest, which, amidst accelerating modern change, offer an image of eternal sameness. This escape is primarily a flight from history into determinism. In the Freudian view man is conditioned, not only by the events of his early childhood but also by an archaic heritage, the distant echoes of the primal crime. History then has no surprises. Men have always known that they killed the primal father. What will happen is what has already happened, granted a slight change in context.

The extent to which Moses Herzog escapes from history into neurosis forms the theme of Bellow's novel, and governs its form. The novel begins and ends with Moses on the couch, going over his past.[5] The opening statement recurs near the close of the novel (p. 332) and the action of the novel is almost entirely retrospective. Herzog's flights, from New York to Martha's Vineyard, to New York, to Chicago, to Ludeyville, offer an impression of whirling movement, but these flights are remembered from a static unchanging point, to which the novel circles back. In his memories Herzog passes from recent memories (a succession of flights on a lecture tour of Europe in the preceding winter) to not so recent memories (Madeleine, Sono, Daisy) to the distant memories of his childhood, turning the clock always further and further back into an ever-receding past.[6] The rapid change of the supposed present, the scenes glimpsed from train and 'plane, is eclipsed by Herzog's immersion in memory, memory which cuts him off from human contact. The circular time scheme of the novel therefore suggests a flight into neurosis, away from the present and into the deepest recesses of the psyche.

Moses is however also a historian and much occupied with, among others, the work of Hegel, for whom history has positive value. Ironically, however, Moses's excursions into the large abstractions of culture history are also a form of escape. Totally isolated in the Berkshires Herzog studies the social ideas of the Romantics, and in particular Hegel's idea of 'concensus and civility' (p. 12). As his marriage to Madeleine founders Herzog immerses himself in Hegel's exposition of the 'law of the heart' (p. 125). The second striking formal device of the novel is the series of letters (unsent) which Herzog addresses to all and sundry, letters which form continual excursions into the meaning of history, addressed amongst others to Hegel, Nietzsche, Nehru, Eisenhower, and Heidegger. The continual counterpoint between Herzog's obsessive memories and the more public rhetoric of the letters, forms an image of his inability to live between the conflicting private and public worlds, the inner world of the self and the external world of culture. The letters therefore represent an alternative flight, flight into history, conceived of as massively dwarfing the individual under its sway. Where the temporal structure displays the flight out of time into the determining realm of the psyche, the letters display the flight into world historical concerns. In both flights the individual is absolved from responsibility for himself, and for his own particular history, surrendering to the determinism of personal psychological time or to that of all encompassing historical movements.

The formal strategies of the novel therefore raise the question of the individual's position in history. Is history essentially neurosis? Or is Herzog's neurosis the product of his involvement in the history of culture? Where the circular temporal structure suggests that history is only repetition, the letters suggest that history is a determinant force. In either case, the individual emerges only as a victim, whether of the rapid change of history or of the timeless psyche.

Each view of the novel has found a forceful proponent in recent critical studies. John J. Clayton[7] understands *Herzog* as primarily a study in psychoanalysis, involving Herzog's retreat from present events into the actions of the distant past. The novel is therefore a case study in neurosis, specifically in sado-masochism. In this (essentially Freudian) reading the action of the novel confirms the view of history as unchanging re-enactment of the past. Herzog's actions depend, not upon the immediate historical situation (his divorce from Madeleine) but upon childhood experiences in thrall to which he must remain. In his actions Herzog therefore fails to act upon the real events of the present, but rather re-enacts the traumas of his youth, so that such major plot events as the court visit, the 'murder attempt' and the automobile accident occur only as fugues from the present, flights into the past as re-enactment. Clayton's argument, briefly summarised, proceeds as follows.

Locating the root of Herzog's problems in 'an Oedipal relationship'[8] Clayton argues that Herzog is governed by the expectation of punishment for his illicit sexual desires from his powerful father, the father who punished him as a boy, and threatened to shoot him as a man, for his disordered life. The consequences of this relationship are twofold. In the first place guilt over his Oedipal feelings leads Moses to masculine women, women who will punish him like his father. Only under such conditions of punishment, only with women like Madeleine who threaten him symbolically with the castration and death which he fears from his father, can Herzog accept pleasure. Herzog therefore allows Madeleine to beat him because he unconsciously desires to be ground under her '*sharp elegant heel*' (p. 82). Other women are conceived in similar terms. Herzog rejects Sono's cheerful polymorphous sexuality in favour of Madeleine. He tends to be drawn to images of aggressive women, to whores in Hamburg in boots and with riding crops, to memories of Madeleine looking at her reflection in a knifeblade, to an imagined knife in Ramona's garter. Sex is continually associated with dirt (Sono) disease (Wanda) and death.

In his childhood Herzog observed that when drunken self-pitying Ravitch told Herzog's father of his sufferings, Jonah pitied and cared for him. In an analogous way Herzog's suffering seeks to produce pity and love. Herzog is aware that

he really had inwardly decided years ago to set up a deal – a psychic offer – meekness in exchange for preferential treatment.
(p. 161)

By adopting the role of helpless victim, Herzog seeks to forestall real punishment, to cast himself as a non-aggressor. He therefore projects his guilt onto others, making Madeleine and Gersbach the scapegoats for his own guilty sexuality. In character he is therefore classically sado-masochistic, alternating between the posture of victim, inviting blows from others, and that of sadist, seeking a revenge upon others which is not really commensurate with their actual guilts.

In this analysis, the action of the novel merely moves inwards into Herzog's psyche, from Madeleine to his father. Moses's terror when deserted by Madeleine, becomes akin to a fear of death. Madeleine's rejection of him is a symbolic repetition of his father's rejection. His father had threatened him with death. Herzog now imputes the same threat to Madeleine. Clayton concentrates his attention on the movement from the court, to the 'murder attempt', to the accident, arguing that in each event Moses moves further into neurosis, never really surfacing from his immersion in the events of the past. Thus, when Herzog witnesses the cases in the courtroom, he sees only his own guilty projections. In the trial of the homosexual he sees only his own sexual indecency, and his latent homosexual leanings. (The feminine passive attitude with which he hopes to cheat death has obvious homosexual components, specifically the desire to be sexually used by the father instead of being castrated or killed by him.) Alice-Aleck presents an image of male whoredom. He carries a toy gun in a holdup, prefiguring Herzog's attempted murder with an antique pistol. Like Herzog, Aleck associates sex with dirt, and he is sentenced by a judge whose authoritative, 'Aleck, if you keep this up you'll be in Potter's Field ... I give you four-five years' (p. 237), may be read as a sentence of death. In the final case a young mother and her lover are tried for the murder of her child by another man who had deserted her. Guilty already as a failed father, Herzog seizes upon the opportunity to transfer his guilt. The obvious parallel with Madeleine and Gersbach, living together with Herzog's child whom he suspects they abuse, contributes to Herzog's belief that Madeleine and Gersbach deserve to die. The court case is therefore seen by Clayton not as a social and public event but as significant only in its relation to Herzog's psyche. Leaving the court, Herzog transforms his own guilt into a death sentence, returns to his father's house, and takes up his father's role, collecting his father's gun which he wraps in the Czarist roubles he had played with as a child. Equipped with his father's values and his father's power, he sets out to kill. In Clayton's view the fact that Moses does not carry out the murder does not mean that he has broken free of his father. Rather,

Herzog continues to act out his father's role. Just as Father Herzog was unable to shoot Moses, he is unable to shoot Madeleine. In Clayton's words:

> If we are correct that at the core of Herzog's guilt is oedipal guilt and resultant fear of castration or death, the attempted murder can be seen as a mime of the father's act of vengeance – mimed by the guilty party to relieve himself? He takes the father's power – the gun – and, becoming the father, goes to seek out revenge on his wife and the villain who has stolen the wife. That the villain is in a number of ways (especially his vanity) a double for Herzog has already been noted. But Herzog does not kill; it is like saying, 'See – father cannot kill, and so, although I am guilty, I am safe.'[9]

Clayton envisages the automobile accident as similarly determined by Herzog's filial guilt. For him, 'the accident [is] no accident. Rather, it is typical of the "accidents" moral masochists arrange for themselves.'[10] Still trapped within the character formed once and for all in his past Herzog arranges the accident as a minor punishment to ward off major punishment, and to free him only temporarily from guilt. Herzog is booked by the police for possession of his father's weapon, for being in possession of his father's phallic power. It is as if he had to sin in a small way to be taken by authority, in order to be released from guilt. Set free, Herzog travels to Ludeyville, to live alone in an Edenic location where he is in harmony with nature and loses track of time completely. This resolution is therefore in Clayton's view a failure:

> Bellow has presented us with a careful unfolding of Herzog's psychological transformation. But the transformation, because it is without a believable lever force, seems likely to be temporary and restricted to Herzog while he is alone. His freedom from the accusation of the father within himself may be lost when he is again exposed to human – and therefore sexual – relationships; it seems likely that guilt and the consequent masochistic mechanism will return.[11]

While this short summary cannot possibly do full justice to the depth and complexity of Clayton's analysis, it is however clear that this reading understands the action of the novel as arguing towards a sense of history as eternal repetition, with the only positive step a temporary return to a timeless realm of nature and childhood. Clayton's argument concedes a determinism which can only be described as Freudian, and presents Herzog's actions in the present as mere repetitions of the all important events and relationships of his past. Herzog therefore appears to be doomed to repeat his past, to project his past onto the present, and to circle always within the boundaries of neurosis. The analysis is percipient, but partial. Herzog *is* fatally drawn towards neurotic behaviour, but as an escape from the pressures of his immediate experience, rather than being determined by the distant past. The Freudian paradigm is being exposed here to irony.

On external grounds alone it seems highly unlikely that Bellow agrees with the Freudian estimation of history. Bellow said of *Herzog* 'I consider *Herzog* a break from victim literature.'[12] Before publishing *Herzog*, Bellow had written a play, *The Last Analysis*, which is an extended spoof of Freudian psychology. Its hero, Bummidge, argues that 'Man is the sick animal. Repression is the root of his madness, and also of his achievements,' and 'In the unconscious, Louie, there is no time, no logic, no death.'[13] Bummidge is however, ironically exposed. Ignoring the problems of his son, he immerses himself in the re-enactment of past traumas, a re-enactment which is televised and makes him a fortune. While the play also, more seriously, deals with the problem of living amidst weltering ideas, the attack on Freudian psychology is wide-ranging and total. (Bummidge's stomach is not rumbling. 'It's doing free association.')[14] The internal evidence of *Herzog* will however suffice to question the validity of Clayton's case, indicating that, while Herzog does flee from the present into the past, this is only a temporary movement. Herzog does see the error of his ways, and in this connection the action does motivate a major change in his character.

Harold J. Mosher argues for precisely this view and also founds his analysis on reactions to history. In his analysis Herzog's problem is not an ahistorical tendency but an excessive commitment to his historical role. In this argument, Herzog has escaped responsibility for his own actions, not by locating their causes in the timeless psyche, but in world history.

At times it seems as if Herzog had taken the responsibility for the faults of Western man to avoid taking responsibility for his own.[15]

Whereas Herzog's first book had made history relevant to the concerns of the present (p. 11) he afterwards buries himself in a mass of abstractions, using the past as a refuge. His country retreat, an antiquated mansion often compared to Versailles, symbolises his activity. Undertaking the enormous labour of restoring the house to its former glory, and writing his historical *magnum opus* are parallel activities. The resultant chaos demonstrates the folly of assuming responsibility for all history. Herzog becomes lost in a mass of abstractions which lead him away from his own essential responsibilities into a monumental absurdity. In Mosher's view, Herzog tends to conceive of history in polarised extremes:

> Like his approach to the present – either accepting too much responsibility or entirely refusing it – Herzog's conception of the past may be divided into two contrasting views: his nostalgia for the past corresponds to a negative view of history, the belief in a golden age from which man is predestined to decline; his repulsion for the past corresponds to a positive theory of history, the belief in continual progress from a dark age. The first theory might be called Christian, or more accurately, Calvinistic, with its emphasis on the Fall. (Herzog is associated several times in the novel with Calvinism, the Elect and Puritanism.) The second theory might be called Romantic with its emphasis on the value of the self and its progress. Thus possibly, the significance of the title of his first book *Romanticism and Christianity*.[16]

Whichever of these polarised ideas he is following Herzog cuts himself off from present reality, minimising his own problems by reference to the larger sweep of cultural history. Under the sway of the Romantic ideas he substitutes, in place of his own moral progress, responsibility for the fate of Western man. Tired of the modern form of historicism which sees his own century as a decline from the past, he attempts to be a '*marvellous* Herzog' (p. 100) to incarnate in his own successes the Romantic possibility. When, inevitably, he fails, he reverts to a pessimistic vision of history as a 'history of cruelty' (p. 297). Yearning for a prelapsarian Golden Age he colours his memories of Napoleon Street with a warm glow of nostalgia. When less pleasant memories of his past intervene he is driven on to the alternative paradigm, in an eternal vicious circle.

In Mosher's view, Herzog's final position at Ludeyville does reveal an acceptance of the present. The action is in the fictional present from the time of Will's arrival, to the end of the novel. Herzog does accept responsibility for himself, in that he refuses dependence on Will. Led by his memories to the realisation that there is both good and bad in the past, as in the present, Herzog accepts the importance of his own actions. No longer bent on a total restoration of the house, nor entirely immersed in the past, he accepts a degree of confusion and a degree of practical action. In saving what is valuable from the past he has strengthened himself. In Mosher's view, the lyrical natural scene at Ludeyville invests the present with an appeal which prevents Herzog from letting it pass. Herzog has been forced to accept responsibility:

> Life compels him to accept it, primarily at the court scenes in New York, and in the police interrogation in Chicago, where Herzog is no longer clothed with his proud air of abstraction.[17]

While Mosher locates the change in the same plot events as Clayton, he does not elaborate further. Clayton, while paying close attention to the actual events of the novel, falls prey to a determinism which finally minimises the force of specific events, assimilating them to a preconceived pattern in which no accidents can occur. Mosher, while acknowledging the force of the historical ideas, neglects to explain how these ideas are functional to the temporal action of the novel. For Clayton Herzog's culture is entirely subservient to his neurosis: the letters are largely the symptoms of his disordered psyche. Mosher's analysis is directed almost entirely to the intellectual 'content' of the novel, seeing plot events as exemplifications of Herzog's cultural inheritance.

But *Herzog* is neither a case study nor an intellectual debate, but a novel with its own logic of events, and its own temporal development. The ambiguities and the ironies of its temporal structure enact the complexity of Bellow's investigation of history, preventing the reader from assimilating its action to a simplistic paradigm. History is neither a curse nor a supreme value, but the medium in which both Herzog and the reader must make difficult moral judgements. In Herzog's memories of Dr Edvig, Bellow satirises both strategies of escape from time. At Madeleine's suggestion Herzog seeks psychiatric treatment, deliberately choosing a man who has written on Barth, Brunner and Tillich, in an effort to understand Madeleine's Christian conversion. In the course of the analysis, however, Edvig becomes more interested in Madeleine. Both Madeleine and Herzog advance their cases by offering their neurosis in historical terms. Intent upon her doctorate in Russian religious history, Madeleine turns her sessions into '*a course of lectures on Eastern Christianity*' (p. 61). Madeleine then accuses Herzog of being a Pharisee. Herzog, however, claims that *he* is the historical victim:

'Do you think that any Christian in the twentieth century has the right to speak of Jewish Pharisees? From a Jewish standpoint, you know, this hasn't been one of your best periods.'

(p. 60)

From this self-justification Herzog flies off into an account of Madeleine's 'case' as the result of a Christian view of history, arguing that neither of them is sick, but merely the victims of cultural and historical conditioning:

'I don't agree with Nietzsche that Jesus made the whole world sick, infected it with his slave morality. But Nietzsche himself had a Christian view of history, seeing the present moment always as some crisis, some fall from classical greatness, some corruption or evil to be saved from.'   (p. 60)

Edvig listens to this disquisition but 'took it all as analytic material' (p. 60). For the psychiatrist, historical speculation is merely more evidence of Herzog's neurosis. The reader, however cannot understand Herzog's problems as historically or psychologically determined. In the letter which precedes the memory of Edvig, Herzog, toying with large historical views, has a moment of clarity. 'You must start with injustices that are obvious to everybody, not with big historical perspectives' (p. 54). The injustice which is clear to the reader, here, is Madeleine's concealed adultery with Gersbach. The time lapse between the events described and the knowledge of their cause operates to throw irony onto both the psychological and the grand historical explanation. When Madeleine imagines that she is being followed by a private detective, Herzog accepts Edvig's description of this as a paranoid episode. The later Herzog realises however that adulterous Madeleine *'had good reason to fear being followed by a private investigator. There was nothing at all neurotic about it'* (p. 71). Madeleine's supposed private investigation by Edvig is carefully designed to forestall more searching private investigators, and to safeguard her own present activities. Embarking on massive spending sprees, for which she is able to claim total amnesia, she uses psychiatry to bolster her bank balance. Directing Herzog to investigate his own past traumas, Madeleine arranges his sessions on the couch to guarantee that her own (with Gersbach) will be uninterrupted. Four afternoons per week the couple know where Herzog is and are therefore safe in bed. Psychiatry offers Madeleine all too easy a means of escaping from detection, and of concealing her real guilt.

One incident crystallises the situation. Herzog makes a sharp remark to Madeleine about the dusty volumes of Russian religious history which are encumbering the marital bed, and an enraged Madeleine attacks him. For Herzog this is further evidence of his historical persecution:

> 'She's built a wall of Russian books around herself. Vladimir of
> Kiev, Tikhon Zadonsky. In my bed! It's not enough they
> persecuted my ancestors!'   (p. 65)

He does not consider Zelda's charge (p. 45) that he has neglected Madeleine, to retreat behind his own wall of books, the study of the social ideas of the Romantics on which he is engaged. While, in a general sense, each party appears equally guilty here, the reader is aware of the specific injustice, adultery, beneath the surface. The discrepancy between the reader's knowledge and Herzog's ignorance generates hilarious ironies. When Herzog recounts the incident to Gersbach, revealing that 'It so happens we had intercourse the night before' (p. 65) he is astonished by Gersbach's sudden anger. The reader is less surprised. As Madeleine's lover, Gersbach's reaction is understandable. When Gersbach promptly accuses Herzog of being 'evasive' (p. 65) swearing that he is for 'truth' (p. 67) the reader knows otherwise. The time structure of the novel underlines Gersbach's amorality. Knowledge of a precise historical event – adultery – reveals that both the psychological and the sweeping historical explanations are flawed. Valentine's reaction to Herzog's plight is to shift with all speed onto his own sad history, claiming a superior degree of victimisation, and offering Herzog religious consolation in the works of Martin Buber. Wryly the later Herzog reconsiders Buber's description of the necessity for spiritual dialogue and brotherhood:

> *God comes and goes in man's soul. And men come and go in each other's souls. Sometimes they come and go in each other's beds, too. You have dialogue with a man. You have intercourse with his wife.* (p. 70)

The chapter, then, castigates the retreat from the historical situation, whether into psychiatry – an image of eternal sameness which becomes dangerously akin to a pseudo-religious position – or into sweeping historical vistas. While the reader is aware of the flaws in both Madeleine and Herzog, the larger time scheme establishes Herzog as not masochistically courting victimhood but actually victimised, not suffering delusions but being in fact deluded by those around him. Herzog is not a victim of large historical trends (anti-semitism, the view of history as Fall) but of a specific injustice. In the Freudian idea, the attachment to the past is neurosis. Indeed in a preceding memory of his father Herzog claims that 'These acute memories are probably symptoms of disorder (p. 39). An acute awareness of the past has its value, however. The reader's full knowledge of past events reveals the real significance of the acts which Herzog so easily dismisses as psychologically defined.

From these memories Herzog moves back to his letter writing. In his letters Herzog is concerned with the question of who governs history. Writing to the defeated Adlai Stevenson, he complains that ideas have no part in public life, that Eisenhower won because he expressed '*low-grade universal potato love*' (p. 72) pandering to the mass psyche. The letters which open the chapter primarily raise the question of the participation open to the intellectual, and to human reason, in the public life. To the Commissioner of the Narcotics conference Herzog laments the decline of civil order. To Martin Luther King he complains that White America is in danger of being depoliticalised, and he applauds King's attempts, in the civil rights campaign, to '*penetrate the hypnotic trance of the majority*' (p. 73). For Herzog culture cannot be written off as mass neurosis, in which individuals are psychologically entranced, drugged by fantasy. '*The political question in modern democracies is one of the reality of public questions. Should all of these become matters of fantasy the old political order is ended*' (p. 73). In opposition to this psychological trend Herzog argues that 'The occupation of a man is in duty, in use, in civility, in politics in the Aristotelian sense' (p. 100). The memories of the chapter, primarily of Shapiro and Himmelstein, dramatise the question raised by the letters. Is there a place for human ideas in history? Or is history governed by mass fantasy? Is there a middle ground in which the individual may assume a civil role and exercise a moral part in history?

In his memory of Shapiro Herzog realises the ineffectuality of intellectuals. At Ludeyville Shapiro and Madeleine discuss ideas. As Gersbach comments, their isolation speaks for itself. 'Nothing interesting had happened here since the Battle of Saratoga' (p. 80). Removed from the problems of twentieth century history Madeleine and Shapiro swap ideas about the revolution of 1848, the Russian church, the concept of *sobornost*. Madeleine has made a particular study of the life and thought of Soloviev and delivers a lecture upon the dead Russian, including his vision in the British Museum. It is an apt subject for Madeleine whose own religious vision is connected to her own escape into dusty books. A cultural magpie, Madeleine has passed through a series of historical enthusiasms: Mirabeau, the French revolution, Schliemann's excavations at Troy, Josephine Tey, Eleanor of Aquitaine. Her only constant interest is murder mysteries, suggesting that her interest in history is entirely the product of a need for immediate present gratification, rather than a serious attempt to apply the ideas of the past to the present. Significantly Rozanov's erotic mysticism figures high on her list of interests. Intellectual conversation excites Madeleine, bringing the blood to her face. She is described as avid for scholarly chat.

Shapiro is similarly avid, but the greed below the surface reveals itself more clearly. As Madeleine turns to Berdyaev's *Slavery and Freedom*, she opens a jar of pickled herring. 'Saliva spurted to Shapiro's lips. . . . Herzog remembered him as a greedy eater' (p. 79). Shapiro refuses the herring on the grounds of 'a stomach condition' (p. 79), unwilling to admit his ulcer because the psychosomatic implications are unflattering. The quality of historian Shapiro's respect for truth is clearly deficient. Shapiro's own monograph on modern history is utterly without a moral or social focus. Entitled *From Luther to Lenin, A History of Revolutionary Psychology* (p. 323) it offers a merely aesthetic critique of modern history and depends upon a vision of history as decline, and as mass psychology. Herzog attacks the vision of decline arguing that the analogies of the classical world will not hold for the modern. History escapes such easy generalisations. For Herzog the problem is that ideas are themselves a potent force causing terror and bloodshed:

> *We mustn't forget how quickly the visions of genius become the canned goods of the intellectuals. The canned sauerkraut of Spengler's 'Prussian Socialism', the commonplaces of the Wasteland outlook, the cheap mental stimulants of alienation.*
>   (p. 81)

Shapiro is drawn to history as a form of social climbing, a way up from his deprived background, much as he is drawn to other canned goods. Madeleine converts the visions of genius into cheap mental stimulants. Ideas appear to assuage animal needs, rather than directing history in accordance with human reason. Herzog realises that ideas are as likely to impoverish a culture as to enrich it: humanity has been the victim of *'engineered famines directed by "ideologists"'* (p. 81). Affected by Shapiro's salivating greed and snarling teeth, Herzog accepts his vision of history as mass psychology. In his review of the work he suggests *'that clinical psychologists might write fascinating histories. Put professionals out of business. Megalomania for the Pharaohs and Caesars. Melancholia in the Middle Ages. Schizophrenia in the eighteenth century'* (p. 83). Herzog turns approvingly to memories of his brother, Shura, for whom 'universal concerns were idiocy. Ask nothing better than to prosper in the belly of Leviathan' (p. 84). Abandoning himself entirely to a Freudian view of history as mass neurosis, in which ideas have no real, or at best only a sinister part, he adopts a Freudian vocabulary to dismiss his affection for his brother as 'his archaic aspect, prehistoric. Tribal, you know. Associated with ancestor worship and totemism' (p. 84).

In the following memory, however, the reader is prevented from accepting the view that civil order is only mass psychology, that the past is valueless, and that the individual had best abandon all but personal concerns, for these ideas are now expressed parodically by Sandor Himmelstein. As a lawyer Sandor assails the ineffectuality of intellectuals. 'What good are those

effing eggheads! It takes an ignorant bastard like me to fight
liberal causes' (p. 87). Sandor enjoys a grandiose pride in his own
civil rights record. He has succeeded in maintaining a Negro,
Tompkins, in the postal service. For Herzog the issue is not so
simple. Tompkins was a drunk. To Sandor this is irrelevant. He
argues, 'It was a question of justice. Aren't there any white drunks
on civil service?' (p. 87). While ostensibly defending an ideal
civility Sandor actually weakens the practical structure of society.
His civility, as his constant foul language implies, is only a pose.
When Sandor wrings a compliment for Bea from Herzog, the
latter comments, 'Among narrow puritans, this is lying; but with
civilized people only civility' (p. 86). For Sandor the rights and
wrongs of a specific case are unimportant. When Herzog consults
him about a custody suit Sandor convinces him that he will lose.
Under the cover of his social conscience Sandor is prepared to
strip his friend of his rights as a parent. 'As the lawyer,' he argues
'I have a social obligation to the child. I've got to protect her.'
'*You*? I'm her father.' (p. 93). Herzog's outraged reaction makes
no impression on Sandor. Wielding his insurance policy he
bludgeons Herzog into accepting his own lack of importance,
screeching, 'What's so great about your effing death?' (p. 93) in
his friend's face. Despite his ostensible faith in civil action Sandor
contends that in this particular civil action Herzog will lose; the
jury will automatically give custody to the beautiful Madeleine.
'That's the jury system. Dumber than cave men, those bastards'
(p. 89). In his view the jury will decide, not on the merits of the
plaintiff, but on archaic psychological grounds. Madeleine will
win because 'She's the mother – the female. She's got the tits.
They'll crush you' (p. 94). On a more immediate level than
Shapiro's monograph, Sandor argues that history is controlled by
psychological motives. By accepting this belief Sandor abandons
all social responsibility. When Herzog leaves emergency money
for June, Sandor at once hands it over to Madeleine to buy
clothes. The quality of Sandor's supposed 'care' for June may be
well imagined from the chaos of his own family relationships.
Surrounded by dirty dishes, Coke bottles and cigarette butts, he
screams, 'they're killing me! Killing their father!' (p. 95). The
parallel with Madeleine's sloppy housekeeping suggests that
Sandor is in similar difficulties to Herzog. He too has discussed his
dirty dishes with a psychiatrist. Sandor imputes murder to his
errant women, argues that Herzog should abandon culture (a

pointless exercise) forget his daughter, revert to Orthodox Judaism, and return to his childhood home. He invokes the younger Herzog as 'My innocent kind-hearted boy' (p. 97). His injunctions are a parody of the Freudian argument – abandoning the present for the timeless past, leaving behind social obligations for individual fulfilment, converting man into child. The real child, June, is to be abandoned in favour of a pseudo-innocence, a specific injustice subsumed beneath a vision of society as primitive and murderous. By placing the argument in the mouth of crass, aggressive, lying Sandor, Bellow effectively undercuts its credibility. Herzog now realises that both psychological and intellectual readings of history depend upon the devaluation of the specific individual. In his view:

> 'History' gave everyone a free ride. The very Himmelsteins, who had never even read a book of metaphysics, were touting the Void as if it were so much saleable real estate. . . . you must sacrifice your poor, squawking, niggardly individuality – which may be nothing anyway (from an analytic viewpoint) but a persistent infantile megalomania, or (from a Marxian point of view) a stinking little bourgeois property – to historical necessity.
>
> (p. 99)

While Herzog recognises that he may have overplayed his own individual value, he refuses to concede that all such values are flawed. He is not willing to abandon June and demands a return to a truer civility based upon the protection of individual rights.

It is at this point that Geraldine Portnoy's letter is introduced, a letter which encapsulates for the reader the implications of the action. Herzog re-reads the letter. The reader, of course, reads it for the first time. The contrast between the two readings is instructive. When Herzog first reads the letter he is impatient with Geraldine's balanced slow style. He skims the letter, trying to swallow it whole. Geraldine concludes, '*a letter gives one a chance to consider – think matters over, and reach a more balanced view*' (p. 107). In Herzog's immediate reaction this is deeply ironic. Rushing through the letter he is filled with the desire to kill. The reader has however previously read the later Herzog's belief that moral values are not merely symptoms of neurosis. '*Charity, as if it didn't have enough trouble in this day and age, will always be suspected of morbidity – sado-masochism, perversity of some sort. All higher or moral tendencies lie under suspicion of being rackets*' (p. 62). Geraldine presents the same view, rejecting Lucas's suggestion of 'something dikey' in her friendship with Madeleine, on the grounds that:

> *any intense feeling between members of the same sex is often, and unjustly, under suspicion. My scientific background has taught me to make more cautious generalizations, and resist this creeping psychoanalysis of ordinary conduct.* (pp. 105–6)

Geraldine goes on to describe a specific incident – June's incarceration in the car – but precedes it with the statement: *Americans have their own craze about child psychology. Everything is done for children, ostensibly* (p. 106). The reader therefore sees Geraldine's interest as distinct from Sandor's ostensible 'care' and motivated by careful attention to the specific case. Our reaction to the letter is akin to the problem of Herzog's letters. Can the individual intervene morally in social events (here to protect June) unmoved by large generalisations? In the immediate time scheme it appears that Geraldine's well meaning letter only engenders madness in Herzog, as the ideas of men of letters engender only horror, as his own letters are only neurotic symptoms. The reader however, as a result of the contrast with the preceding scenes with Himmelstein, recognises some good sense in Geraldine and has to suspend judgement. Importantly Geraldine claims that Madeleine is not a bad mother, and she approves of Gersbach as a playful stepfather. Later in the novel, when Herzog spies on Valentine, playing with June in her bath, he realises the truth of this. Time to consider at first leads him to murder, but eventually to truth. The reader does not of course know of these later events at this point so that the reading of the letter poses the problem of judgement within time. As Herzog's judgement is flawed when first he reads the letter, so the reader's judgement is uncertain until the time of the novel completes itself. It is therefore time which brings truth. While time may appear as only a curse, it is actually valuable. When Herzog first reads the letter he is lost in his immediate concerns. When the reader reads it he has already begun to take a wider view, to set an initial reaction against a larger temporal perspective. In the course of the novel, in the continual counterpoint between past and present, the reader learns to beware of over hasty judgements, or of distancing all judgements into the receding vistas of historical paradigms, but rather to appreciate the full complexity of individual decisions in time.

This process continues in the following chapters. In Chapter

Four Herzog addresses a deceptively moderate letter to Monsignor Hilton. Motivated, he believes, not by his own anger but by the desire for historical objectivity, he offers Hilton '*the true history of one of your converts*' (p. 124). From Madeleine's history, however, Herzog moves back in memory to Daisy, to Nachman and to his father in Napoleon Street. A whole day is lost in the process, as Herzog escapes from his position amidst the rapid change of New York into the deepest individual concerns, in a slow regression back in time. The result of the process appears to be fundamentally amoral. Emerging from his memories Herzog tears up the letter, and expresses less moderate feelings:

> *I want you to know, Monsignor, that I am not writing with the purpose of exposing Madeleine, or to attack you.* Herzog tore up the letter. Untrue! He despised the Monsignor, wanted to murder Madeleine.
> (p. 162)

Given time to consider Herzog turns to murderous thoughts. It is important for the reader that this movement is preceded by Geraldine's letter. From a Freudian point of view Moses is at his most neurotic here, clinging to a past to which he is over-attached. Moses indeed diagnoses his memories as neurotic. 'He was a depressive. Depressives cannot surrender childhood – not even the pains of childhood.' (p. 149). The reader is however distanced from a similar view by the indictment of creeping psychologism in Geraldine's letter. Pondering his father's sad history Herzog also wonders whether the mass cruelties of the twentieth century abolish the interest of his father's case. Is his suffering relevant to a post-Holocaust generation?

> These personal histories, old tales from old times that may not be worth remembering. I remember. I must. But who else – to whom can this matter?
> (p. 155)

As the chapter ends Herzog feels that there is no longer any audience for the dramas of his father's life, as there is no-one to whom he may send his letters; 'to whom would he send the other letters he was drafting?' (p. 155). The question is almost arch, almost daring the reader not to concern himself with specific individual suffering. Herzog writes off the audience to these past dramas, partly because in his view they are relevant only to his individual psyche, partly in terms of the crushing weight of twentieth-century history. By this point in the novel the reader has been well prepared to disregard such disclaimers. The chapter, which closes with them, sets them in ironic perspective, primarily by reference to Hegel, expounded parodically through the characters of Madeleine and Nachman. In so doing, Bellow very carefully constitutes an informed audience for his novel.

Herzog remembers himself 'tragically sipping milk in Philadelphia' (p. 112) while he ponders 'the difference between ancient and modern tragedy according to Hegel' (p. 113). For Hegel history has altered the form of tragedy, so that it is no longer a social expression, but individual in its concerns. Hegel describes ancient tragedy[18] as involving a conflict between two 'rights' represented by two individuals, for example the right of the state versus the right of the family, Creon versus Antigone. Orestes, for example, should avenge Agamemnon by killing Clytemnestra, but the sacred bond of father to son is challenged by the equally sacred bond of son to mother. Both are powers rightfully claiming allegiance. In modern tragedy, he argued, the conflict occurs within the mind of one vacillating individual who is placed in a wide expanse of contingent circumstances. Interest is therefore diverted from ethical conflict to individual characters. Romeo, a modern tragic hero, is not a citizen as well as a lover, he is only a lover. The public or universal dimension of the drama is lost. In modern tragedies we can therefore attribute catastrophe not to justice, but to accident, so that we can only feel that the hero pays the price for existence in a scene of historical contingency.

The contingency of history is of course, precisely what Madeleine wishes to avoid, either by the large determinism of a historical role, or by psychological determinism. When Madeleine accidentally falls on the subway she says, 'I punished myself for my sins,' (p. 124), a hysterical reaction which militates against such a view of Herzog's later accident. Madeleine trips up on her long tweed skirt, a garment donned in accordance with her own self-appointed role as Catholic convert. Madeleine's attraction to Roman Catholicism depends upon her need for a creed in which contingency is denied, in which life has 'rules' (p. 123). The theatrical metaphors of the chapter emphasise Madeleine's self-conscious adoption of a role in a Hegelian ancient tragedy. Madeleine sees herself as caught between warring allegiances – love and her religious faith – each rightfully claiming her. For Madeleine 'Conversion was a theatrical event' (p. 118). Herzog describes Monsignor Hilton as the actor in a drama for which there is still an audience:

> *You see, Monsignor, if you stand on television in the ancient albs and surplices of the Roman church there are at least enough Irishmen, Poles, Croatians watching in saloons to understand you.*   (p. 112)

Rejecting her own bohemian upbringing by Pontritter, impresario and modern tragedian, director of Chekhov and O'Neill, Madeleine hastens into the arms of the Monsignor, who 'made female converts with his burning eyes' (p. 121). Pontritter exercises a similar sway over his female students (p. 120), and over his wife, Tennie, who has sacrificed her life to his artistic genius. Moses meets Tennie on Broadway where he takes a keen interest in the Uptown public: 'its theatrical spirit, its performers – the transvestite homosexuals painted with great originality, the wigged women' (p. 186). Individual existence is being dramatised in modern America. In rejecting this modern drama, however, Madeleine merely turns towards its mirror image. The description of her, making up for her job at Fordham, presents her less as true convert than as actress, carefully applying powder and paint, donning an appropriate costume, and transforming herself into a drab middle-aged woman. Her apartment, 'this setting of disgraced Victorian luxury' (p. 116), replete with backcloths of Flemish altarpieces and mirror panels, forms an appropriate stage set. The roles offered in the past cannot however be repeated at will, for all Madeleine's skill in creating the role of the older woman. Herzog, however, is drawn to Madeleine by his wish to figure, himself, as a great actor on the stage of history, a representative individual. He sets out to save Madeleine, much as he sets out to restore Ludeyville. 'But the parts had been distributed. She had her white convert's face and Herzog couldn't refuse to play opposite' (p. 118). The parallels between Madeleine and Herzog are not entirely complete, however. Madeleine also claims that her conversion is the result of her sexual abuse, as a child, by a grown man. At this point Herzog comments, 'It happens to many, many people. Can't base a whole life on that' (p. 123). Madeleine, however, does base her life upon the past, swinging into polarised extremes of individual drama and social convention. When the reader later learns of Herzog's own childhood abuse, by a homosexual (p. 295), the example of Madeleine prevents the reader from seeing this action as similarly determinant. Madeleine's self-indulgent apportioning of blame – to her abuser, to her parents, to her historical situation – pre-empts the reader from understanding Herzog's situation in similarly reductive terms.

The careful parallelism here forces the reader to make careful distinctions between outwardly similar events, and emphasises the very different way in which each individual reacts to them. There is always the possibility of an individual response to the human tragedy. Where Madeleine argues that she must retreat from the example of her father, into a social consensus, Nachman, in contrast, argues the reverse. A poet, obsessed with modern art, Nachman inveighs against the lack of an audience for his poetry, asserting that bourgeois America yields no place to the artist, and that there is no consensus to which his art can appeal. There are specific parallels between Herzog and Nachman's beloved Laura. Herzog has been described by Tennie as a '*zisse n'shamele*, a sweet little soul' (p. 131). In *The Phenomenology of Mind*[19] Hegel described the life of the 'Beautiful Soul', a spiritual life in which the individual cuts himself off from society in order to pursue goodness and truth in solitary isolation. Nachman describes Laura in similar terms as 'a pure soul that understands only pure things' (p. 139). Nachman believes that Laura has gone insane as the result of persecution by her bourgeois family. '"Why does she keep trying to kill herself?" said Moses. "The persecution of her family. What do you think? The bourgeois world of Westchester!"' (p. 139). In Nachman's view the past is a curse, and Laura's insanity all her father's fault. Her father has taken Laura away and Nachman goes on, 'The old Sorcerer. She'll die without me. The child can't bear life without me' (p. 136). The quality of Nachman's care for his 'child', 'innocent darling', and pure soul is however, undercut. In the service of art and truth Nachman has dragged Laura around the Rimbaud country, reading Van Gogh's letters to her, and sleeping in ditches until Laura's health collapses. Nachman runs from the past to individual art, and the results for Laura are horrendous. (She is last seen in a lunatic asylum, describing the shape of Valéry's images.) Herzog's memory of these facts undermines Nachman's claim to his role as guiltless victim of social and familial persecution. Where the parallels between Herzog and Madeleine undercut

Herzog's pretentions to a grand representative socio-historical role, those between Herzog and Laura indicate the insanity of a purely individual existence. Guilt is laid at the door of bohemian parents (the Pontritters) or conventional parents (Laura's family) only in an attempt to shake off individual responsibility for one's actions. The persecution of the past, the conditioning force of historical circumstances, become a salve for the individual conscience. Madeleine cultivates a social form, stultifying herself in a determined role. Nachman espouses defiant modern individualism, and abandons humanity by the wayside.

The reader is therefore carefully prepared for Herzog's memories of his own family. These are also described as dramatic scenes, but here the Herzogs are the audience. While Herzog notes his father's sense of personal dignity, his father is no posturing actor. That role is taken by Ravitch, 'Like a tragic actor of the Yiddish stage' (p. 141), reeling drunkenly home wailing his melancholy songs. The Herzogs listen, enjoying the comedy of the situation. Moses and his brothers are smiling in the dark. 'It amused the boys to hear how their father coaxed drunken Ravitch to get on his feet. It was family theatre' (p. 142). Father Herzog is also amused. The chapter insists upon the point: he is 'Half laughing' (p. 142), he 'laughed under his breath' (p. 142), and 'laughed with his bare breath' (p. 143). While Ravitch has suffered the blows of history (he has lost his family in the Russian Revolution) and the Herzogs care for him, they do not themselves elevate their own sufferings to the status of tragedy. Jonah, as his name suggests, is presented less as a powerful, strong father, than as a comic failure. He 'failed as a farmer ... failed as a baker ... failed in the dry-goods business; failed as a jobber; failed as a sack manufacturer in the War, when no one else failed' (p. 143). Persecuted as a Jew, imprisoned under Pobedonostsev, beaten up and poverty-stricken in America, Father Herzog has none the less retained responsibility for his children, and for Ravitch, and avoided transferring it elsewhere. Mother Herzog, felled to the ground by the shock of her brother's death, none the less continues the struggle. 'She wept all day. But in the morning she cooked the oatmeal nevertheless' (p. 146). Exhausted by toil Sarah still finds the time to spoil her children (Moses remembers her pulling his sledge) just as she and Jonah find the money for Helen's piano lessons. The supposed 'persecutions' by family and history of Madeleine and Nachman pale into insignificance beside the real sufferings of the Herzogs – Revolution, Anti-semitism, prison, deaths from typhus. Yet the Herzogs have not passed on to their children the urge for revenge. Jonah is distinguished from bitter Zipporah, who unfeelingly castigates the dead Mikhail for making a fortune out of kaffirs, and assails Helen's lessons as a useless luxury. Father Herzog has come to borrow money from Zipporah, who promptly accuses him of being a weakling:

'You can never keep up with these teamsters and butchers. Can you shoot a man?'
Father Herzog was silent.
'If, God forbid, you had to shoot ...' cried Zipporah, 'Could you even hit someone on the head?'   (p. 152)

The answer is clearly negative. Herzog comments, 'all of Papa's violence went into the drama of his life, into family strife and sentiment' (p. 152). When, later in the novel, Herzog tries to borrow money from his father, and his father threatens to shoot him the reader remembers this scene. Jonah is not an all-powerful father figure, but a caring man who has absorbed many blows from history but has largely mastered the urge to strike back. The memory establishes Father Herzog as not a killer, but a victim. When Herzog decides not to kill for the sake of June, when he retires to Ludeyville to paint a piano for her, he does re-enact his father's role, but in a hopeful manner, concentrating upon the future, not the past. It is only at the close of the novel that Herzog fully learns the lessons of his father's life. Jonah is not an actor in a vast social tragedy, nor in an individual psychodrama. He is acting within the confines of his family, for his family, and not for himself. Far from horribly injuring his children's tender psyches he stands up for them against Zipporah's harsh judgements. Remembering these old family events, Herzog is associated with a wider audience: 'But somehow his heart had come open at this chapter of his life and he didn't have the strength to shut it' (p. 149). Listening, 'Engrossed, unmoving in his chair' (p. 150), contemplating the figures from his past, Herzog's position is that of a reader, a member of an audience. Where at the start of the chapter the reader is detached, watching Herzog play his part in the high drama staged by Madeleine, at the chapter's close Herzog has moved towards the audience. The chapter moves us from being spectators on Herzog, to sharing his position. This

movement implies a belief that life is neither a drama of re-
enactment, in which all are individualistic performers, nor a
spectacle the form of which is dictated by sociohistorical conditions alone. History is tragic only when presented in oversimplified terms, governed by the paradigms of Freud or Hegel. In
history the individual may appear to repeat past actions, as
Herzog repeats his father's, but this does not imply a negative
reading of history.

Herzog, however, merely sees the less valuable aspects of
repetition. Tearing up the letter to Hilton he realises that the
Monsignor will not prove a sensitive reader. 'Between the lines of
Herzog's letter the Monsignor would only see a mad, reasoning
face ... Endless repetition threatens sanity' (p. 162). Rejecting the
attempt to present Madeleine's 'true history', Herzog is drawn to
a belief in freedom as the escape from history, as purely private
and inward. He considers de Chardin's description of the inward
aspects of the elements[20] (p. 166), recalls Emerson's belief that
'*The private life of one man shall be a more illustrious monarchy ... than any
kingdom in history*' (p. 167)[21] and dwells on Eisenhower's report on
national aims, wishing that it had pondered '*the private and inward
existence of Americans*' (p. 173). Is freedom the product of an
awareness of history? Or does it consist in ignoring history?
Herzog summarises the positions of Hegel and Tolstoi:

> *Tolstoi (1828–1910) said, 'Kings are history's slaves'. The higher one
> stands in the scale of power, the more his actions are determined. To
> Tolstoi, freedom is entirely personal. That man is free whose condition is
> simple, truthful – real. To be free is to be released from historical
> limitation. On the other hand, G.W.F. Hegel (1770–1831) understood
> the essence of human life to be derived from history. History, memory –
> that is what makes us human, that, and our knowledge of death: 'by man
> came death'. For knowledge of death makes us wish to extend our lives at
> the expense of others. And this is the root of the struggle for power.'*
>
> (p. 169)

The latter position is dramatised in the novel when Herzog,
confronted in court with the death of the murdered child, decides
to extend his own power at the expense of Madeleine and Gersbach. At this point in the novel, however, he is more attracted to
Tolstoi. In Hegel's view knowledge of death confers individuality
upon the human being, and instructs human reason to pursue

freedom in thought. Events, however, undercut this reasoning. As Herzog writes, '*Reason exists*' (p. 172), a crash of disintegrating masonry forms an ironic counterpoint. On the subway Herzog notes obscene, comic graffiti, 'Minor works of Death' (p. 184). Knowledge of death appears only to demystify, to unleash chaotic individual impulses to destruction. The result of thought, of self-awareness is '*An age of special comedy*' (p. 171), of self-revenge and parody. Herzog's own thoughtful earnestness and melancholy thoughts of death have only fostered his exploitation by Madeleine and Gersbach. He tells Ramona, 'I sometimes see all three of us as a comedy team with me playing straight man' (p. 197). Madeleine's comments on Gersbach's toilet habits (p. 200) lead Herzog to see that 'Modern consciousness has this great need to explode its own postures. ... It throws shit on all pretensions and fictions' (p. 201). Pursuing the higher truths of historical thought, Herzog has merely become a target for the excessive demystification of reason, part of a levelling process which converts history not into freedom, but into parody, irony, 'humiliating comedy' (p. 173).

Private existence, however, appears to tend to a similar state. Herzog wonders whether there is any lofty Emersonian enterprise to his life or whether it is only contingency. 'Suppose, after all, we are simply a kind of beast, peculiar to this mineral lump that runs around in orbit to the sun, then why such loftiness, such great standards?' (pp. 169–170). The memory of Sono suggests the deficiencies of private existence, as tending to just such a vision of contingency. Sono offers Herzog personal pleasure, simplicity and a limited form of truth. 'She told me no such broken truths and dirty lies as I heard in my own language' (p. 180). Yet Sono's life is disordered. She lives amidst a chaos of cats, litter and bad smells, and assails Herzog with a succession of random facts – *faits divers* from the Tokyo press, railway accidents, murders. Through a Trade Delegation Sono has met the President, Nasser, Sukarno, the Nizam of Hyderabad, but these contacts with the public world are of no more importance to her than the sight of a three-legged dog, the man who exposes himself to her in the street, or the fat negress with whom she tussles over a bargain. Sono does not fear death (p. 181), and expounds a theology of contingency which Herzog rejects. 'She tried to explain to me once that earth and the planets were sucked from the sun by a passing star. As if a dog should trot by a bush and set free worlds' (p. 181). While she offers

Herzog personal freedom, and makes no demands upon him, Herzog yearns for his old struggles. 'When a man's breast feels like a cage from which all the dark birds have flown – he is free, he is light. And he longs to have his vultures back' (p. 177). As he abandons his memory of her, Herzog finds himself breaking into song, and remembers Lou Holtz, 'the old vaudeville comic' (p. 182) from the Oriental Theatre in Chicago. Sono's cat-like singing, her winking delight in erotic scrolls, are placed by the reference to Holtz as so much comic vaudeville. Wearily Herzog turns to despair. 'But better the void than the torment and boredom of an incorrigible character, doing always the same stunts, repeating the same disgraces (p. 190). A purely personal existence offers, not freedom, but a random life without sense, a life of repetitive comedy.

Comedy of a different kind, however, marks Herzog's relation with Ramona. Prior to visiting Ramona, Herzog predicts the menu (Shrimp Arnaud) the music (Mohammad al Bakkar and his band) and the course of the conversation to come:

> And there would follow another discussion of Madeleine, Zelda, Valentine Gersbach, Sandor Himmelstein, the Monsignor, Dr Edvig, Phoebe Gersbach. Against his will, like an addict struggling to kick the habit, he would tell again how he was swindled, conned, manipulated.   (pp. 163–4)

His imagination is almost a flash-forwards to the visit, which follows the predicted pattern with scarcely a variation. The repetitive character of Ramona's rituals suggests that past and future are all the same. This suggestion is reinforced by Herzog's disorientation in time. Repeatedly (pp. 162, 157, 166) he tries unsuccessfully to fix the time in his mind. Herzog also draws a parallel between his own position *vis à vis* Madeleine, and that of George Hoberly, Ramona's former lover, 'while in New York I am the man inside, in Chicago the man in the street is me' (p. 206). Life appears as a series of repetitions, of acts performed now for one lover, now another. Ramona, however, argues that Herzog is not at all like Hoberly. Ramona's parlour is dominated by Aunt Tamara's clock, on which Herzog comments, 'To own a clock like this you had to have regular habits' (p. 191). Repetition may be seen as senseless, or as assuring a degree of regularity. While Herzog notes Ramona's 'dramatic' (p. 208) appearance in black lace, while he imagines the pair of them, married, as a 'vaudeville show' (p. 210) he none the less finds solace in Ramona's embrace. Superficially it is tempting here to interpret Ramona's appearance, on vicious spiked heels, as confirmation of Herzog's masochism. The text cautions otherwise. In Ramona's bathroom, still thinking of the theatre, Herzog remembers an old joke about a Shakespearean actor in a brothel, 'Madam, we come to bury Caesar, not to praise him' (p. 189). For the Freudian critic[22] the joke emphasises Herzog's connection of sex with death. Herzog however strikes a cautionary note, in a letter to Spinoza.

> *Thoughts not causally connected were said by you to cause pain. I find that is indeed the case. Random association, when the intellect is passive, is a form of bondage. . . .*
> *It may interest you to know that in the twentieth century random association is believed to yield up the deepest secrets of the psyche.* (p. 189)

The preceding rejection of the randomness of Sono implies a deeper rejection of the Freudian paradigm. While Herzog sees a certain sameness in Ramona's actions he does not turn to Freudian beliefs. Explicitly he contends that he is not 'capitulating to the death instinct' (p. 193) and that 'no amount of sublimation' (p. 193) can replace the erotic happiness he shares with Ramona. Far from being based on pain and guilt that happiness depends upon shared laughter. Quipping to Ramona on the 'phone Herzog tells her, 'I never felt less threatened by knives' (p. 157). His supposed masochism is in fact a standing joke between them. When Ramona appears in her heels, 'They both laughed . . . His laughter as it became silent, internal, was all the deeper. . . . He was laughing but it got him' (p. 211). Where in a Freudian view comedy is based upon repression, the shared comedy of Ramona and Herzog is fertile and life-giving in its nature. Ramona, a florist, is repeatedly associated with flowers. As a child Herzog had hated the poisonous smell of roses. In Ramona's bathroom he notes the crimson belladonna compound, made of deadly nightshade. This particular beautiful woman holds no terrors for him, however. Flowering and laughing under Ramona's touch, Herzog feels he 'might be able to stand the roses now' (p. 211), and he finally bids Ramona an uninhibited farewell amidst her flowers. Ramona does not pander to Herzog's 'masochism'. When he remembers her warning him that 'unless you're having a bad time with a woman you can't believe you're being serious' (p. 165) he breaks into spontaneous song and dance. When he threatens a renewed recital of his wrongs, Ramona shuts him up and cautions him against returning to the 'masochistic situation' (p. 203) in Chicago. Herzog agrees to call a halt.

> There is a time to speak and a time to shut up..... Some cry out, and some swallow the thrust in silence. About the latter you could write the inner history of mankind. How did Papa feel when he found that Voplonsky was in cahoots with the hi-jackers? He never said.   (p. 197)

The comment suggests a different lesson drawn from his father's life – not the inevitability of historical repetition, but the ability of the human being to absorb the blows of history and move on. Far from confirming him in masochism, the image of his father allows Herzog to break the thrall of psychological determinism.

Refreshed by his private experience, Herzog now returns to civil action, reaffirming his belief in '*civil usefulness*' (p. 169) without which there can in his view be no freedom. Civil action, however, in the form of his own custody suit, brings him to the courtrooms of New York. In the first cases which Herzog witnesses the description emphasises the dramatic, even operatic, quality of events. The magistrate's 'basso' (p. 232) is counterposed to Aleck's 'soprano voice' (p. 235). Bored by the 'dull routines' (p. 233) of justice, the magistrate diverts himself with a show of temperament, 'rounding up his audience with his glance'(p. 235). Aleck, 'a dream actor' (p. 236), plays up to the judge, 'giving the world comedy for comedy' (p. 236). Repelled, Moses thinks, 'Oh these actors! ... Actors all!' (p. 235). Far from being in the grip of his own fantasy projections here, Herzog is extremely detached from this vaudeville scene, seeing its protagonists not as personae but as impersonators. Social justice in New York appears as a sham, in which detectives theatrically attired in homosexual costumes trap the unwary and deliver them up to the routines of the legal process, routines which may be understood in the sense of both repetition and vaudeville. Herzog has been pondering Hocking's latest book:

> *whether justice on this earth can or cannot be general, social, but must originate within each heart. Subjective monstrosity must be overcome, must*

be corrected by community, by useful duty. And, as you indicate, private
suffering transformed from masochism. .(p. 227)

While social justice appears as a repetitive sham, however, Herzog is surprised when the magistrate shows his human side, taking care to point out to the German intern that if he pleads guilty he will never practise medicine in America. Herzog recognises that for all its flaws social organisation 'has accomplished far more and embodies more good than I do, for at least it sometimes gives justice' (p. 227). Mentally Herzog rejects the view that 'humane feelings were childish' (p. 238), which Edvig, Simkin and Himmelstein have been impressing on him. They are only childish 'if you're looking for the psychological explanation' (pp. 238–9). Herzog clearly, then, sees the court cases in relation to larger social issues, rather than in psychological terms.

In the second court room, a woman and her lover are arraigned for the murder of her child. Here the tone is quite untheatrical. The facts of the case are given in an exceptionally low-key manner; justice is operating objectively and with a proper seriousness. 'All this seemed to Herzog exceptionally low-pitched' (p. 244). There are multiple parallels between the case and Herzog's position. The girl is redhaired and a cripple (Gersbach), has been sexually molested as a child (Madeleine), has a child by one man and lives with another (Madeleine), and has kept her child locked up (Madeleine and Gersbach). On the other hand there are also careful parallels between the witnesses and Herzog. The first witness 'in the storm-window business' (p. 245) wears a stylish suit and cultivates elegant gestures (compare *Herzog* p. 14 and p. 237). A second witness, melancholy like Herzog, describes the crime. Both witnesses were fully aware of the child's suffering. Neither intervened. Herzog's reaction here is less motivated by the parallels between the two unfortunate couples than by his own inability to intervene morally in the present. What he realises is the extent to which, by his strategies of escape from the present, he has failed to act upon its specific injustices. Herzog's reaction to the murder is one of horror. Is this not a perfectly normal reaction? To experience intense horror at the wantonly cruel murder of a small child is hardly a neurotic reaction. The objective, factual court scene focuses closely upon a specific injustice, a fact which cannot be explained away by reference to psychological or historical paradigms. Herzog fails to understand: 'this is the difficulty with people who spend their lives in humane studies and therefore imagine once cruelty has been described in books it is ended' (p. 245).

Each court scene is preceded by a memory, a memory which militates against a psychological reading. In the first, Herzog recalls the delusions of his former mother-in-law. Formerly a suffragette, devoted to social causes, Polina has reverted to her previous existence:

> She had got it into her head that Moses had divorced Daisy because she was a streetwalker, carried the yellow ticket – Polina in her delusions became a Russian again. (p. 228)

Comically Polina begs the highly respectable Daisy to give up her life of shame, her 'social evil' (p. 229). For Polina, Daisy goes out into society and society is whoredom. Herzog considers this view in court (p. 236) but is checked by the kindness of the magistrate to the German intern. The scenes which in Clayton's view dramatise Herzog's sexual guilt are therefore preceded by a memory in which similar accusations are placed parodically in crazy Polina's mouth. Her vision of society as irremediably evil is placed as delusory. Polina is described as 'Tolstoian' (p. 174) implying the deficiencies of private existence outside history.

A second memory occurs before Herzog visits the second court, that of his own mother's death. Even in death Sarah Herzog is still trying to comfort Moses (p. 241). Her impending death is plain, but Moses chooses to ignore it. '*My son, this is death.* I chose not to read this text' (p. 241). The text Herzog does choose to read as his mother lies dying is Spengler's *The Decline of the West.* Ignoring the real example of his mother, Moses plunges into historical determinism. 'I learned that I, a Jew, was a born Magian and that we Magians had already had our great age, forever past.... I had better resign myself to Destiny' (p. 241). It is from Spengler's pages that Moses absorbs 'the bacteria of vengeance', not from his psychological position. In the face of death he retreats into larger vistas of world history.

Now, faced with a child's death, Herzog resolves to act. The court scenes bring home to him the importance of maintaining an awareness of specific sufferings, rather than subsuming these beneath psychological or historical determinism, and of taking preventive action in the present. Herzog is no Polina, nor is he now a historian. (The letters have largely fallen into abeyance now and recur only with the final chapter.) Where previously Herzog had prepared for his outings with Marco by memorising historical facts, he now realises that he had substituted history for personal contact. Turning towards June, the future and the month of the novel's closure, he has at least accepted the need for action in the present, and the need to change his previous habits rather than to reassert them.

While Herzog is now convinced of the need for action, the form which that action takes illustrates the dangers of too short a time scale, too rapid a reaction. Flying west to Chicago, keeping up with the revolutions of the planet, Herzog gains an extension of time, setting his watch back as he reaches Chicago. Stealing a march on time he guns his motor across the town in a headlong rush which almost courts death. 'The thread of life was stretched tight in him. It quivered crazily. He did not fear its breaking so much as his failing to do what he should' (p. 261). He visits Taube, described as 'The living dead' (p. 253), installed in the Herzog 'museum' (p. 250), whose slowness is her weapon against life. 'Taube, a veteran survivor, to be heeded, had fought the grave to a standstill, balking death itself by her slowness' (p. 260). Herzog's hasty actions are clearly contrasted with Taube's retirement and slowness, an image of Herzog's former passivity. Now, however, the house of the past has no hold on him. 'It had no special power over him now. He was another man and had different purposes' (p. 253). Herzog has changed, but he has plunged from one extreme to another, from an excessive concern with history to existence in a timeless heightened present. When Herzog sees Gersbach bathing June the scales fall from his eyes.

> As soon as Herzog saw the actual person giving an actual bath, the reality of it, the tenderness of such a buffoon to a little child, his intended violence turned into *theatre*, into something ludicrous. (p. 265)

The awareness of a specific event – not his own theatrically dramatic projections – stills Herzog's hand on the trigger. Immediately beforehand he had imagined the confrontation, Madeleine shrieking and cursing, Gersbach in tears (p. 262), but his melodramatic imagination is checked by the actual scene. Herzog still loathes the pair. But as people, not as constructions.

He realises that 'only self-hatred' (p. 265) could lead him to ruin himself for such a pair. Back in his car he notes the infinite variety of life, in which '*all the best and all the worst*' (p. 265) are all around him, and he realises that the threat of the father has been finally defused. 'Moses could confidently swear that Father Herzog had never – not once in his life – pulled the trigger of this gun' (p. 266).

Far from yielding to determinism Herzog now perceives in the amorphous streets of Chicago an image of his own freedom. 'Not so much determinism, he thought, as a lack of determining elements' (p. 266). In his following visit to Phoebe Gersbach, Herzog reveals a new awareness of time. He and Phoebe are old friends 'Not by calendar years. . . . You have to think of duration – Bergsonian duration. We have known each other in duration' (pp. 267–8). Time appears now as a vital psychological reality. Phoebe excuses her own lack of intervention in Herzog's life on psychological grounds. 'I was seeing a psychiatrist, and he advised me to keep away' (p. 269). Herzog, however, makes a strenuous effort to call Phoebe's attention to the real facts of Gersbach's adultery, to break her 'trance' (p. 271). Rejected by Phoebe, he wonders if he is now in fact crazy. 'Blood had burst into his psyche, and for the time being he was either free or crazy' (p. 272).

That he is free is powerfully indicated in the visit he pays to Luke Asphalter, in which a loving acceptance of man's historicity is confirmed. Lucas, oppressed by Rocco's death, has engaged in exercises, as prescribed by Tina Zokoly, which involve him in imagining himself dead, in a coffin, with mourners. En route to Luke, Herzog had thrown off his own 'infantile terror of death' (p. 273) and he also rejected the belief that man is only the set of the definitions of him. He goes on to ponder the mystery of life 'only the incomprehensible gives any light. . . . What made it clear? Something at the very end of the line. Was that thing Death? But death was not the incomprehensible accepted by his heart' (p. 273). Immediately his gaze turns to the clock, suggesting that it is a new awareness of time which lies at the heart of his changed condition. The comedy of Luke's death exercises, confirms this impression. On the one hand these form a thorough parody of Freud's 'death instinct'. In *Beyond the Pleasure Principle*[23] Freud understands even death psychologically, not as a bodily event but as willed. He therefore posits the existence of a death instinct. Freud describes the change from the animal need for immediate satisfaction to the human urge for delayed satisfaction as the transference from the pleasure principle to the reality principle. As pleasure is just the sense of transition from an excess to a deficiency of mental energy, it follows that death may be the greatest pleasure, as a total cessation of striving. In his view:

> The dominating tendency of mental life ... is the effort to reduce, to keep constant or to remove internal tension.[24]

The human mind is however infinitely more resilient than the Freudian paradigm allows for. Luke cannot keep his thoughts on death; his mind answers his efforts with images of comedy, pleasure and play. He remembers being rescued from death by firemen, the immense buttocks of his Aunt Rae, the burlesque broads with whom he played softball as a child. The episode bears out Herzog's comment: 'But human life is far subtler than any of its models, even these ingenious German models' (p. 279).

Another German model is touched upon here. When Luke describes his state in the coffin as 'present and absent' (p. 277) and as involving facing death, Herzog comments 'That's Heidegger' (p. 277). In Heidegger's idea[25] being is at once present and absent, manifest and concealed. Being with others is however essential. To be in the world involves the individual in a recognition of his own historicity, the fact that he is deeply grounded in a specific temporal situation. In Heidegger's view, we must live our death in advance, in order to accept our existence in time. Herzog recognises the truth of this. Accepting death need not involve a retreat into individual solipsism.

> I really believe that brotherhood is what makes a man human. ... When the preachers of dread tell you that others only distract you from metaphysical freedom then you must turn away from them.'   (p. 280)

Herzog now reassesses his letters. These products of his mental life are described in terms which reject Freud. 'I go after reality with language. ... I must be trying to keep tight the tensions without which human beings can no longer be called human' (p. 279). Herzog's intelligence works, as Luke's does, against death. The letters, however, are also fictions. 'I conjure up a whole environment and catch them [Madeleine and Gersbach] in the middle. I put my whole heart into these constructions. But they are constructions' (p. 280). The danger lies in allowing these constructions, whether of Herzog's own making, or derived from the dramatic scenarios of Freud and Hegel, to govern life. The novel attests the power of the human intelligence to overcome its problems, only as long as it resists ossifying human beings into simplistic constructions. Freedom in Herzog's view consists in accepting a life with human beings. Time cannot be escaped but the awareness of his own historicity impels the individual to social action.

Before the accident, then, Herzog is clearly established as no longer a prey to self-hatred, no longer turning masochism into a death wish, at peace with his filial role, not determined, and able to accept his own historicity without being enslaved to history. It therefore seems highly unlikely that Herzog as a moral masochist arranges the accident. In contrast to his former behaviour, speeding recklessly towards Harper Avenue, Herzog is here a circumspect and careful driver. Yet the accident occurs. As in *The Adventures of Augie March*, where accidents, and specifically automobile accidents, function as an image of contingency, so this accident is precisely that: a reminder to the reader that history is not determined but involves random events. The accident reveals that Herzog is not alone in a determined world, but part of a society. Society (here represented by the police) does assist the individual. Herzog's reaction to the accident is contrasted to that of the other driver. The latter plunges into self-justificatory lies, accusations and drama:

> He was laying the whole guilt on him, of course. It was very inventive – creative. The story deepened every moment. Oh, the grandeur of self-justification, thought Herzog.   (p. 292)

In his own brief and patient responses Herzog keeps to the facts. Goaded by the police sergeant Herzog 'kept himself steady' (p. 300), he claims no special immunity. In his existence he realises he is subject like everyone else to chance: 'in nine-tenths of his existence he was exactly what others were before him' (p. 294). The parallel between Madeleine's incarceration of a screaming June in her car, and the accident, where June, screaming, is momentarily trapped in the back, implies that Herzog is no better than anyone else. During the visit with June, Herzog, exhausted by the events of the day, had cautioned himself that his trembling sorrow 'should not be imparted to children, not that tremulous lifelong swoon of death' (p. 287). Swooning on the grass, 'looking dead' (p. 289), Herzog *has* presented this image to June. In his behaviour to her he had tried to represent 'the father whose strength and calm judgement she could trust' (p. 286). Fathers are not however all-powerful, and cannot deflect all the accidental blows of life. Society, in the indifferent kindliness of the police, does rescue June. At first alarmed, Herzog had thought, 'The cops could be very bad ... But that was in the old days' (p. 289). Patiently sifting the evidence the cop does see the truth of the accident – that it was not caused by Herzog.

Herzog is however booked for possession of the gun. He recognises the right of this. 'He had made the kind of mistake today that belonged to an earlier period. As of today it was no longer characteristic. But he had to pay an earlier reckoning' (p. 308). As he explains to the sergeant, the gun has only sentimental value to him. Herzog is quite neutral in his responses here. Coolly he asks the questions which reveal Madeleine as she really is. As she departs he realises that she has lost her power over him, and that the definitions which she used against him have lost their force. 'I reject your definitions of me' (p. 306). The story which Herzog tells June cleverly illustrates the idiocy of rigid definitions, with its succession of types: the hairiest bald man and the baldest hairy man, the stupidest wise man and the smartest blockhead. Everyone can be classified in accordance with a definition but the results are ridiculous. In the other fable which he tells, of the boy with stars on his face, amongst them a new star, Herzog emphasises that analysis does not reveal all of men. There are new things to be discovered, though there is also a degree of repetition in man. Importantly June knows the story backwards, and eagerly prompts her father in his repetition.[26] The real neurotic here is not the repetitive father, but Madeleine. '*Her disorder is super-clarity*' (p. 311). Far from espousing a Freudian belief in the ills of society, Herzog now explicitly rejects that view:

Clumsy, inexact machinery of civil peace. . . . If a common primal crime is the origin of social order, as Freud, Róheim et cetera believe . . . then there is some reason why jail should have these dark, archaic tones. . . . But all that is nothing but metaphor. I can't truly feel I can attribute my blundering to this thick unconscious cloud. (pp. 310–11)

It is after the accident that Herzog remembers his childhood abuse by a homosexual, and he moves from this to a further reflection on history. Herzog recalls that he never mentioned the assault to his parents, but turned up for supper as if nothing had happened (p. 296). He recalls Nietzsche's view that 'The strong can forget, can shut out history.... It's true you can't go on transposing one nightmare into another' (p. 296). For all his good intentions Herzog has inflicted a nightmare on June. Now he will be silent, absorb the blows of history and pass on as little of his own suffering as he can. In this also he repeats his father's role, to good purpose: 'And this is the unwritten history of man, his unseen, negative accomplishment, his power to do without gratification for himself' (pp. 296–7). Remembering his own earlier vision of history as the history of cruelty, he now places this view in quotation marks, ascribing it only to the present disillusioned generation.

This is a point to which Herzog returns, at Ludeyville, in his last series of letters, before silence takes their place. Briefly (pp. 326–7) Herzog summarises Nietzsche's views, as expressed in *Nietzsche Contra Wagner*:[27] that pain is ennobling, that destruction has a value, and that man must accept the hardness of life in an acceptance of what occurs, an *Amor Fati*. While Herzog accepts some of Nietzsche's points (particularly the condemnation of the theatrical quality of the educated classes) he adds a disclaimer, '*I also know you think that deep pain is ennobling ... But for this higher education survival is necessary. You must outlive the pain.... No survival, no* Amor Fati' (p. 326). Pain, destruction, are not ends in themselves (though that is the perverted form imposed upon Nietzsche's thought by later German generations) but have a value only in time, not in atemporal metaphor or timeless re-enactment. Nietzsche goes on to describe himself as 'an old psychologist and rat-catcher'.[28] Herzog precedes his letter to Nietzsche with a reflection on the size and number of rats in Panama, and some comic pest control advice. He himself is no psychologist, and no rat catcher. He is eating the remains of a loaf chewed by rats: 'He could share with rats too' (p. 8). A loving acceptance of his own nature, and of nature itself in its different guises, conditions the end of the novel. Herzog moves between the letters and the garden, contemplating the owls above his bed, allowing the spiders to escape from the fire, and admiring the beauty of the roses. 'There, in the same position as in former years, was the rose that used to give him comfort – as shapely, as red (as nearly "genital" to his imagination) as ever. Some good things do recur' (p. 318). At home now with both his animal instincts and his intellectual powers Herzog gains a well-earned peace.

Re-assessing Shapiro's monograph, for example, he concedes that modern power systems offer a resemblance to mass psychosis, and considers Banowitch's view that crowds are fundamentally cannibalistic. Immediately beforehand, however, he writes to Marco admiringly of Scott's expedition, noting that one member of the party willingly sacrificed himself so that others could survive, and how Amundsen's dogs refused to eat the butchered flesh of their own kind. A precise historical example undercuts Banowitch's view, and undercuts with it a vision of nature as vicious and best repressed. Moving between examples Herzog is drawn to a middle ground:

> *this fellow Shapiro is something of an eccentric, and I mention him as an* *extreme case. How we all love extreme cases ... Mild or moderate* *truthfulness or accuracy seems to have no pull at all.*   (p. 323)

At home with history and with nature Herzog begins a new work for June, an insect Iliad. His own heroic image of man imposing himself on history is cheerfully deflated in the Trojan ants, Priam as a cicada and Achilles as a stag beetle.

Ludeyville is no timeless Eden. Herzog discovers both dead animals and the evidence of lovers in its rooms. There are however overtones of fantasy to the house, re-opened, like Sleeping Beauty's castle,[29] and found unchanged. Its location is unclear. Herzog says it is not on the Esso maps (p. 336), though Tuttle and his wife run an Esso station. Tuttle is described as the 'demon of these woods' (p. 341), and his wife has 'tranced grey eyes' (p. 342). On his return, however, Herzog breaks the spell, hacking down the thorns around the house. 'Whatever had come over him during these last months, the spell, really seemed to be passing' (p. 348). He rejects Will's offer of psychiatry and argues that he is no more mad than anyone else. 'Was it any more fantastic for me to have these wives, children, to move to a place like this than for Papa to have been a bootlegger? We never thought he was mad' (p. 340). Assisted by the Tuttles Herzog imposes a degree of order upon the house, and sets his life in motion once again. The fantasy tone has nothing to do with psychology here but much to do with an awareness of human variety. In a recent interview Bellow asked,

> Do you believe the psychoanalytic explanation of your deeper motives? Or do you simply say, 'These are my deeper motives, I don't care what psychoanalysis has to say about them' ... What a woman does for her children, what a man does for his family, what people most tenaciously cling to, these things are not adequately explained by Oedipus complexes, libidos.[30]

Bellow's own reservations about Freud are therefore part and parcel of a wider attack, an attack on the temptation of a 'timeless existence', removed from the present, and upon the dangers of oversubscribing to a belief in history's power. While the attack on the Freudian paradigm dominates the novel, all explanatory definitions of man are tested and found wanting. History is envisaged as grand tragedy, vaudeville routine, mass psychology, contingency, a determining force, or a means to rational freedom. In Herzog's personal history, however, the reader learns to eschew over-rapid and simplistic judgements, to pay careful attention to the specific event, and to maintain a double focus upon the immediate moment and the longer vista of time. While thought reveals its inadequacies it is also a means to wiser judgements. While man is governed to some extent by his animal instincts, he is not totally determined by them. Seen in this light Herzog's change appears to be well-motivated.

5 *Mr Sammler's Planet*: Wells, Hitler and the World State

Mr Sammler's Planet, Bellow's seventh novel, met with a mixed critical reaction. In general critics assailed the novel for its failure to integrate ideas with imaginative action. In *Modern Fiction Studies* David Galloway claimed that the novel displayed 'the bankruptcy of Bellow's novelistic imagination',[1] arguing that the imaginative structure of the novel failed to provide sufficient support for the intellectual structure. Jennifer M. Bailey[2] described the events of the novel as heavy pieces of symbolic machinery, and in 1975 Mas'ud Zavarzadeh reflected the hardening critical position when he lamented the 'aesthetic and ideational thinness' of the novel.[3] These criticisms can however be challenged and completely rebutted by a close study of the relation between the ideas of the novel and the action in which they are inscribed, a study which depends upon an understanding of Bellow's attitude to history in the novel.

In *Mr Sammler's Planet* Bellow's primary interest lies, as the title suggests, in global history. Two historical events govern the action of the novel: the Holocaust, in the past, of which Mr Sammler is a survivor, and the Apollo moonshot which occupies the immediate future of the novel. Each involves a 'planetary' metaphor. The identification of the world of the concentration camps with 'another planet' is a common procedure in the literature of that experience. In a recent article Edward Alexander argues that the 'planet' of Bellow's title is precisely that other world of the Holocaust, and in his support quotes from Hannah Arendt's *The Origins of Totalitarianism*:

There are no parallels to life in the concentration camps. Its horror can never be fully embraced by the imagination for the very reason that it stands outside of life and death. It can never be fully reported for the very reason that the survivor returns to

the world of the living which makes it impossible for him to
believe fully in his own past experience. It is as though he had a
story to tell of another planet.[4]

The second planet of the title is however the moon, identified with
the future. The novel is set shortly before the Apollo moonshot,
from which Dr Lal hopes to gain publicity for his book, *The Future
of the Moon*. Like the world of the camps the moon is another
planet, a world beyond the experience of man. In a general sense
these two opposing planets, past and future, offer the opposition
which dominates the novel, that between history-as-nightmare
and history-as-progress. Where the Holocaust provides a locus for
the discussion of evil in history, a discussion centred on Arendt's
classic study of the war criminal, the moonflight introduces a view
of history as progress, as a Utopian and visionary project, initiat-
ing a discussion which is centred on H.G. Wells's ideas on space
colonisation and technological advance.

Mr Sammler's planet is however also the earth of the present,
described as the novel opens as 'an earth of ideas'.[5] In the action of
the first chapter of the novel, Sammler's conversation with Margotte about Eichmann, his lecture on H.G. Wells, and his encounter with the pickpocket, Bellow develops the opposition
between optimistic and pessimistic visions of global history.
Sammler is invited to lecture at Columbia on the British scene in
the thirties. As a younger man Sammler was a friend of Wells, and
was invited by him to participate in the 'Open Conspiracy',
Wells's Utopian plan for a World State.

> Included, for instance, with Gerald Heard and Olaf Stapledon
> in the *Cosmopolis* project for a World State, Sammler had
> written articles for *News of Progress*, for the other publication,
> *The World Citizen*.   (p. 35)

As Sammler explains in his lecture, the project was based upon
the propagation of the sciences of biology, sociology and history,
'and the effective application of scientific principles to the enlarge-
ment of human life' (p. 35). Wells's Utopia was to involve the
subjection of industry, capital, transport, and population to
world-wide collective control, and the abolition of national
sovereignty and thus of war. When Sammler outlines the plan,
however, he is shouted down by a heckler who yells: 'You quoted

Orwell before.... You quoted him to say that British radicals
were all protected by the Royal Navy.'   (p. 36)

This comment indicates that Sammler's account of the Open
Conspiracy incorporates within it Orwell's pessimistic attack on
Wells. In 'Wells, Hitler and the World State', an essay which
provides an illuminating subtitle to *Mr Sammler's Planet*, Orwell
expresses his revulsion from Wells, whom he identified with the
belief in progress and the faith in science. Orwell points out that,
while sensible men may agree with Wells's view, sensible men
nowhere hold power. In Orwell's view men's motives are not as
reasonable or as progressive as Wells maintains. He points out
that there are immediate problems to be solved in the present,
that of Hitler in particular, and that these problems are being met
from quite unreasonable motives. Atavistic patriotism, he claims,
has kept England on its feet during the war, a type of motivation
which Wells's Cosmopolis would outlaw. Orwell particularly
assails the intellectual's inability to recognise evil:

> The energy that actually shapes the world springs from emo-
> tions – racial pride, leader worship, religious belief, love of war
> – which liberal intellectuals mechanically write off as
> anachronisms.[6]

Orwell goes on to argue that those who perceive Hitler as
Antichrist are closer to the truth than intellectuals who persist in
seeing him as a figure from a comic opera. This latter view is, in
his explanation, a product of the sheltered conditions of English
intellectual life, where 'The Left Book Club was at bottom a
product of Scotland Yard, just as the Peace Pledge Union is the
product of the Navy.'[7] He therefore concludes that Wells is the
victim of a naïve view of history, that 'History as he sees it is a
series of victories won by the scientific man over the romantic
man.'[8]

How far Mr Sammler shares Orwell's sentiments becomes very
evident when he and Margotte discuss Arendt's *Eichmann in
Jerusalem*. Margotte expounds the book as a work which discounts
evil: 'The idea being that here is no great spirit of evil. ... A mass
society does not produce great criminals' (p. 15). Sammler disagrees totally, and the terms of his disagreement suggest a debt to
Orwell:

Intellectuals do not understand. They get their notions about matters like this from literature. They expect a wicked hero like Richard III. But do you think the Nazis didn't know what murder was? Everybody . . . knows what murder is. That is very old human knowledge.   (p. 17)

In Sammler's view, Arendt is 'Making use of a tragic history to promote the foolish ideas of Weimar intellectuals' (p. 17). Sammler is quite clearly Bellow's mouthpiece at this point. In 1975 Bellow restated Sammler's views as his own, dismissing Arendt and arguing that man has an innate sense of evil.[9] Where Wells discounts evil out of progressive futurism, Arendt, in Bellow's view, discounts it from an overactive concentration on historical explanation, seeing man as totally conditioned by his historical circumstances. In 1964 Bellow was asked to comment on an article by Harold Rosenberg which considered Arendt's book, by then a cause célèbre in America. Rosenberg opened with the statement that, in 1963,

> James Baldwin's *The Fire Next Time* raised the question of the future of Western civilisation, Hannah Arendt's *Eichmann in Jerusalem*, that of the nature of its past.[10]

The phrase suggests the range of *Mr Sammler's Planet*. In both works Rosenberg detected the 'groove worn by the reiterated sentiment of the doom of the West.'[11] In his comment, Bellow agreed with Rosenberg in attacking the popular philosophies of doom, anomie and alienation as 'simple-minded historicism'[12] and expressed the hope that 'the imagination will free itself from the clichés of culture history.'[13]

When Mr Sammler wakes in America, his first impulse is to lament the dominance of historical explanations. Eying his books he surmises that,

> they were the wrong books, the wrong papers. . . . Being right was largely a matter of explanations. Intellectual man had become an explaining creature. Fathers to children, wives to husbands, lecturers to listeners, experts to laymen, colleagues to colleagues, doctors to patients, man to his own soul explained. The roots of this, the causes of the other, the source of events, the history, the structure, the reasons why.   (p. 5)

Just as Sammler is now less than certain of Wells's Utopian views, so he discounts the writers of culture history, on the grounds that looking only backwards to historical conditions is as morally paralysing as the longsight gaze into the future. In America Sammler 'had been reading historians of civilization' (p. 32) (he names Ortega, Valéry, and Burckhardt among others) but now wants to read only thirteenth century mystics – Suso, and Eckhart. As we shall see Bellow does draw upon these historians in *Mr Sammler's Planet* but as a part of a critical evaluation of historicism. The opposition between the governing planets of optimism and pessimism is contained within this larger question. Bellow rejects historicism, in the sense in which Karl Popper understands the term, as the appeal to history as a determined order.[14] Yet he accepts the phenomenon of historicism as the sudden hypersensitivity of modern man to the sense of history.

Mr Sammler is particularly influenced by Ortega. When he visits Israel he is struck by its confusion of cultures, as demonstrated in the person of a Bessarabian-Syrian-Spanish-speaking Israeli from the Argentine. He comments:

> The many impressions and experiences of life seemed no longer to occur each in its proper space, in sequence, each with its recognizable religious or aesthetic importance, but human beings suffered the humiliations of inconsequence, of confused styles, of a long life containing several separate lives. In fact the whole experience of mankind was now covering each separate life in its flood. Making all the ages of history simultaneous.   (p. 23)

Sammler's stress on the mass and multiplicity of life, and the rise of the historic floodwaters to cover man, takes its metaphors from Ortega. In *The Revolt of the Masses*, Ortega argued that historicism is intimately connected with the rise of the mass-man, that, 'Now the average man represents the field over which the history of each period acts; he is to history what sea level is to geography . . . the level of history has suddenly risen.'[15] We recall that Sammler, overwhelmed by pullulating historical explanations, opened the novel by describing the mind as 'A Dutch drudgery . . . pumping and pumping to keep a few acres of dry ground. The invading sea being a metaphor for the multiplication of facts and sensations' (p. 5). Ortega also sees modern life as planetary:

Life has become, in actual fact, worldwide in character; I mean
that the content of existence for the average man of today
includes the whole planet; that each individual habitually lives
the life of the whole world.[16]

Unlike Wells, however, Ortega views this new Cosmopolis with
unalloyed disgust. The widespread dissemination of culture, of
information and technology, produces in his view only a new
barbarian: the mass-man. For Ortega there are two fundamental
traits of the mass-man:

the free expansion of his vital desires and therefore of his
personality, and his radical ingratitude towards all that has
made possible the ease of his existence. These traits together
make up the well known psychology of the spoilt child.[17]

Bellow introduces these spoilt children of the West in Sammler's
pervasive hostile comments on the youth culture of America, and
in particular, in the characters of Angela and Wallace Gruner,
spoiled children of Elya Gruner, each expressing their vital
desires without restraint, neither showing gratitude. Ortega argues that the spoilt child is unable to distinguish the works of
history from nature. When Wallace floods the Gruner house he
makes this point himself, intrigued to discover that he cannot shut
off the water because he has no idea of its source. He says,

It's supposed to be a sign of the Mass Man that he doesn't know
the difference between Nature and human arrangements. He
thinks the cheap commodities – water, electricity, subways,
hot-dogs – are like air, sunshine, and leaves on the trees....
Ortega Y Gasset thinks so.   (p. 196)

The point of Ortega's argument is that civilisation demands
continual vigilance; it is neither infinite advance or regress:

Civilisation is not 'just there', it is not self-supporting. It is
artificial and requires the artist and artisan. If you want to
make use of the advantages of civilisation, but are not prepared
to concern yourself with the upholding of civilisation you are
done. In a trice you find yourself left without civilisation. Just a
slip, and when you look around everything has vanished into
air. The primitive forest appears in its native state.[18]

Ortega founds his morality on the assertion that human nobility involves, not the passive enjoyment of rights, but the active attempt to meet one's obligations to civilisation. Mr Sammler's own life illustrates the point. As a young aristocrat in Poland, Sammler enjoyed, as of right, his cultural privileges, flattered by the gift to him on his sixteenth birthday of Schopenhauer's *The World As Will and Idea*, delighting in its cosmic pessimism. In London Sammler is equally flattered by his entrée into Bloomsbury intellectual circles, and in particular by his involvement in Wells's Utopian schemes. While Sammler plays with ideas of cosmic pessimism and Utopian Cosmopolis, however, the Second World War is looming. In Poland he suddenly discovers that civilisation has disappeared, and finds himself, a murderous savage, in the Zamosht forest.

Sammler now relates this experience to modern America. Around him he sees only an unthinking acceptance of civilised plenitude – 'No scarcity was acknowledged' (p. 30) – and a stress on rights – 'the rights of women, the rights of children, the rights of criminals' (p. 28). Sammler is conscious of the barbarism of America as the scatological and animal imagery of the novel emphasises, keenly aware of Wallace's faecal smell, of Angela's musk odour, of Shula's yak and baboon hair wig, of the dog turds which beset his path through dangerous subways, past smashed telephone kiosks. Confronted with one of the latter he paraphrases Ortega's views:

You opened a jewelled door into degradation, from hypercivilised Byzantine luxury straight into the state of nature, the barbarous world of colour erupting from beneath. . . . The thing evidently, as Mr Sammler was beginning to grasp, consisted in obtaining the privileges, and the free ways of barbarism, under the protection of civilized order.   (p. 8)

Ortega's concept of the mass-man as planetary has a double sense: as the worldwide quality of the phenomenon, and as the flawed individualism on which it depends. While enjoying all the advantages of the world the mass-man is atomistic in his own self, concerned only with his egotistic desires. In one sense the world is unified. In another it contains only 'planetary' individuals, without obligations, describing their own selfish orbits. Thus Wallace, his eyes like 'bony orbits' (p. 72) is 'Unto himself a roaring centre' (p. 214). Lal is a 'flying sort of man' (p. 166) whom Sammler imagines as a 'planet-buzzing Oriental demon' (p. 179). Shula appears daubed with a Hindu caste mark which has 'lunar significance' (p. 167). Angela, weeping, suggests 'earth tremors' (p. 126) while Eisen is 'orbiting a very different foreign centre' (p. 232).

Ortega's conception of the mass-man as super-individual, and as member of a mass, encloses the discussion of Wells and Arendt. In Arendt's thesis the Holocaust is the result of mass organisation. Orwell also drew attention to the similarity between Nazi Germany and Wells's projected World State:

> Much of what Wells has imagined and worked for is physically there in Nazi Germany. The order, the planning, the state encouragement of science, the steel, the concrete, the aeroplanes are all there, but all in the service of ideas appropriate to the Stone Age.[19]

Mr Sammler, however observes also in the Holocaust the results of overblown individualism. Eichmann has his counter-example in Chaim Rumkowski, dictator of the Lodz ghetto, on whom Sammler is said to have written an article. Unlike Eichmann, a cog in a machine, Rumkowski is 'A man with a bit to play, like so many modern individuals' (p. 185). Within the little world of the Lodz ghetto Rumkowski saw himself as king, with his own institutions, currency, postal system and state coach. Sammler describes him as a parodic king, 'King of rags and shit, Rumkowski, ruler of corpses' (p. 87). The rise of the atomistic individual has created, in Sammler's opinion, a world populated with Rumkowskis, each a king in a circumscribed sphere only by dint of ignoring the existence of a wider moral universe in which their actions occur. While society moves forward technologically, its moral gears are set in reverse. Technological progress releases barbarian urges, and the World State is ruled by parodic kings.

It is only in the action of the novel, however, that Sammler learns the full lesson of his past: the dangers of intellectual distance, and the obligations of the present. The novel begins and ends with scenes involving a black pickpocket. In the first chapter Sammler watches the pickpocket at work but does not intervene. Intellectually he condemns the thief, refusing to see him as a social rebel, and telling Angela that, 'He didn't give a damn for the glamour, the style, the art of criminals. They were no social heroes to him' (pp. 10–11). He is similarly impatient with Margotte's historicist speculations: 'Who was this black? What were his origins, his class or racial attitudes, his psychological views, his true emotions, his aesthetic, his political ideas?' (p. 14). And yet Mr Sammler seeks out opportunities to watch the thief in action. He connects the experience with a detail of his reading:

> the moment in *Crime and Punishment* at which Raskolnikov brought down the axe on the bare head of the old woman, her thin grey-streaked grease-smeared hair, the rat's-tail braid fastened by a broken horn comb on her neck. That is to say that horror, crime, murder, did vivify all the phenomena, the most ordinary details of experience. In evil as in art there was illumination. (p. 11)

Watching the pickpocket Sammler dwells upon every tiny detail of the crime – the scallop clasp of the victim's purse, the manicured nails of the thief, the leafy green of dollar bills. After being heckled at Columbia Sammler admits to a similar 'intensification of vision' (p. 37). A precise parallel exists between the two events. At the lecture the heckler had taunted Sammler in terms of phallic pride, 'Why do you listen to this effete old shit? What has he got to tell you? His balls are dry' (p. 36), to which there is a cry of 'Shame. Exhibitionist' (p. 36). The cry also applies to Sammler, of course, exhibiting his pride in his Bloomsbury contacts on the lecture stand. After the lecture Sammler converts the experience into matter for intellectual diversion, pondering the heckler's comment from a safe distance. Bellow comments, 'individuals like Sammler were only one stage forward, awakened not to purpose but to aesthetic consumption of the environment' (p. 38). When Sammler is seen by the pickpocket he adopts a similar strategy. 'confronted by the elegant brute . . . he adopted an English tone. A dry, a neat, a prim face declared that one had not crossed anyone's boundary; one was satisfied with one's own business' (p. 7). 'Mr Minutely-Observant Artur Sammler' (p. 12) enjoys registering the details of the world around him, converting them into matter for intellectual and aesthetic diversion, but he does not feel called upon to act. In exposing himself to Sammler, the Negro mimics Sammler's own position: he does not cross Sammler's boundaries or assault him, he does not speak, he merely gives Sammler something to look at. Ironically catering to Sammler's desire to observe, he displays his penis. 'Sammler was required to gaze at this organ. No compulsion would have been necessary. He would in any case have looked' (p. 42). When the thief leaves, Sammler is for once singularly unilluminated by his experience, unable to convert it into 'safe' intellectual material. He feels only 'a temporary blankness of spirit. Like the television screen in the lobby, white and grey, buzzing without image' (p. 43). For once Sammler gains nothing from an experience, finding that rather than vivifying the phenomena, it erases them altogether.

Sammler is, however, fatally attracted to distancing strategies, ways of escaping from the present. In the novel the image of the moon serves as a focus for each of his three principal strategies: imaginative vision, an ironic perspective, and mystic transcendence. Here Sammler is attracted to the latter. Collapsing onto his bed he finds Lal's book under the pillow.

> 'How long,' went the first sentence, 'will this earth remain the only home of man?'
> How long? Oh, Lord, you bet! Wasn't it the time – the very hour to go? For every purpose under heaven. A time to gather stones together, a time to cast away stones. Considering the earth itself not as a stone cast but as something to cast oneself from – to be divested of. To blow this great blue, white, green planet, or to be blown from it.   (p. 43)

Sammler's description of the earth as stone borrows its terms from Ecclesiastes 3, suggesting that the earth is a place of stony confinement, burying the individual soul in earthly matter, as opposed to the changeless eternal moon, where 'Stone crumbles but without the usual erosion' (p. 44). History reappears as nightmare, the horror of man's confinement within space and time. The central experience of Sammler's life, his burial, choking on stones and earth, in a mass grave, has reinforced Sammler's vision of the finite world as confinement, its concerns merely irrelevant in the light of mystic vision. In America pedantic Sammler had lectured his students on etymology: '*Lapis*, a stone. Dilapidate, take apart the stones. One cannot say it of a person' (p. 31). After the Columbia lecture, however, his distance is threatened, and he sees himself as eroded, 'As if he had been cast by Henry Moore. With holes, lacunae.... Particles in the bright

wind, flinging downtown, acted like emery on the face'
(pp. 37–8). In Sammler's fancy these 'holes' are eroded by the
ceaseless pressure of his mental preoccupations, one of which is
with murder. In Israel, Sammler saw himself as reflecting the
landscape around him:

> there were mental dry courses in his head, . . . wadis, he be-
> lieved such things were called, small ravines made by the
> steady erosion of preoccupations. The taking of life was one of
> these. (p. 116)

Sammler now realises that his confinement within time may have
a positive value, in that his experiences in time erode his intellectual distance and give him a greater sense of moral issues.

Sammler now confronts his own ambivalence towards the
attempt to transcend the present, an ambivalence which he
expresses in a reflection on Kierkegaard. In the passage which he
paraphrases from *Fear and Trembling*[20] Sammler connects the
question of finite and infinite with that of travel to other worlds:

> And this brought to mind Kierkegaard's comical account of
> people travelling around the world to see rivers and mountains,
> new stars, birds of rare plumage, queerly deformed fishes,
> ridiculous breeds of men – tourists abandoning themselves to
> the bestial stupor which gapes at existence and thinks it has
> seen something. This could not interest Kierkegaard. He was
> looking for the Knight of Faith, the real prodigy. That real
> prodigy, having set its relations with the infinite, was entirely at
> home in the finite. (pp. 51–2)

Sammler sees in Kierkegaard's theology a possible solution to the
problems of space and time. By accepting that his life is finite, a
mere preamble to infinity, the Knight of Faith accepts that life as
his duty, a contract to be honoured, and has no need for other
non-physical worlds. Yet there is a difficulty for Sammler in
accepting Kierkegaard's ideas:

> Mr Sammler was worried. He was concerned about the test of
> crime which the Knight of Faith had to meet. Should the
> Knight of Faith have the strength to break humanly appointed

laws in obedience to God? Oh yes, of course! But maybe
Sammler knew things about murder which might make the
choices just a little more difficult.   (p. 52)

What Sammler knows of murder includes of course his own
murder of the German straggler. Before Sammler murders the
German, he has come to the conclusion that the world is only a
spatial-temporal prison, and when the man pleads for his life, he
sees 'the soil already sprinkled on his face. He saw the grave on his
skin. The grime of the lip, the large creases of skin descending
from his nose already lined with dirt – that man to Sammler was
already underground' (p. 112). Sammler's vision of the earth on
this man's face, of the finitude of the individual confined in the
earth, actually assists him in the act of murder. Acting with one
eye on eternity appears as radically immoral. Kierkegaard distinguishes in *Fear and Trembling* between the moral realm and the
realm of faith, using as his example Abraham's readiness to
murder Isaac at God's command, an act which is immoral by
human standards. Feffer describes the heckler as a product of the
divorce between the ethical and the religious realms, a man who
thinks himself 'a pure Christian angel because you commit murder' (p. 88). Sammler is now not so sure that the two realms can be
so easily divorced. Sammler is an exponent of Meister Eckhart, a
German mystic. The choice of this particular figure underlines the
ambiguity. Eckhart was adopted by the Nazi party as giving
religious sanction to its racist views. While this is based on a
vulgarisation of Eckhart's writings,[21] it is a reminder to the reader
that mysticism may also foster amoral and violent energies. The
transcendental, while not entirely discarded, is subjected to moral
criticism here.

The action of the novel develops the point. At the bedside of
Elya Gruner, Sammler meets his son, Wallace. Wallace's adventures clearly illustrate the description by Kierkegaard of those
who are ill at ease in the finite. When Sammler lends Wallace
Burckhardt's *Force and Freedom*,[22] a work which attacks on moral
grounds the belief in historical determinism, Wallace ignores the
moral message to rush off to Turkey, Morocco and Albania to
observe peoples at different stages of historical development.
Farcical and spectacular events dog Wallace's trajectory as he
rushes from project to project, and from world to world. Wryly
Sammler sees in Wallace an alternative sense of the lunar
metaphor:

Wallace was genuinely loony. For him it required a powerful effort to become interested in common events ... so often he seemed to be in outer space. *Dans la lune.*   (p. 76)

To be distant may be merely folly. Wallace, as befits the mass-man, is particularly obsessed by numbers, by sporting statistics and research in mathematics. He seeks his transcendence of the limits of human life in plenitude, amassing experiences and ideas, understanding infinity as a mathematical quality.

Elya Gruner, however, presents an image of the man who is entirely at home in the finite, accomplishing his daily tasks to the best of his ability and meeting his obligations in the present. Sammler dismisses Elya's faults – his obsession with business, his need for approval, his vanity in his elegant clothes and manicured nails – defects which Sammler describes as 'dust and pebbles, as rubble on a mosaic which might be swept away. Underneath, a fine, noble expression' (p. 70). Contemplating Elya's face Sammler sees the 'dirt' of ordinary human existence as unimportant, arguing that 'A few may comprehend that it is the strength to do one's duty daily and promptly that makes saints and heroes' (p. 76). As Knight of Faith, however, Elya has met the test of crime all too well. Wallace reveals Elya's Mafia involvement to Sammler. Suddenly Sammler sees Elya as akin to the pickpocket, whose manicured nails and elegant attire he had also registered. The pickpocket is in fact described as a surgeon at three separate points, (p. 6, p. 10, p. 39) reinforcing his kinship with Elya. Sammler's next moon vision reveals the ambiguity of his feelings. 'Drop a perpendicular from the moon. Let it intersect a grave. Inside, a man till now tended, kept warm, manicured. Those heavy rainbow colours came' (p. 85). In the rainbow image Sammler suggests the contract which Elya has kept in his life, yet the rainbow colours are also those of decay and putrescence. Sammler retreats again from his vision of Elya as Knight of Faith to take refuge in distant thoughts:

> He could not cope with the full sum of facts about him. Remote considerations seemed to help – the moon, its lifelessness, its deathlessness.   (p. 85)

From Elya's bed Sammler retreats once more to a planetary position, to describe a lonely orbit around Stuyvesant Park, 'an ellipse within a square' (p. 85) immersing himself in Lal's book.

The novel began with Sammler's decision not to attempt to 'resolve certain difficulties imaginatively' (p. 5) in sleep. No longer certain of the value of mystic transcendence, however, Sammler returns to the imagination, approving of Lal's description of it. Sammler's next moon vision appears in response to Lal's suggestion that 'The imagination is innately a biological power seeking to overcome impossible conditions' (p. 87). Sammler feels a red flush pervading his mind:

> This assumed a curious form, that of a vast crimson envelope, a sky-filling silk fabric, the flap fastened by a black button. He asked himself whether this might not be what mystics meant by seeing a mandala ... As for the black button, was it an after image of the white moon? (p. 94)

Sammler's position in the square, in an ellipse within a square, is mandalic as is his vision of spherical button within square envelope. For Jung, seeing a mandala in dreams, or creating an artistic representation of one, was evidence that psychic conflicts were being resolved imaginatively.[23] In Eastern mysticism the form of the mandala, square within circle or circle within square, expresses the dynamic tension between the oppositions of life, and is itself an aid to overcoming them, by meditation. For a moment Sammler yields to these suggestions, feeling 'Bliss and mystic joy' (p. 95). Feffer, however, who now accosts Sammler, offers less than comforting evidence of the ability of the human imagination to create new forms. In the past, as he explains, Feffer had been delighted by his psychiatrists' ability to give new names to his problems. Labelled as 'manic' 'reactive-depressive' or 'Oedipal', Feffer had felt like a new man. As he explains 'When you set up a new enterprise, you redescribe the phenomena and create a feeling that we're getting somewhere' (p. 90). New names, however, don't alter old problems. Wallace and Feffer are planning a new business enterprise, flying over suburban gardens to identify and label their shrubs, an enterprise which ends in old fashioned disaster when Wallace crashes his 'plane into a house. This lunatic flight of Wallace's imagination casts an ironic light on Sammler's new optimism in relation to the moonshot as evidence of the triumph of the creative imagination.

Feffer does bring news to Sammler, but of an unpalatable kind. He reveals that Shula, Sammler's daughter, has stolen Lal's manuscript. Shula has committed this crime out of a belief in the imagination; she sees her father as a 'Prospero' (p. 93) able to conjure up wonderful cultural visions, and hopes that Lal's book will remind Sammler of his own projected book on Wells. Apologising to Dr Lal, Sammler describes Shula as a believer in the scientific future who is also anachronistic. 'Psychologically archaic – all the fossils in her mental strata fully alive (the moon, too, is a kind of fossil) – she dreams about the future' (p. 104). In Shula's action, Sammler sees evidence that the human imagination cannot be counted upon to transform itself and the world. The way in which he makes this point significantly develops his assessment of Utopian writers:

> New worlds? Fresh beginnings? Not such a simple matter. ...
> What did Captain Nemo do in *20,000 Leagues Under the Sea?* He sat in the submarine, the Nautilus, and on the ocean floor he played Bach and Handel on the organ. Good stuff, but old.
> (p. 110)

The remark is remembered from Paul Valéry's essays on politics and history, in which Valéry considers the imagination as irremediably backward-looking:

> What would an inventor of imaginary worlds, such as a Wells or a Verne do today? Please observe that though they invented imaginary worlds, neither of them tried anything in the realm of the mind. For instance they never attempted to picture the arts of the future. The famous Captain Nemo, whom everybody knows, played the organ in his Nautilus at the bottom of the sea, and on it he played Bach and Handel.[24]

As Valéry sums it up, man is entering the future backwards. The danger of history is that it acts upon the present with violence. According to Valéry

> Our feelings and ambitions are stirred by memories of what we have read, memories of memories, to a far greater extent than they result from our perceptions and the data of the present moment. The real nature of history is to play a part in history itself.[25]

Thus, in his view, history fatally dictates the actions of the present; Louis Seize, for example, would not have died on the scaffold without the previous example of Charles I. Anachronistic Shula, lost in her memories of H.G. Wells and of Sammler's long abandoned memoir, steals Lal's book, a vision of the future. Lal sketches the future as a realm of transformed minds. 'A shared consciousness may well be the new America. Access to central data mechanisms may foster a new Adam' (p. 109). Sammler, however, remembers at this point only the old Adam within him, recalling the murder of the German. Sammler has already experienced the anachronism of history. Saved by Polish partisans he had fought alongside them. Yet as peace drew near the Poles returned to older loyalties, to anti-Semitism, and massacred the Jewish fighters. Saved once again by another Pole, Sammler corresponds with him for a time until a tinge of anti-Semitism creeps into Cieslakiewicz's letters. Sadly Sammler considers the persistence of outdated historical ideas – the Russian desire for a Mediterranean port in an era of air power, the stupid sultanism of Louis Quatorze reproduced in General de Gaulle, the Arabs in Israel once more killing Jews. The fact that the ideas are anachronistic makes little difference:

> No more than the disappearance of Jews from Poland made a difference to the anti-Semitism of the Poles. This was the meaning of historical stupidity.   (p. 115)

It is a measure of Sammler's development that, when he confronts Shula, he is able firmly to reject all her attempts to minimise her crime by distancing strategies. When she tries to excuse the crime by reference to her past history, speaking Polish and assuming a guise of childishness, Sammler demands that she answer in English. When she attempts to redefine the crime, to give it a new label, Sammler is obdurate. 'It wasn't actually stealing', says Shula. Sammler replies:

> Well, what word do you prefer, and what difference does it make? Like the old joke: what more do I learn about a horse if I know that in Latin it is called *equus*?   (p. 159)

Shula then argues that she stole from concern for the future, switching to an appeal to the creative imagination, maintaining that 'For the creative there are no crimes' (p. 159). Sammler, however reiterates his belief that human beings know what is right and wrong, and that these categories are not redefinable. Crime is crime, whether committed under the influence of a nightmare past, out of desire for the future, or as a means of bringing to birth the 'new' thing, creatively redefined. Gently, by a demythologising of Wells, Sammler communicates to his errant daughter that the world cannot be made afresh by the efforts of the imagination, that he is no Prospero, and that, in his words, 'There is nothing left remarkable/Beneath the visiting moon' (p. 157).

Shula's theft, however, leads Sammler to the last of his distancing strategies – that of cosmic irony. The alternation between the planets of moon and earth now appears as an image of the meaningless recurrence of history, its errors cyclically repeated. The plot of the novel suggests the farcical nature of this repetition. Shula actually steals Lal's book twice, once from Lal and again from Sammler's room. When Sammler discovers the second theft, he connects Shula in his mind with the pickpocket. In the plot Shula's theft, and Sammler's pursuit of her, forms a comic parody of his involvement with the black thief. The low, farcical tone of the chase, culminating in the discovery of Shula, naked in the Gruner tub, discredits the view that crime has overtones of glory. Murder and intense sexuality may be seen as vivifying the phenomena. Low pilfering by the grotesquely bewigged Shula can have no such overtones. Confronted with Shula's second theft Sammler gains a horrified awareness that 'humankind kept doing the same stunts over and over' (p. 141). Whirled off by the lunatic Shula into the circus of her fancy-dress activities, Sammler sees life as a cyclic dance in which:

> Anyone can clutch anyone, and whirl him off. The low can force the high to dance. The wise have to reel about with leaping fools. (p. 141)

Images of cyclic action, of circles and circuses, multiply in the text.[26] In the structure each major idea is encircled, ironically, by parodic re-enactment. Wells celebrates technology and space travel. Lunar Wallace, looking for money to insure his future as a flyer, prepares a technological blueprint before searching the plumbing of the Gruner house, thus causing a flood. In his desire to 'crash out of the future my father has prepared for me' (p. 197) Wallace crashes his 'plane into a house. Apocalyptic visions of flood and fire yield to domestic engulfment. Oriental mysticism is horribly parodied by Shula in a sari. Sammler's own life is repetitive. He 'dies' in Poland in a mass grave, emerging to a second life in which he merely repeats the errors of the former, assuming once again the position of distant intellectual. This distance, tragically irrelevant in the thirties, becomes merely comical in America. The novel conveys a sense of future-in-past and past-in-future, as technological progress is accompanied by anachronistic urges, as Wells, prophet of the future, becomes the mainspring of anachronistic action in the present.

Superficially events in the Gruner house appear to confirm the senselessness of cyclic activity. The house is described as a moon world, bathed in moonlight (pp. 153, 154) and a technological desert, a house where 'nothing really functioned except the mechanical appliances' (p. 153). Travelling towards it in the Rolls Sammler makes an analogy between car and space ship. 'Outer-space voyages were made possible by specialist-collaboration. . . . Totality was as much beyond his powers as to make a Rolls-Royce, part by part, with his own hands' (p. 145). Overhead the moon looms, large and full, as if Sammler and Wallace were travelling towards it. 'The moon was so big tonight that it caught the eye of Wallace ... leaning back, he pointed moonward' (p. 146). In the car, Wallace, who has already booked his moonflight with Pan-Am, asks Sammler if he would like to travel beyond the earth, but Sammler now demurs:

> if I had my choice, I'd prefer the ocean bottom. . . . I seem to be a depth man rather than a height man. I do not personally care for the illimitable. The ocean, however deep, has a top and bottom, whereas there is no sky ceiling. (p. 147)

Events in the house confirm Sammler's belief that there is quite enough lunacy in the world already. The geography of the house is comically symbolic. Wallace, the height man, retires to the attic, while Sammler and Lal take up positions in the sunken living-room, variously described as tank, well and pool. While the two intellectuals discourse, Wallace prepares his own action, an action which reduces them to farcical activity. Sammler has just taken flight when he is interrupted:

> 'when we had an earth of saints, and our hearts were set upon the moon, we could get in our machines and rise up ...' 'But

what is this on the floor', said Shula. All four rose about the
table to look. Water from the back stairs flowed over the white
plastic Pompeian mosaic surface. (p. 190)

A child crying for the moon Wallace has encircled Sammler's
views in his own irony. Sammler has to set to work bailing, to
safeguard literal rather than metaphoric ceilings; the need for
practical action in the present to maintain the structure of the
house takes precedence over abstract considerations. Emerging
from the house into the 'moon-purged air' (p. 204) Sammler's
thoughts turn to his memories of the Six Day War, which checks
Elya's vision of Israel as a new world for the Jews. Not only are the
Jews once more threatened, but they have also become themselves
aggressors. In Israel Sammler sees the marks of Israeli napalm,
and recognises only another society gone the way of its predeces-
sors. He recognises that human aspiration and human evil are
linked, that the one flows from the other as inevitably as day
succeeds night, as the moon controls the tides. Contradictory
purposes crew Sammler's own planet, the earth, as scientist and
brute, good and evil, old and new, repeat themselves:

> The waking, like a crew, worked the world's machines, and all
> went up and down and round about with calculations accurate
> to the billionth of a degree, the skins of engines removed,
> replaced, million-mile trajectories laid out. By these geniuses,
> the waking. The sleeping, brutes, fantasists, dreaming. Then
> they woke and the other half went to bed. And that is how this
> brilliant human race runs this wheeling globe. (p. 204)

And yet this cycling is not entirely without value, as Sammler's
monologue reveals. It may also be necessary. Sammler begins his
lengthy exposition of his views by inveighing against those historical writers who have, he feels, in their analysis of the past,
violently conditioned the present: 'history follows their words.
Think of the wars and the revolutions we have been scribbled into'
(p. 170). Supposed progress is ambivalent, as Sammler sees the
manner in which revolutions cycle back, ending in more violence
and terror than that which they sought to remedy. When he thinks
of Wells he recalls only the despair of Wells's last books and he
wonders whether in the last analysis, anything is accomplished by
such prophets:

When they begin to call for blood, and advocate terror, or proclaim a general egg-breaking to make a great historical omelet, do they know what they are calling for? When they have struck a mirror with a hammer, aiming to repair it, can they put the fragments together again?   (p. 171)

Yet Sammler does speak, engaging in an activity which he acknowledges as cyclic. 'Once you begin talking, once the mind takes to this way of turning, it keeps turning, and it dips through all events' (p. 172). 'Like a Ferris wheel' (p. 173), comments Lal. Sammler's monologue describes the sea of ideas around man, the anachronistic savagery of the mass-man, the dangers of the transcendental view, the horrors of individualism without obligations. These ideas have already been expressed, even repetitively, in the novel. Yet Sammler makes no apology for this repetition. He argues that:

it is sometimes necessary to repeat what we know. All mapmakers should place the Mississippi in the same location and avoid originality. It may be boring, but one has to know where he is. We cannot have the Mississippi flowing towards the Rockies for a change.   (p. 183)

The point of Sammler's monologue, circling back to his previous arguments, restating and repeating, is precisely that while these ideas may appear to be boringly known, there is a need for continual restatement, lest they go into eclipse; much as in the life of the individual there is a need for constant vigilance, for repeated moral activity. Continual restatement is necessary to keep such truths as have been attested before men's eyes. The cyclic dance of human activity, advancing only to retreat, may appear as a circle of 'black irony' (p. 9) but it may also express the essential truths of human existence. Significantly, Elya, the moral touchstone of the novel, now appears, in Sammler's mind, in cyclic motion. 'Elya reappeared strangely and continually, as if his face were orbiting – as if he were a satellite' (p. 179).

The monologue is interrupted by the flood which flows over a mosaic floor. Elya's face has previously been compared to a noble mosaic (p. 70) and when the mosaic floods there is the clear implication that this is the moment of Elya's aneurysm, a flooding of the brain in blood. While events in the Gruner household attest the necessity of human repetition, they also stress the importance of immediate, practical action within time. In the final chapter of the novel Sammler is forced out into the present. The action emphasises the pressure of time. Sammler wakes the next morning to find that everyone has left, and that he is stranded in New Rochelle, unable to rush to Elya's bedside. Formerly scornful of modern technology and rapid communications, Sammler now finds that the cars have left, the telephone is engaged, and that patience and waiting, far from the centre of events, is now forced upon him. His former detachment is replaced by furious irritation as Sammler admits that 'I should have realised that returning might present problems' (p. 206). Further events delay his return: Emil takes the car to fetch the cleaner, Shula sets his shoes on fire, Elya asks him to pick up some clippings before his visit. While Sammler has now realised that he cannot attempt to live outside the world, in philosophical detachment, he has realised this too late to allow him to reach Elya's bedside before he dies. Time has run out for Elya and for Sammler who has missed the opportunity to speak to Elya. Life does not always offer a second chance. By his concern with essentials, with large utterances and intellectual debate, Sammler has lost the chance to say something, however imperfect, in time.

In its final violent scene the novel circles back to its starting point, the black pickpocket, but this time Sammler is determined to act in the present, to intervene, rather than remaining at a safe distance. The fight between Feffer and the thief is the result of the former's attempt to 'observe' the thief in action. Feffer's plan to arrest the thief's activities involves the use of high technology and media publicity: he intends to take a 'candid camera' shot of the thief at work which he will then show to the world, on television. Technology does not, however, serve these moral purposes. The crowd who *do* see the thief caught remain detached spectators, aroused not to moral purpose, but to passive observation. Their somnambulistic attitude is an ironic reflection of Sammler's own earlier mystic detachment:

> what united everybody was a beatitude of presence. As if it were – yes – blessed are the present. They are here and not here. They are present while absent. So they are waiting in that ecstatic state. (p. 232)

Sammler, maddened by the 'tone of discussion' (p. 230) in which Eisen ponders what to do, sees that immediate action is called for.

Physically powerless himself, Sammler turns to Eisen. Eisen, Sammler's wife-beating son-in-law, is clearly a Yeatsian barbarian, a rough beast whose second coming is a horror. Shambling on his mutilated feet, his long curls fusing head and neck, Eisen prepares to save the day. In Russia, in the war, Eisen had seen men having their heads smashed in. Rescued from the Holocaust, trained as a craftsman, Eisen had reached security in Israel. Yet, as Sammler comments, 'you could not tell recovery where to stop. He had gone on to become an artist' (p. 135). In New York he carries with him his crude medallions, inscribed with Jewish symbols, stars of David, rams' horns, scrolls, candelabra, even a Sherman tank. To restrain the violence before him Sammler has to turn to Eisen who wields the symbols of atavistic patriotism, clubbing the thief with his bag of medallions. Orwell's analysis of the motives which restore civilised order – patriotism, love of violence, leader worship – is horrifically realised in this scene as Eisen acts on Sammler's dictates. Once unleashed, however, Eisen is quite unable to stop, and prepares to beat the Negro to death. Sammler's comment in his monologue, on the prophets of violence, unable to restrain the revolutions their words initiate, finds its correlative in the action. Sammler recognises that he has his existence in time, that the present is before him in all its horrors and obligations, and that he must act. Action, however, is not once and for all, but continuous. Feffer acts to restrain the pickpocket. His action leads to Eisen's intervention. Sammler then has to intervene to restrain Eisen. Eisen sees events in simplistic terms, arguing that he must hit the black hard if he is not himself to be killed. He tells Sammler:

'You know. We both fought in the war. You were a Partisan. You had a gun. So don't you know? ... If in – in. No? If out – out. Yes? No? So answer.' It was the reasoning that sank Sammler's heart completely.   (p. 234)

Human decisions are not as simple as Eisen implies. Sammler has been 'in' the world, and has killed. He has also been 'out' of the world, distant, yet morally no better. Sammler 'knows' that there is at times a need for violence. He also knows the need for its restraint. In this the role of time is important. Man is neither 'in' nor 'out', doomed by the finite world, or perfectible beyond it, but has to make the best of his existence in time. Moral decisions have a temporal dimension, and cannot be taken in a spirit of calm discussion or simplistic logic. The complex logic of the events of *Mr Sammler's Planet* belies simplistic thinking, constructing a novel which, while it asserts the importance of intellectual discrimination, based on the awareness of history, also responds to the pressures of the present. The art of Wells, with its enthronement of the future, the art of Eisen, with its symbols of the past, are deployed in the service of an altogether more complex, morally active novel. The worlds of past, present and future are inextricably interwoven, and amidst them the best that man can do is to maintain moral vigilance.

The novel closes with Sammler's recognition of the ambiguity of human action and of human knowledge. Contemplating the face of criminal Elya, he says that:

> he did meet the terms of his contract. The terms which, in his inmost heart, each man knows. As I know mine. As all know. For that is the truth of it – that we all know, God, that we know, that we know, we know, we know. (p. 252)

For Bellow, unlike his critics, the relation of ideas, what we know, to action, is not merely a literary, formal problem, but a moral one. Mr Sammler, exponent of Valéry, Burckhardt, Ortega, Wells, Orwell, Arendt, and Kierkegaard, finally learns their lessons in action. While the complex logic of events demonstrates the importance of careful intellectual discrimination, the repetitions and recurrences of the plot subject each idea to moral criticism, founded upon the demands for action in time. Long-distance views of human history, whether optimistic or pessimistic, give way to present, ethical imperatives. The opposition of moon and earth, variously figured as between infinite and finite, eternal and temporal, Utopia and apocalypse, vision and nightmare, is not finally encircled in ironic detachment. Rather, the novel argues that amidst the change and contingency of the sublunary sphere there is only one fixed pole: the moral imperative. By a sense of longer perspectives, by an understanding of what is owed to the past, the individual may be able to maintain his precarious knowledge and carry it forward into a civilised future. He can only do so by neither abdicating from the demands of the present, nor by surrendering totally to its standards. Unsubmerged by the sea of ideas, the novel emerges as a pro-

foundly moral construction, carrying both aesthetic and intellectual conviction, a statement which is a restatement of important,
if not original, human truths.

6 *Humboldt's Gift*: The Comedy of History

In *Humboldt's Gift* Bellow explores an encyclopaedic assortment of different approaches to history, both in terms of literary stereotypes and of culture readings, parodying the hero's attempts to escape from time. A critical relation to myth is the starting point of the novel. To comprehend Bellow's view of history in this novel we have to refer back to the committed criticism of the forties and in particular to Philip Rahv. Writing in 1953, in his essay 'The Myth and the Powerhouse',[1] Rahv argued that the concern with myth in modernist writing resulted not from a lack of history, but from the fear of history. History is feared because:

> modern life is above all a historical life producing changes with vertiginous speed, changes difficult to understand and even more difficult to control. And to some people it appears as though the past... were being ground to pieces in the powerhouse of change, senselessly used up as so much raw material in the fabrication of an uncertain future. One way intellectuals have found of coping with their fear is to deny historical time and induce in themselves through aesthetic and ideological means a sensation of mythic time... confounding past, present, and future in an undifferentiated unity, as against historical time which is unrepeatable![2]

Rahv refers to the mythicism of Pound and Eliot as primarily a retreat from historicism, and in some ways a reactionary distortion.[3] Rather than demonstrating the workings of the mythic imagination they provide an aesthetic simulacrum of it. Such a retreat is essentially a retreat from the hazards of freedom. Art achieves independence as it detaches itself from myth. The mind's recognition of its own creations as such, can only be an advance. It

157

is my contention that Bellow is occupied in *Humboldt's Gift* with this freeing of the mind by confronting it with its own creations, and thus with the relationship of art and history. To Bellow, as to Rahv,

> Nietzsche was surely right in his observation that the development of the historical sense in the modern epoch represents what is virtually a new faculty of the mind, a sixth sense.[4]

Rahv characterises the retreat into myth in the following terms:

> To [the mythmakers] as to Stephen Dedalus in *Ulysses* history is a nightmare from which they are trying to awake. But to awake from history into myth is like escaping from a nightmare into a state of permanent insomnia.[5]

To turn to *Humboldt's Gift* is to find that the novel practically opens with these words of Rahv's. Humboldt quips that, 'history was a nightmare during which he was trying to get a good night's rest'.[6] Insomniac Humboldt is contrasted with Citrine, a sleeper through the events of history, relentlessly in flight from involvement. In a recent essay Bellow discussed the modern faith in progress by technological innovation and lamented with Paul Valéry the cultural amnesia which is its byproduct:

> The new era will produce men who are no longer attached to the past by any habit of mind. For them history will be nothing but strange, incomprehensible tales.[7]

Citrine's technocrat brother, Julius, suffers from this very condition, his cultural amnesia extending even to the events of his personal past. As the novel advances, the initial presentation of the forties and fifties as richly textured historical periods, yields to a series of 'strange incomprehensible tales' – the various film scenarios, the Thaxter kidnapping, the Cantabile plot. Parody becomes the dominant mode of the novel as Bellow explodes ossified 'fictions' – both historical and literary – to free the past as experience. Bellow is concerned with two alternative problems: the dangers of avoiding history, paralysed by fear of it, and the danger of embracing it too fondly.

Humboldt's character is marked less by amnesia than by an

overactive memory and a relentless desire for individual status in history, a desire which Bellow has described in the following terms:

> Everyone wants to be the friend and colleague of history. And consciously or not intellectuals try hard to be what Hegel called World Historical Individuals... They may denounce the nightmare past, but they have also an immortal craving to be in the line of succession and prove themselves historically necessary.[8]

Humboldt is continually identified with the World Historical Individual. In the flashback trip to New Jersey which opens the action, Humboldt's conversation is described as being on a grand scale, ranging from the Napoleonic disease, Julien Sorel, Balzac's *jeune ambitieux*, and Marx's portrait of Louis Bonaparte, to Hegel's World Historical Individual. 'Humboldt was especially attached to the World Historical Individual' (p. 18). The Napoleonic myth of intelligence in action, understanding and controlling events in the thick of battle, is satirised here. The text insists on Humboldt's power brakes and power steering, on his muddy 'staff car from Flanders Field' (p. 21) and on the desolation all around him: 'a filth artillery, fired into the Sunday sky with beautiful bursts of smoke. The acid smell of gas refineries went into your lungs like a spur' (p. 22). The intellectual discoursing on his self-appointed task – to pull together technology, capitalism and poetry – is linked to the tyrant and destroyer, oblivious to the fate of those in his power. The description is highly reminiscent of Nicola Chiaromonte's definition of the modern 'historical' individual:

> The most striking image of the egomaniacal inflation of the individual produced by modern society and indiscriminate extension of his physical power is the face of the man behind a steering wheel. Tensed in his effort to sustain the weight and prestige of the power at his command and arrogantly shooting ahead at full speed, overbearing and scornful of anything slow or stationary he has all the appearance of a super-normal or if one prefers, abnormal being.[9]

As a poet, Humboldt inclines towards a belief in his Orphic role. As a World Historical Individual he fails to remain the instru-

ment of any larger purpose but sets out to wage war on society. In
his need to escape from becoming the victim of history he becomes
one of the aggressors. The social cost of such a philosophy is
implicit in the description of his surroundings, a 'pauperised' area
in which chickens resemble immigrant women, trees are 'under-
privileged' and 'orphaned looking' and 'The very bushes might
have been on welfare' (p. 24) to all of which Humboldt, posturing
as poet-king is oblivious, blithely reciting that 'This castle hath a
pleasant seat' (p. 23).

The cost to Humboldt's poetry is demonstrated through a
second historical parallel – with Tolstoi. Humboldt's attitude to
Tolstoi is instructive. 'As for great men and kings being History's
slaves, I think Tolstoi was off the track' (p. 7). Bellow's novel
restates what Isaiah Berlin, in a seminal work on Tolstoi's theory
of history, has described as the hedgehog and the fox – the
opposition between the craving for one absolute idea and the
multiplicity of individual events which constitute life. Humboldt
lives in the realm of large abstractions. He 'lived out the theme of
Success. Naturally he died a Failure. What else can result from
the capitalization of such nouns?' (p. 6). Humboldt's conversation is peppered with references to particular historical facts, in a
manner which levels all it touches. No distinctions are made
between the Age of Gold and the Gilded Age, the gold death mask
of Agamemnon and the golden scandals of yesteryear. Historical
events are just so much raw material from which literary capital
can be made. The alliterative phrasing of the account of Humboldt's youth and his father's adventures 'Whores and horses'
'boots, bugles and bivouacs' (p. 4) creates a jingling rhythm
foreshadowing the decline of Humboldt's poetic art. Whereas
previously Citrine had described Humboldt in terms of contradictory qualities, 'He was fine as well as thick, heavy but also light,
and his face was both pale and dark' (p. 11), a device which, like
the often repeated strings of unpunctuated epithets in the novel
serves to explode categorisation, he now labels Humboldt as
'Poet, thinker, problem drinker, pill-taker, man of genius, manic
depressive' (p. 25). The 'tinker-tailor' rhythm, with its allitera-
tion and internal rhymes is repeated in Humboldt's conversation
'Rich boys, poor boys, jewboys, goyboys' (p. 31). The trivial and
childish jingle suggests the effect on his poetry of the obsession
with social categories. Humboldt becomes, himself, merely a
succession of categories. Where his father rode with Pershing's

cavalry, Humboldt approaches poetry in martial fashion, as raids between the lines to bring back beauty. In personal terms Humboldt's obsession with historical and literary categories, seeing Kathleen as Albertine, or as a Christian maiden in the hands of a Jew, leads to such jealousy that he loses Kathleen. By attempting to pin down an individual Beauty within an imprisoning category, he loses hold of it. Citrine notes that Humboldt 'was pondering what to do between *then* and *now*, between birth and death, to satisfy certain great questions' (p. 6). In Humboldt's poetic grammar, however, 'now' has become 'then'. The idea that he can make history implies the self-conscious casting of himself in the role of a historical character, and a consequent transformation of the present moment into a historical moment. The present becomes, indeed, an abstract idea; the individual life is therefore foreshortened, almost erased.

Citrine begins the novel as a reverse Humboldt. During his New York apprenticeship to Marxism Citrine finds it impossible to fit human beings into historical categories. Meeting housewives he tries to see them as petty-bourgeois, husband killers, social climbers, within the definitions of Marx and Freud, but this doesn't destroy the fascination of their human stories. Citrine is paired with Demmie, in a reverse parallel to Humboldt and Kathleen. While insomniac Humboldt watches horror movies, Kathleen sleeps. Humboldt had 'surrounded her with the whole crisis of Western Culture. She went to sleep' (p. 28). Citrine represents a similar retreat from history, while Demmie is the insomniac, preferring horror movies to her own nightmares. Demmie's horrors are fundamentalist in origin, the product of an earlier American culture. She is caught between overpolarised alternatives, between grace and depravity, a role as a 'good' girl or a 'bad' girl. Humboldt's long monologue in New Jersey reveals a similar overpolarisation in his reading of history. The monologue deals with the reverse of the 'World Historical Individual', what has been called the 'Furtive Fallacy'.[10] Humboldt dwells on such topics as the secret sex lives of great men, the perversions of the military, the secret police. For Humboldt, either history is made by great men with great motives, or it is created out of secret conspiracies, dire psychological needs, and wicked plots. Nothing however, is the result of chance; everything forms part of the pattern. Unable to measure up to the ideal, Demmie and Humboldt plunge into its obverse.

In the Cantabile plot, the events of the present which are interrupted by Citrine's memories, the opposition between 'high' and 'low' readings of history is continued. Where the New Jersey episode focused on insomniac, history-obsessed, nightmare-bound Humboldt, the fourth section of the novel returns to the present, to 'a different side of life – entirely contemporary' (p. 34), to the awakening of Citrine, the sleeper, by Cantabile, and the battering of his car. Like Humboldt's, Citrine's car is a symbol of an inflated self-image, bought in 'an Antony and Cleopatra mood. Let Rome in Tiber melt. Let the world know that such a mutual pair could wheel through Chicago in a silver Mercedes' (p. 36). The car is battered by baseball bats, suggesting the low culture of the crowd, its windows 'spat on all over' (p. 35) as if it had suffered a 'crystalline internal hemorrhage'. Citrine's car has been 'bled' because he set himself up as a great man and therefore incurred the wrath of the mass. 'How could such a thing happen on a public street?' he asks (p. 36). But the answer is plain. Other people also like to sleep through violent events, to transform pistol shots into backfires. The attack on his car symbolises the historical event, and public indifference to it. The attacker, Cantabile, emerges from the underworld, the secret evil beneath life, to use Humboldt's terms. In the poker game, which forms the catalyst for the Cantabile plot, Citrine is exposed to low life. Cantabile introduces him as a contrast-gainer, a term he uses of couples where one ugly partner makes the other look good in contrast, but which becomes a portmanteau expression. The novel is structured around such pairs – grace and depravity, high and low plots – in such a way that each part of the duality is exposed to irony. Citrine, for example, may look less noble than Humboldt but feels superior to Cantabile. At the poker game he is shown attempting to occupy a 'high' position, discoursing on art and culture, provoking the lower elements to cheat him. Unlike the Humboldt plot, in which man's pretensions to heroic or superhuman status were explored, the Cantabile plot explores the less than human, and the stereotypes of 'low' life. Cantabile lectures Citrine on Robert Ardrey, the territorial imperative, paleontology in the Olduvai gorge and the views of Konrad Lorenz. The game itself takes place under webs of power lines, in an urban environment which has reverted to the wild. (Citrine notices odd natural survivals in the area, carp and catfish in its polluted ponds.) Even George's outrage at the cheating is the result of the violation of his own territorial instinct. 'They don't get away with that on my turf,' he roars (p. 63). The territorial imperative sheds new light on the attraction exercised by categories, suggesting that the attraction to closed philosophical systems or forms of ordering is only a refinement of a basic biological drive. The tuxedo man, for example, is astonished by Charlie's suggestion that he should have married his girlfriend. 'What, marry a hot broad who turns on in hotel rooms?' he exclaims, and his friend the undertaker explains to Charlie that 'you don't mix things up. That's not what a wife is about. And if you have a funny foot you have to look for a funny shoe' (p. 63). The episode foreshadows Charlie's own problems. Renata, repeatedly described as Citrine's funny shoe, a hot broad who turns on in hotel rooms, later marries an undertaker, and is also mourned by Citrine. Citrine fails to marry Renata largely because she does not meet up to his impossibly high moral demands. He is a victim of a black and white morality, a lack of moral sophistication. It is at this point in the novel that he recalls the T.B. ward (p. 65) to which 'good' people donated comics, where Charlie read the Bible all day, surrounded by dying children. The white geometry of the ward, with its graphic illustrations of good and evil, represents the naive Manichaeanism of America. It is as a consequence of the sanatorium episode that Citrine is consumed by a desire for 'pure' love.

Bellow creates an image of American society as a series of closed spheres, in which the 'bad social game' (p. 125) is played by very different rules. Uncle Moochy Cantabile, cop turned murderer, murders because he is humiliated by two hoodlums who make him grovel and gobble sawdust like an animal. Moochy's supposed allegiance to a higher code does not withstand this threat to his individual status in the biological pecking order. He therefore loses his place in both the 'good' legal system, and the 'bad' underworld, as both systems reject him for not conforming to the moral (or immoral) stereotype. Similarly when Charlie attempts to operate in both 'high' and 'low' cultural spheres he is cheated out of his money, both in the poker game, and the social game. Uncertain where he stands Citrine tries to consult Vito Langobardi, a gangster at the top of the underworld hierarchy, 'so high in the organisation that he had become rarefied into a gentleman' (p. 67). In the 'nude democracy' (p. 67) of the locker room Charlie had identified with Vito. At the club, however, he realises that Langobardi is playing a different game from him. While Charlie

worships vitalist George as a hermetic personality, Vito represents a different and equally vital force. At the Club, on the
telephone to other gangsters, he 'gave instructions, made rulings,
decisions, set penalties' (p. 69). In the game, cut-throat, the third
player, Hildenfisch, drops dead in the midst of the game. Citrine
realises that he and Vito 'had a relationship in the same way that
the Empire State Building had an attic' (p. 70). The fact that
Langobardi is at the top of one social hierarchy does not mean
that the hierarchies form a continuum.

Seeking advice in dealing with Cantabile Citrine travels
through decaying Chicago to the Russian bath. The scene around
him is like a speeded up film of the historical process. 'It's like a
film montage of rise fall and rise' (p. 71), he comments, gazing at
the demolished rubble of fallen apartment blocks. 'Eternity got no
picturesque interval here. The ruins of time had been bulldozed,
scraped, loaded as fill' (p. 75). Charlie is horrified by this destruction amidst which the Russian bath alone stands untouched. The
bath is deliberately described in mythic terms. Its denizens are
cast in antique form, eat epic meals, and appear to be engaged 'in
a collective attempt to buck history' (p. 78). Bellow undercuts this
mythic quality however. The bath may appear to resemble the
underworld – its occupants lie panting and groaning on hot
planks as if in Hades – but two senses of the term 'underworld' are
exploited here, the criminal and the mythic. With a shock Citrine
realises that the bath may in fact be owned by the Mafia. Myron
Swiebel, who visits the bath each day, is also a car enthusiast, but
more dangerous than Humboldt or Citrine, because the cataracts
on his eyes give no side vision. Committed to one way of seeing
Myron forges ahead, swiping other cars. Bellow suggests here that
the attempt to idolise the elemental nature of man, to enthrone the
biological imperative and natural forces as mythic beings is as
dangerous as to isolate man from them as saint or hero. The scene
in the toilet forms an ironic coda to this mythic view of man.
Cantabile's noble savagery turns out to be the product of loose
bowels. The mythic is revealed as not only squalid, but, worse,
trivial. While Cantabile roars, Citrine notices his buttons and
comments that Circe might have had buttons like that in her
sewing box.

While Bellow wishes to avoid imprisoning the contingency of
events within narrow ideological categories – in Citrine's terms,
joining the 'metaphysical-historical' (p. 76) thought police – he

does not underestimate the difficulty inherent in attempting to see events as they really occur. Leaving the bath, Citrine asks Cantabile what he did in the war. Cantabile produces his war history – a squalid tale – with the words 'I'll tell you what you want to hear' (p. 88). At the same time he dwells on his cousin Emil's participation in the 1968 riots. Emil was 'twigged out and didn't even know which side he was on' (p. 87). The actual events of history are lost either through the confusion of the participants or by their attempt to give the expected answer to the enquirer. It is almost impossible therefore to see history in Ranke's terms, '*wie es eigentlich gewesen*'. This is dramatised in the following meditation which returns to Humboldt, to whom Citrine devotes a morning of meditation. Charlie contemplates the postcard poem which Humboldt sent him, and realises that, far from being nonsensical, the poem dramatises the chronic war between 'sleep' and waking nightmare, detailing a hierarchy of violence in which the 'heedless' sleep of the lions follows gory butchery. The poem insists on the interconnection of each level in the hierarchy. Citrine realises that his failure to help Humboldt stemmed from his belief that they were in different categories; his last sight of him followed a morning with the topmost of the political hierarchy in a helicopter over New York, part of the overview in every sense. Fleeing New York he runs to Chicago, a Chicago which embodies the nightmares of history. Formerly 'slaughter-city' (p. 114), its soil breathing out the reek of death, its buildings constructed on a base of pulverised bones, Chicago is a place where 'billions' died. The references to the smell of burnt hair and soap suggest a human holocaust. The city is described as if still in a state of crisis; it is a 'rape and murder' night (p. 115) with fire trucks and ambulances screaming past. Paralysed by the horrors of public life Citrine allows his individual moral commitment to lapse. Instead of succouring Humboldt he runs into the arms of the crisis mentality incarnate – Denise, who lives in a constant state of operatic crisis. Overaware of the duty owed to politics and ideas, obsessed with his own relation to the horrors of history, Charlie loses sight of its real components – individual suffering and death.

Nor is he alone in so doing. Like Citrine, Humboldt allowed the demands of public life to dwarf his personal ideals. 'To Humboldt the Eisenhower landslide of 1952 was a personal disaster' (p. 120). Citrine, less committed then to the need for public recognition comments that 'We'll have to mark time,' (p. 120) but Humboldt is determined to make his mark on it before it marks him. Historical nightmares oppress him. He refuses a lectureship in Germany on the grounds that it is dangerous. On occupying Sewell's office he replaces Sewell's Toynbee with Rilke and Kafka, reflecting his own status as poet and persecuted artist on trial. Humboldt is unwilling to accept even a temporary setback, since this irremediably damages his self-image as man of destiny, historical individual. The association of writing with war is underlined in Humboldt's accoutrements (he is described as 'bandoliered' (p. 129) with pens) in his initiation a power struggle with Sewell, and his forcing Citrine into the blood-brother pact. When Citrine signs the cheque his arm jerks as if he were signing in blood. When Humboldt tells him to keep the cheque safe because 'It's dangerous. I mean it's valuable' (p. 130) the Freudian slip is apt, revealing that for Humboldt value is inseparable from the ability to harm others. For him the pen is mightier than the sword *as a weapon*.

The consequences of this on his poetry are illustrated in the interview Citrine has with Ricketts, which makes two points – firstly that the division of society into different closed spheres has led to different languages, and therefore a loss in communication, and secondly that poetic language itself has been debased in the process. Charlie and Ricketts are unable to communicate. Ricketts begins with the language of finance for which Charlie needs an interpreter, 'Table of organization? Translate, please' (p. 134). When Charlie uses a Jewish idiom, describing himself as a 'compulsive-*heimischer* type' it is Ricketts's turn to be baffled. He tries again with his personal idiom, hard-boiled naval slang, welcoming Charlie aboard his 'shakedown cruise' and mentioning the 'scuttlebutt' (rumour) that 'you guys are going great in Sewell's program,'. Charlie tries to bridge the gap with a poetic use of nautical terms, 'you should have heard Humboldt speak on *Sailing to Byzantium*' (p. 131), but the visionary, like the emotional, founders on the rocks of the business ethic. The conversation becomes an empty ritual with no real exchange of information, a salesman's pitch for Humboldt in which words are merely content-free linguistic counters in a commercial game. Charlie eulogises Humboldt in exaggerated terms. 'Oh, Humboldt! Wise warm gifted Humboldt!' (p. 132) reverting to the tinker-tailor rhythm 'poet, critic, scholar, teacher, editor, original', (p. 132) which Ricketts helpfully completes, echoing the earlier internal rhyme.

'He's just a man of genius' (p. 132). The rhythm of their exchanges becomes progressively more pronounced:

> The only thing is the dough!
> If only we had enough dough!   (p. 134)

Citrine's earlier scorn for the academic music box is fully borne
out, by this empty tinkling language, of popular jingle, which is
the only idiom they share. When Citrine returns the message to
Humboldt, the hollowness of Ricketts's interest in poetry, as
opposed to the heavy respect which money commands, is underlined by the rhythm of Citrine's speech [The lines are not
typographically arranged like this in the text of course.]:

> You're famous.
> he loves you,
> admires you,
> desires you,
> but he can't create a chair without the dough.   (p. 135)

Even worse, Humboldt picks up the rhythm in lines which not
only echo the lyrics, but also the rhythm of a song from *My Fair
Lady* ![11]

> 'And that's what he said?'
> 'Exactly what he said.'
> 'Then I think I've got him!
> Charlie, I've got him!
> We've done it!'
> 'How have you got him?
> How have we done it?'   (p. 135)

Charlie's comment that Humboldt 'looked Mother-Goosey when
he did this. The cow jumped over the moon. The little dog
laughed to see such fun' (p. 135) pushes home our awareness of
the debasement of poetry into jingle. Humboldt has become an
animated cliché. He sets off for New York 'Like a silent-movie
hero taking his invention to the big city' (p. 136). In short he has
lost his own language by becoming the hero of a form of culture
dedicated to the go-getter and the fortune hunter. The empty
artistic forms of a money-minded society have taken him over.

In New York, while Citrine is involved in the production of his historical melodrama, *Von Trenck*, Humboldt launches himself into a superdrama of his own – also historical in its plot. Unable to find the next 'new' thing to do, 'Instead he did a former thing. He got himself a pistol, like Verlaine, and chased Magnasco' (p. 155). Humboldt becomes a mere figure of a poet, enacting the 'Agony of the American Artist' (p. 156), staging 'mad-scenes' at Bellevue. Citrine, meanwhile, stages his own Humboldt-based historical drama, and occupied with this falsification of emotion, discards the emotional reality, failing to visit his friend. Humboldt's construction of a case history, legal for the lawyers, psychological for the psychiatrists, reveals the extent to which he has become 'historical'. The audience adore his performance, flocking to Bellevue, reminding Citrine of 'the residents of Washington who drove out in carriages to watch the Battle of Bull Run and then got in the way of the Union troops'(p. 158). The audience prevent Humboldt winning his battle with madness, delighted by Humboldt's drama, much as they would be by war, or any other crisis as a relief from their dull lives. His narrative has moreover a sexual theme, titillating to the psychiatrists. His evasion is therefore two-fold, like Citrine, who takes refuge from later events in the arms of both 'crisis mentality' and a sexually gratifying woman. Humboldt's re-enactment is described in terms which link him with pioneer-faced Demmie:

> I saw Humboldt whipping his team of mules and standing up in his crazy wagon like an Oklahoma land-grabber. He rushed into the territory of excess to stake himself a claim.   (p. 155)

The territorial imperative can be linked to excessive emotionalism, as easily as to the constriction of emotion by ideological limits. Humboldt's sexual show is paralleled by Demmie's elaborate wedding plans with the Littlewoods as best man and maid of honour. A double irony is intended here. Not only are the wife-swapping Littlewoods depraved, but their depravity was offered by Littlewood as a 'good show' (p. 165) and 'Eskimo wife deal' (p. 145). The polar and theatrical metaphors suggest that America has polarised morality into pairs of alternative roles to be played.

The meditation ends with Citrine complaining at the timing of Humboldt's action in cashing Citrine's blank cheque. Humboldt cashes the cheque immediately on the death of Demmie Vonghel, and Citrine complains that 'he reads the papers. He knows she's gone!' (p. 168). The meditation follows the events of the Cantabile plot in terms of narrative time, but of course precedes them in terms of the supposed historical order of events. When Citrine accuses Humboldt in terms of 'he reads the papers' the reader remembers Cantabile's preceding accusation that Citrine should have known of the death of Bill's brother from the papers. In both cases the individual is unaware of the public version of the events he is living through. The reader's judgement of Citrine largely depends upon the imaginative presentation of the total time scheme. Historical events are used by Citrine to justify his betrayal of down-and-out Humboldt, but the imaginative narrative counters and reverses this justification by positioning the betrayal first, before we learn of Humboldt's own betrayal. The impossibility of living up to the image of man as controller of time leads Citrine to live in a sensationalised present. Whirled along in the present by Cantabile, however, the present becomes a re-ordering of his past. Only the awareness of a personal relation to the past can supply a true moral perspective. Man is neither totally bound to the past nor able to ignore it; rather he exists in a complex relation to it, forced to make moral distinctions between outwardly similar events. The timing of Humboldt's betrayal of Citrine is morally culpable in terms of the public record of events, but this is not the only temporal perspective from which the event can be judged. The personal and emotional becomes as important as the cultural overview. The construction of the novel up to this point may effectively be said to respect Whitehead's dictum: that history can be read in two directions, forwards and backwards, but that the thinking man must do both.

From this point on in the novel the tone becomes increasingly comic. Events are summed up in oblique fashion by the Caldo-freddo filmscript which Citrine describes to Cantabile. In order to survive in a polar world, Caldofreddo turned cannibal just as Citrine and Humboldt, caught between overpolarised codes of behaviour, are seen as cannibals in the imagery of the blood-brother cheques, and the feeding off each other's reputation.[12] Caldofreddo's action is set within the context of two rival explorers one of whom fails to rescue the other. Caldofreddo is then used by the Russian political machine as proof of the failure of Capitalism, seen merely as the adjunct to an ideology. In later life

Caldofreddo is faced by a journalist investigating his past, much as Mrs Cantabile questions Citrine. Given the choice of killing the threat to his peace, Caldofreddo refrains, as Citrine resists the temptation of having Denise killed. Humboldt envisaged the scenario in terms of 'vaudeville and farce but with elements of *Oedipus at Colonus* in it' (p. 182) and the novel takes its key from the filmscript. Indeed its form may be said to reflect Hegel's view of the historical process, as described by Marx.

> Hegel remarks somewhere that all acts and personages of great importance in world history occur, as it were, twice. He forgot to add: the first time as tragedy the second as farce.[13]

The double reading of history is extended also in terms of the style in which events are presented. The form of the novel avoids the danger of offering the reader simplistic moral judgements upon events, as similar historical events occur within very different stylistic modes. In a second deflation of myth Myron Swiebel meets Gaylord Koffritz in the Russian bath. Gaylord's glittering beard and piercing eye promise significant revelations – but when he speaks this particular Ancient Mariner launches into a sales pitch for tombs, which is distinctly low-poetic. 'Has your last rest been arranged? Is there a family plot? Are you provided? No? but why not?' (p. 195). Koffritz sells the tombs in terms of art, moreover. They range in style from early Etruscan to Art Nouveau, fitting monuments for those who have lived their lives according to ready-made styles, myths and ideologies. From death, Bellow turns to the re-enactment of past roles in love, dealing with Citrine's first encounter with Renata. The meeting is arranged by Szathmar, a poseur whom Citrine indulges, aware of what he describes as:

> the middle-class endeavour of two centuries to come out look-
> ing well, to preserve a certain darling innocence – the innocence
> of Clarissa defending herself against the lewdness of
> Lovelace.   (p. 209)

The escape from history is also an attempt to whitewash moral failings, to preserve a myth of innocence. In the scene which follows, Citrine casts himself as Lovelace, with Renata, drugged by Martini, as Clarissa, in a hilarious burlesque of the melodrama of seduction. Charlie begins by justifying himself in terms which, by now, destroy his moral credibility in the eyes of the reader:

> we couldn't evade History, and that this was what History was doing to everybody. History had decreed that men and women had to become acquainted in these embraces.　　(pp. 210–11)

The capitalisations and the juxtaposition of sexual needs with an appeal to history automatically form a '*caveat lector*'. The scene veers between melodrama and Goldoni farce as Charlie struggles with the folding bed, in the mix-up over the key, and in the re-appearance, at this of all moments, of Charlie's childhood sweetheart. Seeing her alone at the bar Charlie jumps to the hasty conclusion that she has become a hooker. Were he really a Lovelace, this confrontation between the seducer and the wronged girl now sunk in shameful depths would not be so very unlikely. Charlie however clings to his darling innocence, and turns the tables on Naomi, accusing her of 'ruining' him. 'I lost my character altogether because I couldn't spend my life with you' (p. 213).

The court scene which follows explores the polarisation and subsequent stereotyping of the roles of good and evil, in public life. Although ostensibly deployed in Charlie's support, his own lawyers won't hear criticism of the opposition because of their allegiance to a code of 'professional ethics'. Since Charlie is also paying both sets of lawyers, the supposed legal battle is only an empty ritual, with no real commitment from either side. In Charlie's words, 'History had created something new in the USA, namely crookedness with self-respect or duplicity with honor' (p. 221). Although the judge's order of *Ne exeat* leaves Charlie fighting mad, he swallows his impulse to burst out in impassioned speech, 'like Shylock telling off the Christians' (p. 232). The intuitive sense of right and wrong, and meaningful appeals on behalf of the human bond are out of place in a court which deals only in ideas of justice, and where everyone, including Cannibal Pinsker, is entitled to his pound of flesh. Citrine keeps silent 'out of respect for the real thing' (p. 232) – real suffering and persecution. His own 'bleeding' is after all only a metaphor, and Citrine is now alert to the dangers of allowing a metaphor to govern reality. Abjuring the melodramatic he opts instead for silence. 'The name of the game was silence, hardness and silence' (p. 232).

As we might expect silent manly control is no more valid than any other stereotyped role. The novel directs its ironies against the hard-boiled, tough hero, firstly through the character of Tigler, then through Charlie himself. Retiring to the men's room, Charlie reads Kathleen's letter, recounting the death of Tigler, a result of his attempt to live on the margin of society, 'a little outside the law' (p. 238). Tigler's attempts to reincarnate the Western hero are only a step backwards, a re-enactment of an outworn social pattern, seen through an outworn artistic convention. When Charlie saves Tigler from drowning (off a horse Tigler is helpless) no acknowledgements are made. 'It was an incident between two men. I mean, I felt it to be the manly silent West' (p. 238). Tigler's sunburnt figure is not so much vital, as statuary however, as if he 'were cast in bronze' (p. 238). Charlie pulls him from the water, while around them the Indians fish out toobie-fish, living fossils like Tigler. The cruelty of the silent West is underlined by the Indians' behaviour to Winnemucca, whom they watch bleeding to death. Silent detachment can be taken too far. The past now holds no nostalgic value for Citrine. 'I can't think what made those old days so good. I doubt that Humboldt had had a single good day in all his life' (p. 240). Tigler's finances were saved by a movie company wishing to film the Mongol hordes on his property – saved from one dramatic stereotype only by the adoption of another.

If Tigler's eventual fate leans somewhat towards the tragic, the scenes in Stronson's office replay the 'hard-boiled' role in a comedy. Charlie is forced by Cantabile into the role of hit-man. Melodrama, this time of the *roman noir* type, recurs, from the coded sets of knocks, to Charlie's slouch hat and tightly belted raincoat, from the FBI agent in disguise to Thaxter's mysterious CIA immunity. Charlie plays out his role in a cops and robbers drama, the twentieth-century version of the strong silent Westerner. Ironically, Charlie had already diagnosed, in his relentless fashion, the connection between the 'shrinking of investment opportunities and the quest for new roles or personality investments' (p. 269). Yet his own analysis does not prevent him being cast in a new role in order to recoup Cantabile's investment losses. Both Cantabile and Thaxter use the idea of a cultural Overview in order to cheat Charlie, through the plans for *The Ark*, and the cultural Baedeker, in Thaxter's case. The establishment of analytical versions of life is a form of trap, casting the individual into false roles, exposing him to misunderstandings of the events in which he acts. Analysis of events does not protect from events. The fact that Charlie is an internationally known historian cuts no ice with the Chicago police. He is rescued from the consequences of his false role by the daughter of his childhood sweetheart, Maggie Lutz. Maggie is quite uninterested in Charlie's historical works. 'I understand they're history books and history has never been my bag' (p. 290). What motivates her is the memory of her mother's past love for Charlie. Charlie is rescued then, not by rational historical analysis, but by the real force of remembered emotion.

In the final movement of the novel Charlie embarks on a spiritual quest in an attempt to resolve his problems, a quest which Bellow treats in primarily comic terms. Before leaving, Charlie takes his children to a historical pageant in which the figure of Rip Van Winkle suggests a parallel to his own position, as sleeper suddenly awoken. 'Great world events pass him by. . . . Decades of calendars drop their leaves on him just as the trees dropped leaves and twigs on Rip' (p. 294). Charlie rationalises his desertion of his children, a further retreat from life, by reference to *Pilgrim's Progress*:

> Christian in *Pilgrim's Progress* had taken off, too, and left his family to pursue salvation. Before I could do the children any real good, I had to wake up. (p. 294)

This is undercut however by the children's screams of terror as Rip wakes up. Charlie cannot expect to wake up suddenly and find all his problems solved by a bolt of revelation. The tables are also turned on Charlie by Renata, whose quest for what Charlie always calls 'the riddle of your birth' parodies Charlie's own somewhat more ethereal quest. In attempting to escape the complications of his life – Denise and the children – Charlie finds himself ending up as *paterfamilias* to the loathsome Señora and Roger. If he can abandon his children for the supposed good of his soul (actually to engage in sexual shenanigans with Renata) so Renata can abandon Roger to go in quest of Biferno (actually to engage in similar shenanigans with Flonzaley.) Although Charlie does finally propose to Renata, the Señora's comment says it all. ' "I congratulate you on finally making sense," . . . She didn't say, mind you, that I had done this in time' (p. 419). Abstract problems may be resolved by 'making sense'. For human beings the solution may come too late. Charlie cannot re-negotiate the terms of his existence from scratch. In Marx's words:

> Men make their own history, but they do not make it just as they please; they do not make it under circumstances chosen by themselves, but under circumstances directly encountered, given and translated from the past.[14]

Given this inheritance from the past, does this reduce life to a meaningless cycle of repetitions? This is the question faced by Charlie on Demmie's death when he meets the missionary Vonghels. Not only are they a second group, the first having been eaten by cannibals, but they all look exactly alike. Wearily Charlie comments that

> The whole thing is disintegrating and reintegrating all the time, and you have to guess whether it's always the same cast of characters or a lot of different characters. (p. 301)

The repetitive and parallel structures within the novel pose the same question. Does the individual merely repeat past errors, or does he gain wisdom from a broader time perspective? Is the pattern of history merely bleed-or-be-bled, Toynbee's rout-rally-rout view of history? The second of the two film scenarios sums up the negative effects of the attempt to repeat events, to return to a state of primal innocence, akin to myth. The hero of the scenario, Corcoran, a successful writer like Charlie who has been barren for some years, and has a dominant wife, meets and falls in love with a beautiful woman and escapes with her to foreign climes. He then attempts to repeat the experience in order to write a book. Corcoran's experience is seen in terms of American mythicism. Coming to a Paradisal island he feels renewed, but when he tries to repeat the process he is forced into a false role and ruins the paradise itself, forced to bribe the natives with technological marvels. On Corcoran's second trip 'All now is parody, desecration, wicked laughter' (p. 345). The events of history are not repeatable at will: repetition implies not timelessness, but parody. To attempt to repeat events is to fail to act upon them. In Spain Citrine dwells on the resemblance between the Spaniards and his immigrant Jewish forbears. 'We were parted when the Jews were expelled in 1492. Unless you were very stingy with time, that wasn't really so long ago' (p. 421). The date is of course resonant with other implications – the year in which Columbus sailed the ocean blue. Where Augie March determined to cling to his ideals, to become a 'Columbus of those near-at-hand', Citrine rejects New World optimism. The American faith in beginning again is belied when seen in the larger historical context of persecution and expulsion. In Spain Citrine finally accepts his place in history, wryly adopting the persona of a historian of the Spanish-American war.[15]

Is the reader then to finish the novel in a spirit of cynicism, of wicked laughter? Bellow is aware of the danger of reducing historical speculation to mere entertainment, to 'pop history', such as E.L. Doctorow's *Ragtime*. The point is discussed by reference to Orlando Huggins, Humboldt's executor, and to Thaxter's kidnapping by terrorists. Although Orlando, a top journalist, forever analysing public events, seems committed to the maintenance of certain standards, his presentation undercuts his status. We note that although he covers a political convention, he does so for *Women's Wear Daily*, although he discourses on McCarthyism, he does so nude on a log opposite a naked woman. The suggestion is that even the élite of New York culture approach questions of morality and history in a time-killing spirit akin to that of their sexual activities. The point is made even clearer by the description of Huggins's 'shirt of Merrymount stripes, broad crimson and diabolical purple, like the ribbons of the revelers' Maypole' (p. 322). In Hawthorne's story, the revellers' frolic is not only sexual, but also a reversion to former customs. The Merrymount colonists were led by men who 'had sported so long with life that when Thought and Wisdom came, even these unwelcome guests were led astray'.[16] Huggins, supposedly one of the thinkers of the age, has had a much gayer time in New York with his parties – of either type – than gloomy Puritan Citrine in Chicago. Huggins may think he is pursuing the new, a representative of the avant garde, but in fact he is moving backwards. Hawthorne described the colonists as having 'made their true history a poet's tale'.[17] Huggins's syllabic stammer, 'ch-ch-charm' (p. 324) 'twi-twi-twink' (p. 323) 'ago-go' (p. 323), lends a ragtime quality to his speech, and recalls the rhythms of Humboldt's poetry. Although our inheritance from the past is inescapable, it is a mistake to view it as mere entertainment, trivialising its content. Moral and political questions raised by history should not have the same status as sexual revelry. Thaxter should not be able to make a fortune out of his kidnapping by writing a work of 'instant history' about it. Should such a book be written the reader would suffer intensely with Thaxter, but at one remove. In Citrine's words: 'the powers of compassion are now being weakened by an impossible volume of demands' (p. 472). Thaxter's excessive emotionalism blunts the moral sensibilities as much as the detached comic view of history.

Bellow's own ability to avoid the pitfalls offered by black comedy and sensationalism is demonstrated by the film *Caldofreddo* which Citrine watches in Paris. Two points are emphasised – the historical nature of the film with its 'old newsreel manner' and 'Time marches on' style, and the audience reaction to it. For the audience the film is primarily comic. 'The plane sank. Thousands of people were laughing' (p. 461). Events in the film are stylised, particularly the opposition between the rival explorers. Only Citrine, who is aware of Humboldt's personal tragedy behind the events, weeps uncontrollably. History is comic only when presented in stylised oversimplified and over-rapid terms, without the awareness of individual suffering involved in it. Citrine has a horrified vision of

> humanity either laughing its head off as pictures of man-eating
> comedy unrolled on the screen or vanishing in great waves of
> death.   (p. 462)

Earlier in the novel Citrine espoused Tolstoi's belief that 'it's time we simply refused to be inside history and playing the comedy of history, the bad social game' (p. 125). Humboldt has taught Citrine that he cannot step out of history but that this doesn't reduce history to a joke. The ending of the film is a choric scene of reconciliation and forgiveness, reminiscent of *Oedipus at Colonus*, which points to a different view of the social game. Society is not an audience, comically detached from history, but a participant in the drama. Approached with this sense of shared responsibility, the awareness of past evils doesn't polarise society but unites it. The novel ends on a less than affirmative note[18] – at the graveside – but this is to be expected if we accept its thesis: that there can be no totally 'new' beginning but that the past can be handled responsibly.

The novel therefore explores different approaches to history and retreats from history: pop history, instant history, history as nightmare, as tragedy, as farce, the retreat into myth or transcendence, or into the eternal present of the crisis mentality. By the novel's various structurings of time, Bellow succeeds in avoiding any one style of approach and thereby liberates the event to be judged in its total context, as it affects its participants, as it is recorded in public records, and as it is inherited, transformed and translated by succeeding generations. That he does so in a novel which is both emotionally and intellectually satisfying makes this his *tour de force*.

7 Conclusion

While it is, of course, always advisable to trust the tale and not the teller, Bellow's own non-fictional writings offer cautionary advice to the critic and address themselves repeatedly to the problems of historical understanding. In his critical essays Bellow has expressed deep reservations about contemporary criticism, in which he discerns two major failings: an excessive interest in symbolic detail, and an over-readiness to subsume complex literary works to the dictates of ideology. In 'Culture Now',[1] for example, in a survey of literary periodicals, Bellow laments the extent to which individual readings of novels have been swallowed up by crudely ideological interpretations. In an interview, Bellow rejected the idea of writing in accordance with preconceived ideological intent, whether affirmative or skeptical:

> Writers who tell you life is beautiful or writers who tell you life is vile are, alike, imbeciles. Beautiful and vile have nothing to do with the matter; what does have something to do with the matter is something that is demonstrated in fact, an independent detail in the telling of the story. But as for matters on the ideological side, there is very little to be said for them.[2]

In 'Deep Readers of the World, Beware!', however, Bellow cautioned against too obsessive an interest in the particular detail of the story, a critical practice which may degenerate into naive symbol-hunting and a failure to confront major social and moral issues. Such symbol-mongering depends upon the inflation of realistic detail into abstraction. The 'deep reader'

> falls wildly on any particle of philosophy or religion and blows it up bigger than the Graf Zeppelin ... Are we to attach meaning to whatever is grazed by the writer? Is modern literature Scripture? Is criticism Talmud, theology? Deep readers of the world beware![3]

At the same time, Bellow has regretted the lack of care in the reading of fiction, pointing out that in *Mr Sammler's Planet,*

> Each word is very carefully weighed and connected, closely connected, to the man. The internal processes of Mr Sammler require the very narrowest attention.[4]

Bellow therefore clearly indicates the desirability and importance of careful, even close, reading, with due attention to detail, though without symbolic over-inflation. In addition he describes himself as disappointed with readings of novels which do not take into account the full density of the experience presented:

> One of the troubles with criticism is that it's simply linear, if you know what I mean – sketchy. The novelist never feels he's got anything until he has it in all the density of actual experience. Then he looks at a piece of criticism and all he sees is the single outline of thought. It's not the same thing. And you can't deal with a phenomenon that way. So he never really trusts criticism, because it lacks the essential density.[5]

The terms of this criticism, the objection to linear and schematic readings, and the concern with the experiential and actual facts, suggest the importance of the historical dimension in Bellow's own work.

Indeed, Bellow has described himself as a historical writer, telling an interviewer, 'After all, I am a historian. Every novelist is a historian, a chronicler of his time.[6] Bellow does not understate the importance of historical conditioning. To Chirantan Kulshrestha he conceded that

> Nine-tenths (to guess at a fraction) of what a man writes is determined for him unconsciously by social circumstances and by historical forces of which he is unaware.[7]

He is, however, wary of espousing too complete an identification between the writer and his historical conditions, in particular in modern America where an obsession with history is itself a fact of history. Bellow frequently laments the manner in which public interest in immediate events, race riots, political scandals, campaigns, rumour and news, looms over the writer, converting serious moral and political questions into crisis mentality, agitation and public entertainment:

> These are considered the Action, the Centre of common experience. This is History, in which we live. To many it seems that nothing can be more important than this History.[8]

This overriding interest produces two analogous reactions. Firstly the major facts of Western history appear to swamp the writer's art, leaving him nothing to say:

> How can a writer compete with the great events of this century? What is he going to say after the revolution of 1905, World War I, the Russian revolution, the rise of Fascism, the great depression, World War II, the atomic bomb and all these other tremendous movements of destiny?[9]

Secondly his readers tend to demand that the writer register contemporary events, and transform his fiction into reportage, for which there is an expanding market. Americans, Bellow argues, are beginning to place themselves in history, and are absorbed in the immediate details of this new form of existence, to the point of valuing only the contemporaneous and the 'relevant'.[10] Worse, history is valued only as prediction:

> We're all engaged in historical analysis ... For about a hundred and fifty or two hundred years we have been obsessed with the notion that unless you stand at the crossroads of history you're going to become obsolete.[11]

This obsession with history also conditions the ideological quality of much modern writing. Baldly Bellow declares that 'Ideology is a drag.'[12] Arguing that literature has been swallowed up by sociological, political and psychological models of reality, he locates the phenomenon in the contemporary attitude to time, amongst literary critics in particular.

> Common to all of them is a certain historical outlook. All that is not *now*, they say, is obsolete and dead. Any man who does not accept the historical moment as defined by the only authoritative interpreters is dead.[13]

Bellow goes on to object forcibly to the wilful recasting of the past into simplistic patterns. Literary critics, he complains, consume the culture of the past in order to turn it to their own purposes.[14] In particular, both writers and critics are too ready to subordinate the imagination to thought, to float with the current of intellectual history, and to accept without question such definitions of their situation as are offered by leading historical thinkers. The novel thus appears to be entirely determined by historical analysis:

> Hegel, Marx, Nietzsche, Husserl, Einstein, Schrodinger, Heisenberg, and others made further disclosures which evidently determined the form of the novel for such writers as Gide, Mann, Musil, Camus, Sartre, Beckett.[15]

Bellow, however, is as unwilling to see his own art as determined by intellectual analysis of history as he is to yield to the weight of specific contemporary events. He is especially attached to a belief in the value of the individual self, whereas modern writers (Gide and Mann are cited) 'have accepted the obliteration of the personal as the historical fact (to be unhistorical is a fate worse than death).'[16]

Bellow's interest in history is altogether more complex than a concern for a place in the immediate orthodoxy. Repeatedly Bellow refers to the more distant historical past to criticise contemporary understanding of history. Thus, Bellow takes issue with the Romantic emphasis on the original and 'smashingly new'[17] by calling attention to the repetitive patterns of history. In our lives, he argues,

> We simply do again what has already been done, marvellously. The fact is that most stories have been told, and told again, and again . . . The individuals are different, the story tends to be the same.[18]

Turning to his own personal past Bellow describes his childhood as independent of the conditions of his particular time, but steeped in history:

> I was born into a medieval ghetto in French Canada (Lachine, Quebec). My childhood was in ancient times which was true of all orthodox Jews.[19]

In his own past, Bellow sees evidence to counter the Romantic view of history. In his view, 'the Jewish feeling resists Romanticism and insists on an older set of facts.'[20] Bellow understands this Romantic attitude as veering between the belief in newness and originality, as a break from the past, and apocalyptic nihilism, the conviction that the world must be destroyed in order to rise again.[21] In *Mr Sammler's Planet*, by his own admission, he attempted, among other things, to construct an argument against 'the absurd ideas of originality which belong to the Romantic tradition.'[22] He emphasises that man derives much of his being from the past, and he cites, approvingly, the belief, current in the seventeenth and eighteenth centuries in the necessity of imitating past models of conduct.[23] While Bellow recognises that men do not always learn by the past, that the individual 'does not easily correct himself but forgets what he has felt and seen'[24] he none the less maintains that 'History has given us the means to act more wisely.'[25] While historical change cannot be completely controlled he contends that it must be squarely faced:

> We can't master change. It is too vast, too swift. We'd kill ourselves trying. It is essential, however, to try to understand transformations directly affecting us.[26]

The adoption of simplistic attitudes to change is not helpful. Bellow is especially disturbed by apocalyptic attitudes, and the urge towards violent change.[27] For him, it is as pernicious to lament the decadence of the present by comparison with the past as it is to exalt it as the new and the beautiful. He is particularly repelled by sceptical, impersonal readings of history, and by an age where it is 'thought blessed to see through to the class origins of one's affection for one's grandfather.'[28] Bellow castigates an unexamined belief in market ideologies, whether Marxist, Freudian, or aesthetic. He includes modernism as a similar ideology. In an essay on the relation of the writer to his public he concludes:

> A final word about the avant-garde. To labour to create vanguard conditions is historicism. It means that people have been reading books of culture history and have concluded retrospectively that originality is impossible without such conditions.[29]

Bellow deplores the retreat to the ivory tower of aestheticism as thoroughly as he registers his distaste for the obsession with contemporary relevance. In his opinion many modern writers, whether novelists or historians, follow a purely aesthetic standard. Describing Burckhardt's aesthetic conception of history as the product of a loss of faith, he argues that 'a sharp sense of disappointment and aestheticism go together.'[30] In much modern fiction he therefore detects an unearned wretchedness, a bitterness about existence which is merely fashionable. These are, of course, themes which recur in the novels, in particular in *Herzog* and in *Humboldt's Gift*.

Indeed what emerges from a study of the novels is the high degree of cohesion in Bellow's works. Different approaches to history are outlined, explored, reassessed, and reintroduced with modifications. Interesting links appear between outwardly dissimilar novels. Thus, cyclic models of history dominate both *Henderson the Rain King* and *Mr Sammler's Planet*. The opposition between history and nature which is extensively developed in *The Adventures of Augie March* recurs in *Henderson the Rain King* where it is more narrowly defined in relation to social taboo. The philosophy of Ortega, critically assessed in *The Adventures of Augie March*, surfaces again in *Mr Sammler's Planet*, where its central tenets are accepted with fewer reservations. Psychoanalytical approaches to culture, strongly dominated by their historical implications, constitute the focus of *Henderson the Rain King* and *Herzog*. Where the logic of the former tends towards a cautious acceptance of the Freudian over the Reichian, the latter novel proceeds to a more direct consideration of Freud's attitude to history. The Romantic attitude, a major piece of Herzog's mental luggage, is systematically challenged in *Mr Sammler's Planet*. History as determinism (whether economic, psychological or cultural), history as progress (whether material or religious), history as fall and decline recur at different points in each of the novels.

At the same time, while the novels are closely connected, evincing clear evidence of a continuing debate with the different modes of historical understanding, some degree of development is discernible in Bellow's career. Augie and Henderson may be characterised as questing heroes, leaving their own society to confront their problems in exotic environments, in Mexico, in Africa, in desert and ocean. In addition the form of these two novels is, at least ostensibly, picaresque, creating the impression of a sequence of linked episodes. In contrast Herzog, Sammler and Citrine, all historians, are altogether less naive and more informed. Intellectual history occupies more of the foreground to their experiences. Their movement is largely internal, circling between memories and ideàs, and there is an increased sense of mental debate, complex evaluation and finely drawn distinctions. Parody also comes increasingly to the fore, and the range of tone is wider, extending from high tragedy to low comedy, irony and parody.

A return to the critical assumptions with which this study opened is now informed by an increased awareness of their insufficiencies. In the first place, while it is clear that psychology is of importance in the novels, psychoanalytical theories are always enclosed within a social and moral framework which attacks the vision of man as isolate. While the possibility of eventual trans-cendence is never discounted, the irony to which it is exposed becomes, if anything, more trenchant. Henderson's delight in mystic awareness of the infinite is checked by the reader's uneasy knowledge of the implications of his social role as Sungo. Herzog observes the similarity between the false religiosity of Madeleine and her attempts to exploit him by psychoanalytic therapy, between her conversion and her attraction to a star role. Mr Sammler's uncertainty in regard to Kierkegaard, the reader's unease in relation to Eckhart, and the logic of the action suggest that contemplation *sub specie aeternitatis* may be a strategy of avoiding moral action in the present. Citrine's Steineresque mission to save his soul is wickedly parodied by Renata's antics. Transcendence is always subordinated to the demands of social and moral action in time. While there are often two worlds in the novels, they are more often the worlds of past and present than of atemporal and time-bound. Structurally the novels tend to be organised into polarised alternatives, the double narration of *The Adventures of Augie March*, the two tribes of Henderson's Africa, Mr Sammler's second chance, and the high and low plots of *Humboldt's Gift*. This dualism operates, however, always to highlight the importance of a middle ground, the area of the individual's action in time.

In addition the novels display an extremely precise attention to the specificity of history. Augie's adventures are permeated by accurate notations of the Depression in Chicago, replete with details of political regimes, gang wars and labour agitation. *Herzog* extends from the Russian revolution to the Kennedy era, with letters addressed to presidents, generals, economicians, and political figures. *Mr Sammler's Planet*, drawing upon a *cause célèbre* of the sixties, refers to the Holocaust, the space race and the debates of European intellectuals in the Thirties. In a panorama from the Thirties to the Seventies, *Humboldt's Gift* weaves a richly textured tapestry of historical detail. This specific historical dimension is not, however, merely ancillary to the fiction. As the carefully organised temporal scheme of *The Adventures of Augie March* demonstrates, the sense of history is always of functional importance in the organisation of plotting, structure and theme. The formal duplicity of first person narration is designed to dramatise the opposition of nature and history in *The Adventures of Augie March*. The excursion into an atemporal world, in Africa, externalises and magnifies the conflicts of Henderson's psyche. Where Herzog's letters offer a series of historical debates, his memories provide a sense of a personal past. The attention to the time of the reader mediates between the two, challenging both foreshortened and overdistanced responses to history. In *Mr Sammler's Planet*, the repetitive nature of the action is reflected in the circling motion of the protagonist's mind, to highlight cyclical visions of history. In *Humboldt's Gift* the reader is once again called upon to make careful distinctions between the implications of narrative time and the interpretation of events in their chronological sequence. Even quite minor temporal notations – Augie celebrating Passover, Herzog setting his watch back, the moon rising over Sammler – are of major functional importance. Time is therefore both the formal backbone to Bellow's novels and the thematic centre. In the independent details of the story, and in the ideas considered, Bellow succeeds in probing extremely complex social and historical questions within a satisfying fictional realisation.

Notes and References

CHAPTER 1 INTRODUCTION

1. Friedrich Nietzsche, 'Beyond Good and Evil', in *The Complete Works of Friedrich Nietzsche*, ed. Oscar Levy (London: Foulis, Allen & Unwin, 1909–13) XII, p. 167.
2. Francine Lercangée, *Saul Bellow: A Bibliography of Secondary Sources* (Brussels: Center for American Studies, 1977); Marianne Nault, *Saul Bellow: His Works and His Critics* (New York: Garland, 1977); Robert G. Noreen, *Saul Bellow: A Reference Guide* (Boston: G.K Hall, 1978).
3. Keith M. Opdahl, *The Novels of Saul Bellow: An Introduction* (London: Pennsylvania State University Press, 1967) p. 6.
4. Ibid., p. 26.
5. John J. Clayton, *Saul Bellow: In Defense of Man* (London: Indiana University Press, 1968, revised 1979) p. 4.
6. M. Gilbert Porter, *Whence the Power? The Artistry and Humanity of Saul Bellow* (Columbia, Missouri: University of Missouri Press, 1974).
7. Robert R. Dutton, *Saul Bellow* (Boston: Twayne, 1971) pp. 163–4.
8. Tony Tanner, *Saul Bellow* (Edinburgh: Oliver & Boyd, 1965).
9. Brigitte Scheer-Schäzler, *Saul Bellow* (New York: Ungar, 1972).
10. Howard M. Harper, *Desperate Faith* (Chapel Hill: University of North Carolina Press, 1967) p. 7.
11. Ibid., p. 50.
12. Irving Malin, *Jews and Americans* (Carbondale: Southern Illinois University Press, 1965), and *Saul Bellow's Fiction* (Carbondale: Southern Illinois University Press, 1969).
13. Jeff H. Campbell, 'Bellow's Intimations of Immortality: *Henderson the Rain King*', *Studies in the Novel*, 1, No. 3 (Fall 1969) 323–33; Robert Fossum, 'The Devil and Saul Bellow', *Comparative Literature Studies*, 3, No. 2 (1966) 197–206; Herbert Gold, 'Fiction of the Fifties', *Hudson Review*, 12 (Summer 1959) 192–201; Anthony Quinton, 'The Adventures of Saul Bellow', *London Magazine*, 6 (December 1959) 55–9.
14. Robert Detweiler, *Saul Bellow: A Critical Essay* (Grand Rapids, Michigan: Eerdmans, 1967).
15. Ihab Hassan, 'Five Faces of a Hero', *Critique: Studies in Modern Fiction*, 3, No. 3 (Summer 1960) 28–36.
16. Abraham Chapman, 'The Image of Man as Portrayed by Saul Bellow', *College Language Association Journal*, 10 (June 1967) 285–98.
17. Irwin Stock, 'The Novels of Saul Bellow', *Southern Review*, 3, No. 1 (Winter 1967) 13–42.

18. Robert D. Crozier, 'Theme in Augie March', *Critique: Studies in Modern Fiction*, 7, No. 3 (Spring 1965) 18–32.

19. Albert J. Guerard, 'Saul Bellow and the Activists: On *The Adventures of Augie March*', *Southern Review*, 3 (Summer 1967) 582–96.

20. Max F. Schulz, *Radical Sophistication* (Athens, Ohio: Ohio University Press, 1970) pp. 110–53.

21. Helen Weinberg, *The New Novel in America: The Kafkan Mode in Contemporary Fiction* (Ithaca, New York: Cornell University Press, 1970) pp. 29–54.

22. Joseph Baim, 'Escape From Intellection: Saul Bellow's *Dangling Man*', *University Review*, 37, No. 1 (October 1970) 28–34.

23. Steven M. Gerson, 'Paradise Sought: The Modern American Adam in Bellow's *Herzog*', *McNeese Review*, 24 (1977–78) 50–57, and 'The New American Adam in *The Adventures of Augie March*', *Modern Fiction Studies*, 25, No. 1 (Spring 1979) 117–28; Donald W. Markos, 'Life Against Death in *Henderson the Rain King*', *Modern Fiction Studies*, 17, No. 2 (Summer 1971) 193–205; David Noble, *The Eternal Adam and the New World Garden* (New York: Braziller, 1968) 216–23.

24. Sanford Pinsker, 'Moses Herzog's Fall into the Quotidian', *Studies in the Twentieth Century*, 14 (Fall 1974) 105–16.

25. Ralph Ciancio, 'The Achievement of Saul Bellow's *Seize the Day*', in *Literature and Theology*, ed. Thomas F. Staley and Lester F. Zimmerman (Tulsa, Oklahoma: University of Tulsa, 1969) pp. 49–80.

26. Nathan Scott, *Adversity and Grace: Studies in Recent American Literature* (Chicago: University of Chicago Press, 1968) pp. 27–57.

27. Franklin R. Baruch, 'Bellow and Milton: Professor Herzog in his Garden', *Critique: Studies in Modern Fiction*, 9, No. 3 (1967) 74–83.

28. James D. Boulger, 'Puritan Allegory in Four Modern Novels', *Thought*, 44, No. 174 (Autumn 1969) 413–32.

29. Robert F. Capon, 'Herzog and the Passion', *America* 112, (27 March 1969) 425–7.

30. Harold Kaplan, 'The Second Fall of Man', *Salmagundi*, 30 (Summer 1975) 66–89.

31. Chester E. Eisinger, 'Saul Bellow: Love and Identity', *Accent*, 18 (Summer 1958) 179–203; Irving Malin, *Jews and Americans* (Carbondale: Southern Illinois University Press, 1965); Nathan A. Scott, *Adversity and Grace* (Chicago: University of Chicago Press, 1968); Dan Vogel, 'Saul Bellow's Vision Beyond Absurdity: Jewishness in *Herzog*', *Tradition*, 9 (Spring 1968) 65–79.

32. Robert Boyers, 'Nature and Social Reality in Bellow's Sammler', *Critical Quarterly*, 15 (Autumn 1973) 251–71.

33. Blanche Gelfant, 'In "Terror of the Sublime": Mr Sammler and Odin', *Notes on Modern American Literature*, 2, No. 4 (Fall 1978) Item 25, unpaginated.

34. Stephen R. Maloney, 'Half-way to Byzantium: *Mr Sammler's Planet* and the Modern Tradition', *South Carolina Review*, 6, No. 1 (November 1973) 31–40.

35. James N. Harris, 'One Critical Approach to *Mr Sammler's Planet*', *Twentieth Century Literature*, 18, No. 4 (October 1972) 235–50.

36. Nathan A. Scott, *Three American Moralists: Mailer, Bellow, Trilling* (Notre Dame: University of Notre Dame Press, 1973) pp. 99–150.

37. Herbert J. Smith, '*Humboldt's Gift* and Rudolf Steiner', *Centennial Review*, 22 (1978) 478–89.

38. Malcolm Bradbury, 'The It and the We: Saul Bellow's New Novel', *Encounter*, 45, No. 5 (November 1975) 61–7.

39. Jennifer M. Bailey, 'The Qualified Affirmation of Saul Bellow's Recent Work', *Journal of American Studies*, 7, No. 1 (April 1973) 67–76.

40. Maxwell Geismar, *American Moderns: From Rebellion to Conformity* (New York: Hill and Wang, 1958) pp. 210–24.

41. Theodore J. Ross, 'Notes on Saul Bellow', *Chicago Jewish Forum*, 28 (Fall 1959) 21–7.

42. Kingsley Widmer, 'Poetic Naturalism in the Contemporary Novel', *Partisan Review*, 26, No. 3 (Summer 1959) 467–72.

43. John Updike, 'Draping Radiance with a Worn Veil', *The New Yorker*, 51, No. 30 (15 September 1975) 122 and 125–30.

44. Stanley Trachtenberg (ed.), *Critical Essays on Saul Bellow* (Boston: Hall, 1979) p. ix.

45. C.J. Bullock, 'On the Marxist Criticism of the Contemporary Novel in the United States', *Praxis*, 1, No. ii (1976) 190.

46. David D. Galloway, *The Absurd Hero in American Fiction* (Austin: University of Texas Press, 1966); Ihab Hassan, *Radical Innocence: Studies in the Contemporary American Novel* (Princeton: Princeton University Press, 1961); Helen Weinberg, *The New Novel in America* (Ithaca, New York: Cornell University Press, 1970).

47. Sanford Pinsker, 'Saul Bellow's Cranky Historians', *Historical Reflections*, 3, No. 2 (1976) 35.

48. Ibid., p. 38.

49. Ibid., p. 43.

50. Ibid., p. 43.

51. Alexandre Maurocordato, 'Les quatre dimensions du *Herzog* de Saul Bellow', *Archives des Lettres Modernes*, No. 102 (Paris: Lettres Modernes, 1969).

52. Harold J. Mosher, 'The Synthesis of Past and Present in Saul Bellow's *Herzog*', *Wascana Review*, 6, No. 1 (1971) 28–38.

53. Gabriel Josipovici, *The World and the Book* (London: Macmillan, 1971) Chapter 9.

54. James M. Mellard, 'Consciousness Fills the Void: Herzog, History and the Hero in the Modern World', *Modern Fiction Studies*, 25, No. 1 (Spring 1979) 86.

55. James Gindin, *Harvest of a Quiet Eye: The Novel of Compassion* (Bloomington: Indiana University Press, 1971) pp. 305–36.

56. Tony Tanner, *City of Words: American Fiction 1950–1970* (London: Cape, 1971) Chapter 13.

57. C.W.E. Bigsby, 'Saul Bellow and the Liberal Tradition in American Literature', *Forum*, 14, No. 1 (Spring 1976) 56–62.

58. Malcolm Bradbury, 'The It and the We', *Encounter*, 45, No. 5 (November 1975) 61–7.

59. Brian Way, 'Character and Society in *The Adventures of Augie March*', *British Association for American Studies Bulletin*, No. 8 (June 1964) 36–44.

60. Robert Alter, 'The Stature of Saul Bellow', *Midstream*, 10, No. 4 (December 1964) 3–15.

61. The proceedings of the symposium were later published: Edmond Schraepen (ed.), *Saul Bellow and His Work* (Brussels: Centrum voor taal – en literatuurwetenschap, Vrije Universiteit, 1978).
62. Ibid., p. 31.
63. Ibid., p. 43.
64. Ibid., p. 48.
65. Ibid., p. 85.
66. Ibid., p. 106.
67. Ibid., p. 118.
68. Ibid., p. 62.
69. Ibid., p. 63.
70. Ibid., p. 125.
71. Ibid., p. 95.
72. Ibid., p. 96.
73. Ibid., p. 97.
74. Ibid., p. 100.
75. Ibid., p. 16.
76. Ibid., p. 131.
77. Ibid., p. 131.
78. Ibid., p. 135.
79. Ibid., p. 134.
80. Saul Bellow, *To Jerusalem and Back* (London: Secker & Warburg, 1976) p. 80.
81. Bellow has himself commented on the change which occurs with the novel. See Gordon Lloyd Harper, 'Saul Bellow – The Art of Fiction. An Interview', *Paris Review*, 9, No. 37 (Winter 1966) 49–73.
82. Alice Albright Hoge, 'Saul Bellow Revisited, At Home and At Work', *Chicago Daily News* (18 February 1967) 5.
83. Chirantan Kulshrestha, 'A Conversation with Saul Bellow', *Chicago Review*, 23–24 (Spring–Summer 1972) 12.
84. Saul Bellow, 'The Mexican General', *Partisan Review*, 9 (May–June 1942) 178–94. See Judie Newman, 'Saul Bellow and Trotsky: "The Mexican General"', *Saul Bellow Newsletter*, 1, No. 1 (Fall 1981) 26–31.
85. Saul Bellow, *Mosby's Memoirs and Other Stories* (London: Penguin, 1971).

CHAPTER 2   HISTORY, NATURE AND FREEDOM: *THE ADVENTURES OF AUGIE MARCH*

1. Saul Bellow, 'How I Wrote Augie March's Story', *New York Times* Book Review (31 January 1954) 3.
2. José Ortega Y Gasset, *Towards A Philosophy of History* (New York: W.W. Norton, 1941) p. 217. The other works by Ortega to which I here refer are *The Revolt of the Masses* (New York: W.W. Norton, 1932) and *The Dehumanisation of Art and Other Writings on Art and Culture* (Garden City, New York: Doubleday, 1956). The latter collection postdates *The Adventures of Augie March*, but the five essays collected in it predate the novel. They are 'The Dehumanisation of Art' and 'Notes on the Novel', previously published in 1948 by Princeton University Press: 'On Point of View in the Arts', *Partisan*

Review (August 1949); 'In Search of Goethe From Within', *Partisan Review* (December 1949); 'The Self and The Other', *Partisan* Review (July–August 1942). Bellow refers to Ortega by name in *Mr Sammler's Planet* (London: Penguin, 1971) p. 196; in 'Cloister Culture', in *Page Two*, ed. E.F. Brown (New York: Holt, Rinehart & Winston, 1969) p. 6; in 'Skepticism and the Depth of Life', in *The Arts and the Public*, ed. J.E. Miller and P.D. Herring (Chicago: University of Chicago Press, 1967) p. 25, where Bellow refers to Ortega's notion of 'shipwreck'; and in 'Where Do We Go From Here: The Future of Fiction', in *Saul Bellow and the Critics*, ed. Irving Malin (New York: New York University Press, 1967) p. 214 where he refers to Ortega's theories of novelistic form. While these references to Ortega postdate *The Adventures of Augie March*, Bellow can hardly have failed to encounter his ideas at an earlier date, firstly as I demonstrate here, because the internal evidence of the novel reveals a close familiarity with them, and secondly because during the period in which Ortega's essays were published in *Partisan Review*, Bellow was himself an active contributor to the journal, publishing in it the excerpts from the work in progress which was to become *The Adventures of Augie March:* 'From the Life of Augie March', *Partisan Review* (November 1949) and 'The Einhorns', *Partisan Review* (November–December 1951).

3. Saul Bellow, *The Adventures of Augie March* (London: Penguin, 1966) p. 7. All subsequent page references are to this edition.

4. H.P. Rickman (ed.), *Meaning in History: Wilhelm Dilthey's Thoughts on History and Society* (London: George Allen & Unwin, 1961) pp. 85–6.

5. The reader who wishes to pursue the point will find an illuminating analysis of the formal aspects of autobiography in Patricia Drechsel Tobin, *Time and the Novel* (Princeton: Princeton University Press, 1978) pp. 22–5.

6. Saul Bellow, 'The Writer As Moralist', *Atlantic Monthly*, 211 (March 1965) 58.

7. *The Chicago Herald Examiner* (25 May 1931) 3.

8. Ortega, *Towards A Philosophy of History*, p. 210.

9. Ibid., p. 220.

10. Karl Jaspers, *The Origin and Goal of History* (London: Routledge & Kegan Paul, 1953) p. 234.

11. Saul Bellow 'The Writer As Moralist', *Atlantic Monthly*, 211 (March 1965) 59.

12. Ortega, *Revolt of the Masses*, pp. 173–4.

13. Enid Starkie, *Arthur Rimbaud in Abyssinia* (Oxford: Oxford University Press, 1937) pp. 134–5.

14. Jaspers, *Origin and Goal of History*, p. 272.

15. See Dan Mannix, 'Hunting Dragons with an Eagle', *Saturday Evening Post* (18 January 1941) 20–21, 38, 40–41, 43, and Jule Mannix, *Married to Adventure* (London: Hamish Hamilton, 1954). Full details of Bellow's debt to the Mannixes appear in Eusebio L. Rodrigues, 'Augie March's Mexican Adventure', *Indian Journal of American Studies*, 8, No. 2 (July 1978) 39–43.

16. Jule Mannix, *Married to Adventure*, p. 11.

17. Ortega, *Towards A Philosophy of History*, p. 191 and p. 198.

18. Ibid., p. 203.

19. I am indebted for this observation to Stan Smith, in an unpublished paper, 'A Sadly Contracted Hero: The Comic Self in Post War American Fiction'.

20. Ortega, *Dehumanisation of Art*, p. 173.
21. Ortega, *Revolt of the Masses*, pp. 108–9.
22. Ortega, *Dehumanisation of Art*, p. 48.
23. Ibid., p. 164.
24. Ibid., p. 175.
25. Ibid., pp. 126–27.
26. Ibid., p. 68.
27. Ibid., p. 69.
28. Ibid., p. 86.
29. Ibid., pp. 87–8.
30. Saul Bellow, 'The Writer As Moralist', *Atlantic Monthly* 211 (March 1965), 61.

CHAPTER 3   *HENDERSON THE RAIN KING*: A DANCE TO THE MUSIC OF TIME

1. Saul Bellow, 'Deep Readers of the World, Beware!' *New York Times Book Review*, 15 February 1959, 1 and 34.
2. These elements of literary parody have been detailed by Jeff H. Campbell, 'Bellow's Intimations of Immortality: *Henderson the Rain King*', *Studies in the Novel*, 1 (Fall 1969) 323–33.
3. Saul Bellow, *Henderson the Rain King* (London: Penguin, 1966) p. 7. Subsequent page references are to this edition.
4. John J. Clayton, *Saul Bellow: In Defense of Man* (London: Indiana University Press, 1968) p. 185.
5. These objections are summarised by Tony Tanner, *Saul Bellow* (Edinburgh: Oliver and Boyd, 1965) pp. 80–81.
6. Saul Bellow, 'Deep Readers of the World, Beware!' p. 1.
7. Saul Bellow, *Dangling Man* (London: Penguin, 1963), p. 7.
8. Bellow's debt to Burton and others has been detailed by Eusebio L. Rodrigues, 'Bellow's Africa', *American Literature*, 43, No. 2 (May 1971) 242–56. Rodrigues points to Melville J. Herskovits, Bellow's anthropology tutor and author of major works on both the cattle cultures of Africa and the kingdom of Dahomey (the sources of the Arnewi and Wariri episodes respectively) as Bellow's point of access. The details taken from these sources include all aspects of the Arnewi relation to their cows, their adoration of fat women, and keenness on wrestling, the lion religion of the Wariri, though not the hunt in the hopo, Dahfu's dress, details of the palace, gibbets, skulls, the bridge table brought out in Henderson's honour, the Y-shaped gag, umbrellas, hammocks, Amazons and wives, but not the skull throwing. I would add to these the details taken from Sir James George Frazer, *The Golden Bough* (London: Macmillan, 1911–1915). These form the basis of the rain ritual: hauling heavy stones into trees to represent clouds, insulting of gods, cutting on the chest so that blood imitates rain, dressing of the king in leaves, throwing the deity or his representative into water. This high degree of borrowing from sources suggests a deliberate attempt by Bellow to forestall the 'deep reader'.

9. In his essay 'The Antithetical Sense of Primal Words', in James Strachey (ed.), *The Standard Edition of the Complete Psychological Works of Sigmund Freud* (London: The Hogarth Press, 1954–1966) Freud remarks that primitives may use the same word for opposites. The Wariri, however, do know change and therefore make the distinction between 'lucky' and 'unlucky' in 'Wariri ibai', 'Arnewi nibai', (p. 156).

10. T.S. Eliot, *Four Quartets* (London: Faber & Faber, 1959) p. 14.

11. Reichian overtones in the novel have been detailed by Eusebio L. Rodrigues, 'Reichianism in *Henderson the Rain King*', *Criticism*, 15, No. 3 (Summer 1973) 212–34. This article credits Bellow with an allegiance to Reich which I challenge.

12. Philip Rieff, 'The World of Wilhelm Reich', *Commentary*, 28, No. 3 (September 1964) 53.

13. The phrase is that of Sarah Blacher Cohen, *Saul Bellow's Enigmatic Laughter* (London: University of Illinois Press, 1974) p. 122.

14. Stephen Toulmin and June Goodfield, *The Discovery of Time* (London: Hutchinson, 1965) p. 19.

15. Delmore Schwartz, *What Is To Be Given* (Manchester: Carcanet New Press, 1976) pp. 36–7.

16. T.S. Eliot, *Four Quartets* (London: Faber, 1959) p. 15.

17. M. Gilbert Porter details musical images without connecting them to the question of time, and invents a Hallelujah chorus at the close of the novel, in his *Whence the Power?* (Columbia, Missouri: University of Missouri Press, 1974).

CHAPTER 4   *HERZOG*: HISTORY AS NEUROSIS

1. Saul Bellow, *Herzog* (London: Penguin, 1965) p. 7. All subsequent page references are to this edition.

2. Norman O. Brown, *Life Against Death: The Psychoanalytical Meaning of History* (London: Routledge & Kegan Paul, 1959) pp. 91–3.

3. Philip Rieff, 'The Meaning of History and Religion in Freud's Thought', *The Journal of Religion*, 31 (1951) 115.

4. Ibid., p. 118.

5. Robert R. Dutton, *Saul Bellow* (Boston: Twayne, 1971) p. 121. 'Bellow's protagonist is going through a form of psychoanalysis.'

6. The time scheme of *Herzog* has been analysed by Alexandre Maurocordato, *Les quatre dimensions du Herzog de Saul Bellow*, Archives des Lettres Modernes, No. 102 (Paris: Lettres Modernes, 1969).

7. John J. Clayton, *Saul Bellow: In Defense of Man* (London: Indiana University Press, 1979).

8. Ibid., p. 197.

9. Ibid., p. 219.

10. Ibid., p. 221.

11. Ibid., p. 229.

12. David Boroff, 'The Author', *Saturday Review* (19 September 1964) 38.

13. Saul Bellow, *The Last Analysis* (London: Weidenfeld & Nicolson, 1966) p. 126. An early version of the play opened in 1964, and an excerpt was pub-

lished in 1962: Saul Bellow, 'Scenes From Humanitis – A Farce', *Partisan Review*, 29 (Summer 1962) 327–49.

14. Saul Bellow, *The Last Analysis*, p. 46.

15. Harold J Mosher, 'The Synthesis of Past and Present in Saul Bellow's *Herzog*', *Wascana Review*, 6, No. 1 (1971) 28–38.

16. Ibid., p. 32.

17. Ibid., p. 36.

18. G.W.F. Hegel, *The Philosophy of Fine Art* (London: G. Bell and Sons, 1920) pp. 338–42. Hegel's theory of tragedy has been clarified by A.C. Bradley, *Oxford Lectures on Poetry* (London: Macmillan, 1909) pp. 69–95.

19. G.W.F. Hegel, *The Phenomenology of Mind*, trans. J.B. Baillie (London: George Allen & Unwin, 1910).

20. Pierre Teilhard de Chardin, *The Phenomenon of Man* (London: Collins, 1959) chapter 2.

21. Ralph Waldo Emerson, 'The American Scholar', in *The Complete Works of Ralph Waldo Emerson* (Cambridge, Mass.: Harvard University Press, 1971) I, 65–6.

22. Clayton, p. 196.

23. James Strachey (ed.), *The Standard Edition of the Complete Psychological Works of Sigmund Freud* (London: The Hogarth Press, 1954–1966) XVIII.

24. Ibid., pp. 55–6.

25. See Jean Wahl, *Les philosophes de l'existence* (Paris: Librairie Armand Colin, 1959).

26. Strachey, p. 35. Freud describes children's demand that stories be repeated exactly to them, but argues that adults seek pleasure in novelty, not in repetition.

27. Friedrich Nietzsche, 'Nietzsche Contra Wagner', in Oscar Levy (ed.), *The Complete Works of Friedrich Nietzsche* (London: Foulis, Allen and Unwin, 1909–1913) VIII.

28. Ibid., p. 98

29. Madeleine is described as 'Sleeping Beauty' by Pontritter, p. 14.

30. Jo Brans, 'Common Needs, Common Preoccupations: An Interview with Saul Bellow', *Southwest Review*, 62 (1977) 3–4.

CHAPTER 5   *MR SAMMLER'S PLANET*: WELLS, HITLER AND THE WORLD STATE

1. David Galloway, '*Mr Sammler's Planet:* Bellow's Failure of Nerve', *Modern Fiction Studies*, 19 (1973) 17–28.

2. Jennifer M. Bailey, 'The Qualified Affirmation of Saul Bellow's Recent Work', *Journal of American Studies*, 7 (1973) 63–73.

3. Mas'ud Zavarzadeh, 'The Apocalyptic Fact and the Eclipse of Fiction in Recent Prose Narratives', *Journal of American Studies*, 9 (1975) 69–83.

4. Edward Alexander, 'Imagining the Holocaust: *Mr Sammler's Planet* and Others', *Judaism*, 22 (1972) 300.

5. Saul Bellow, *Mr Sammler's Planet* (London: Penguin Books, 1971) p. 5. Subsequent page references, given in the text of this study, are to this edition.

6. George Orwell, 'Wells, Hitler and the World State', in *Collected Essays* (London: Secker and Warburg, 1961) p. 162.
7. Ibid., p. 162.
8. Ibid., p. 163.
9. Robert Boyers et al., 'Literature and Culture: An Interview with Saul Bellow', *Salmagundi*, 30 (1975) 16–17.
10. Harold Rosenberg, 'Form and Despair', *Location*, 1 (1964) 7.
11. Ibid., p. 9.
12. Saul Bellow, 'A Comment on Form and Despair', *Location*, 1 (1964) 10.
13. Ibid., p. 12
14. See Karl Popper, *The Poverty of Historicism* (London: Routledge & Kegan Paul, 1961) p. 17.
15. José Ortega Y Gasset, *The Revolt of the Masses* (London: W.W. Norton, 1932) p. 26.
16. Ibid., p. 41.
17. Ibid., p. 63.
18. Ibid., p. 64.
19. Orwell, *Collected Essays*, p. 164.
20. Søren Kierkegaard, *Fear and Trembling* (Princeton: Princeton University Press, 1941) p. 52.
21. Notably in Alfred Rosenberg, *Der Mythus des 20. Jahrhunderts* (Munich: Hoheneichen Verlag, 1930). For a complete analysis of Rosenberg's misinterpretation of Eckhart, see Albert R. Chandler, *Rosenberg's Nazi Myth* (Ithaca, New York: Cornell University Press, 1945).
22. Published in Britain as *Reflections on History* (London: George Allen & Unwin, 1943).
23. See Herbert Read, Michael Fordham and Gerhard Adler (eds), *The Collected Works of Carl Gustav Jung* (London: Routledge & Kegan Paul, 1953–1967) IX.
24. Paul Valéry, *Reflections on the World Today*, trans. Francis Scarfe (London: Thames and Hudson, 1951) p. 150.
25. Ibid., pp. 12–13.
26. A recent essay lists cyclic images which are seen as emphasising the fated necessary limits of life. See William J. Scheik, 'Circle Sailing in Bellow's *Mr Sammler's Planet*', *Essays in Literature*, 5 (1979) 95–101.

CHAPTER 6 *HUMBOLDT'S GIFT*: THE COMEDY OF HISTORY

1. Philip Rahv, 'The Myth and the Powerhouse', in *Literature and the Sixth Sense* (Boston: Houghton Mifflin, 1969).
2. Ibid., p. 210.
3. Malcolm Bradbury has also referred to Rahv in this connection in ' "The Nightmare in which I'm Trying to Get a Good Night's Rest": Saul Bellow and Changing History,' in Edmond Schraepen (ed.), *Saul Bellow and His Work* (Brussels: Centrum voor taal – en literatuurwetenschap, Vrije Universiteit, 1978) pp. 11–30. We have reached this conclusion independently. See

Judie Newman, 'Saul Bellow: *Humboldt's Gift* – The Comedy of History', *Durham University Journal*, 72, No. 1 (December 1979) 79–87.

4. Rahv, p. vii.

5. Ibid., p. 208.

6. Saul Bellow, *Humboldt's Gift* (London: Secker & Warburg, 1975) p. 4. All subsequent page references are to this edition.

7. Saul Bellow, 'Literature in the Age of Technology,' in *Technology and the Frontiers of Knowledge: The Frank Nelson Doubleday Lectures* (Garden City, New York: Doubleday, 1973) pp. 9–10.

8. Ibid., p. 11.

9. Nicola Chiaromonte, *The Paradox of History* (London: Weidenfeld and Nicolson, 1970) p. 143.

10. David H. Fischer, *Historians' Fallacies* (London: Routledge and Kegan Paul, 1971).

11. Frederick Loewe, *My Fair Lady* (London: Chappell, 1956) pp. 55–8. As Eliza sings 'The Rain in Spain' Higgins comments, 'I think she's got it! I think she's got it!'

12. The need to accept the past without being swamped by it is emphasised in the structure of the novel, in the cannibal imagery, the contracts and the exchanges of gifts, all of which must be understood in terms of the sociological analysis of gift-exchange. See Judie Newman, 'Bellow's Indian Givers: *Humboldt's Gift*', *Journal of American Studies*, 15, No. 2 (August 1981) 231–8.

13. Karl Marx, 'The Eighteenth Brumaire of Louis Napoleon', in Karl Marx and Friedrich Engels, *Selected Works* (London: Lawrence and Wishart, 1968) p. 96.

14. Ibid., p. 96.

15. Charlie's Steineresque exercises occupy much of his time in Spain. It is a mistake to see the teachings of Steiner as a transcendent solution to Charlie's problems. Rather it is a system which offers a means of articulating his newfound moral and temporal perspective. The manner of meditation expresses moral imperatives without Manichaeanism. The first contact with the dead leads the meditator to sexual thoughts which must be accepted but not dwelt upon. Also anthroposophy offers a new concept of time.

> The time to ask the dead something is in the last instant of consciousness before sleeping. As for the dead they reach us most easily just as we awaken. These are successive instants in the time-keeping of the soul, the eight intervening clock hours in bed being only biological.
>
> (*Humboldt's Gift*, p. 441.)

Thus, without being either a nightmare insomniac or a sleeper through the events of history the individual may in this view strike a balance between overawareness of his role in history or total withdrawal from it. For details of Bellow's debt to Steiner see Herbert J. Smith, '*Humboldt's Gift* and Rudolf Steiner', *Centennial Review*, 22 (1978) 478–89.

16. Nathaniel Hawthorne, *Selected Tales and Sketches* (New York: Rinehart, 1964) pp. 138–49.

17. Ibid., p. 143.

18. The ending, set in a cold cemetery with only crocuses showing any sign of life, deliberately evokes the ending of George Orwell's *Nineteen Eighty-Four*, where Winston and Julia meet in a cold park, on 'a vile biting day in March, when the earth was like iron and all the grass seemed dead, and there was not a bud anywhere except a few crocuses which had pushed themselves up to be dismembered by the wind'. George Orwell, *Nineteen Eighty-Four* (London: Penguin, 1976) p. 233. The film which Winston watches (*Nineteen Eighty-Four*, p. 10) in which the audience laugh as a man drowns, is strongly reminiscent of *Caldofreddo*; Winston's reaction is similar to Citrine's.

CHAPTER 7   CONCLUSION

1. Saul Bellow, 'Culture Now: Some Animadversions, Some Laughs', *Modern Occasions*, 1 (Winter 1971) 162–78.
2. 'Literature and Culture: An Interview with Saul Bellow', *Salmagundi*, No. 30 (Summer 1975) 14.
3. Saul Bellow, 'Deep Readers of the World, Beware!' *The New York Times Book Review*, 15 February 1959, p. 1.
4. Chirantan Kulshrestha, 'A Conversation with Saul Bellow', *Chicago Review*, 23–4 (Spring–Summer 1972) 8.
5. Jo Brans, 'Common Needs, Common Preoccupations: An Interview with Saul Bellow', *Southwest Review*, 62 (Winter 1977) 15.
6. Ibid., p. 14.
7. Kulshrestha, 'A Conversation with Saul Bellow', p. 9.
8. Saul Bellow, 'Are many modern writers merely becoming actors who behave like writers?' *Chicago Sun Times*, 15 September 1968, 10.
9. 'Literature and Culture', p. 11.
10. Saul Bellow, 'Are many modern writers', p. 10.
11. Sanford Pinsker, 'Saul Bellow in the Classroom', *College English*, 34 (April 1973) 980–1.
12. Alice Albright Hoge, 'Saul Bellow Revisited, At Home and At Work', *Chicago Daily News*, 18 February 1967, p. 5.
13. Saul Bellow, 'Culture Now', p. 171.
14. Ibid., pp. 174–5.
15. Saul Bellow, 'Literature', in *The Great Ideas Today*, ed. Mortimer Adler and Robert M. Hutchins (Chicago: Encyclopaedia Britannica, 1963) p. 173.
16. Ibid., p. 155.
17. 'Literature and Culture: An Interview with Saul Bellow', *Salmagundi*, No. 30 (Summer 1975) 9.
18. Ibid., p. 9.
19. Nina A. Steers, ' "Successor" to Faulkner?: An Interview with Saul Bellow', *Show*, 4 (September 1964), 36.
20. Ibid., p. 38.
21. Ibid., p. 37.
22. Sanford Pinsker, 'Saul Bellow in the Classroom', p. 979.
23. Ibid., p. 980.

24. Saul Bellow, 'Foreword', in Feodor M. Dostoevsky, *Winter Notes on Summer Impressions*, trans. Richard Lee Renfield (New York: Criterion Books, 1955) p. 19.
25. Saul Bellow, 'The Jewish Writer and the English Literary Tradition', *Commentary*, 8 (October 1949) 367.
26. Saul Bellow, 'Cloister Culture', in *Page Two*, ed. E.F. Brown (New York: 1969) p. 3.
27. Saul Bellow, 'Culture Now', p. 174.
28. Saul Bellow, 'Cloister Culture', p. 8.
29. Ibid., p. 9.
30. Saul Bellow, 'The Sealed Treasure', *Times Literary Supplement*, 1 July 1960, 414.

Bibliography

The bibliography which follows is selective. For a full bibliography the reader is referred to:

Lercangée, Francine, *Saul Bellow. A Bibliography of Secondary Sources* (Brussels: Center for American Studies, 1977).

Nault, Marianne, *Saul Bellow: His Works and His Critics. An Annotated International Bibliography* (London: Garland, 1977).

Noreen, Robert G., *Saul Bellow: A Reference Guide* (Boston: G.K. Hall, 1978).

Francine Lercangée lists interviews, secondary criticism and book reviews, accurately, alphabetically and without annotation. With similar accuracy, Robert G. Noreen lists and annotates secondary criticism, arranged chronologically by year of publication. Marianne Nault lists Bellow's novels, short stories, plays, non-fiction, manuscripts and works in translation, together with reviews, interviews, doctoral dissertations, and criticism of Saul Bellow's works. Critical entries are annotated but are not always accurate.

A. BELLOW'S WORKS

MAJOR WORKS

In each case the first edition is listed, followed by the edition referred to in this study.

Dangling Man (New York: Vanguard, 1944; London: Penguin, 1963).

The Victim (New York: Vanguard, 1947; London: Penguin, 1966).

The Adventures of Augie March (New York: Viking, 1953; London: Penguin, 1966).

Seize the Day (New York: Viking, 1956; London: Penguin, 1966).

Henderson the Rain King (New York: Viking, 1959; London: Penguin, 1966).

Herzog (New York: Viking, 1964; London: Penguin, 1965).

The Last Analysis (New York: Viking, 1965; London: Weidenfeld and Nicolson, 1966).

Mosby's Memoirs and Other Stories (New York: Viking, 1968; London: Penguin, 1971).

Mr Sammler's Planet (New York: Viking, 1970; London: Penguin, 1971).

Humboldt's Gift (New York: Viking, 1975; London: Secker & Warburg, 1975).

To Jerusalem and Back; A Personal Account (New York: Viking, 1976; London: Secker & Warburg, 1976).

The Dean's December (New York: Viking, 1982; London: Secker & Warburg, 1982).

UNCOLLECTED WORKS

'The Mexican General', *Partisan Review*, 9 (May–June 1942) 178–94.

'A Sermon by Dr Pep', *Partisan Review*, 14 (May–June 1949) 455–62.

'The Jewish Writer and the English Literary Tradition', *Commentary*, 8 (October 1949) 366–7.

'From the Life of Augie March', *Partisan Review*, 16 (November 1949) 1077–89.

'The Trip to Galena', *Partisan Review*, 17 (November–December 1950) 769–94.

'The Einhorns', *Partisan Review*, 18 (November–December 1951) 619–45.

'How I Wrote Augie March's Story', *New York Times Book Review*, 31 January 1954, 3 and 17.

'Foreword', Feodor M. Dostoevsky, *Winter Notes on Summer Impressions*, trans. Richard Lee Renfield (New York: Criterion Books, 1955).

'Deep Readers of the World, Beware!', *New York Times Book Review*, 15 February 1959, 1 and 34.

'The Sealed Treasure', *Times Literary Supplement*, 1 July 1960, 414.

'Scenes From Humanitis – A Farce', *Partisan Review*, 29 (Summer 1962) 327–49.

'Literature', *The Great Ideas Today*, ed. Mortimer Adler and Robert M. Hutchins (Chicago: Encyclopaedia Britannica, 1963) 135–79.

'A Comment on Form and Despair', *Location*, 1 (Summer, 1964) 10–12.

'The Writer as Moralist', *Atlantic Monthly*, 211 (March 1965) 58–62.

'Skepticism and the Depth of Life', *The Arts and the Public*, ed. J.E. Miller and P.D. Herring (Chicago: University of Chicago Press, 1967) pp. 13–30.

'Where Do We Go From Here: The Future of Fiction', *Saul Bellow and the Critics*, ed. Irving Malin (New York: New York University Press, 1967) pp. 211–20.

'Are many modern writers merely becoming actors who behave like writers?', *Chicago Sun Times*, 15 September 1968, 10.

'Cloister Culture', *Page Two*, ed. E.F. Brown (New York: Holt, Rinehart and Winston, 1969) pp. 3–8.

'Culture Now: Some Animadversions, Some Laughs', *Modern Occasions*, 1, No. 2 (Winter 1971) 162–78.

'Literature in the Age of Technology', *Technology and the Frontiers of Knowledge*, Frank N. Doubleday Lecture Series (New York: Doubleday, 1973) pp. 1–22.

'An Interview with Myself', *New Review*, 2, No. 18 (September 1975) 53–6.

B.   OTHER WORKS CITED

Alexander, Edward, 'Imagining the Holocaust: *Mr Sammler's Planet* and Others', *Judaism*, 22 (Winter 1972) 288–300.

Alter, Robert, 'The Stature of Saul Bellow', *Midstream*, 10, No. 4 (December 1964) 3–15.

Bailey, Jennifer M., 'The Qualified Affirmation of Saul Bellow's Recent Work', *Journal of American Studies*, 7, No. 1 (April 1973) 67–73.

Baim, Joseph, 'Escape from Intellection: Saul Bellow's *Dangling Man*', *University Review*, 37, No. 1 (October 1970) 28–34.

Baruch, Franklin R., 'Bellow and Milton: Professor Herzog in his Garden', *Critique: Studies in Modern Fiction*, 9, No. 3 (1967) 74–83.

Berlin, Isaiah, *The Hedgehog and the Fox* (London: Weidenfeld and Nicolson, 1953).

Bigsby, C.W.E., 'Saul Bellow and the Liberal Tradition in American Literature', *Forum*, 14, No. 1 (Spring 1976) 56–62.

Bloom, Solomon F., 'Director of the Lodz Ghetto', *Commentary*, 8 (May 1949) 111–22.

Boroff, David, 'The Author', *Saturday Review*, 19 September 1964, 38.

Boulger, James, 'Puritan Allegory in Four Modern Novels', *Thought*, 44, No. 174 (Autumn 1969) 413–32.

Boyers, Robert, 'Nature and Social Reality in Bellow's Sammler', *Critical Quarterly*, 15 (Autumn 1973) 251–71.

Boyers, Robert *et al*, 'Literature and Culture: An Interview with Saul Bellow', *Salmagundi*, No. 30 (Summer 1975) 6–23.

Bradbury, Malcolm, 'The It and the We: Saul Bellow's New Novel' *Encounter*, 45, No. 5 (November 1975) 61–7.

Bradley, A.C., *Oxford Lectures on Poetry* (London: Macmillan, 1909).

Brans, Jo, 'Common Needs, Common Preoccupations: An Interview with Saul Bellow', *Southwest Review*, 62 (1977) 1–19.

Brown, Norman O., *Life Against Death: The Psychoanalytical Meaning of History* (London: Routledge and Kegan Paul, 1959).

Bullock, C.J., 'On the Marxist Criticism of the Contemporary Novel in the United States', *Praxis*, 1, No. 2 (1976) 189–98.

Burckhardt, Jacob, *Reflections on History* (London: George Allen and Unwin, 1943).

Campbell, Jeff H., 'Bellow's Intimations of Immortality: *Henderson the Rain King*', *Studies in the Novel*, 1, No. 3 (Fall 1969) 323–33.

Capon, Robert F., 'Herzog and the Passion', *America*, 112, 27 March 1965, 425–7.

Chapman, Abraham, 'The Image of Man as Portrayed by Saul Bellow', *College Language Association Journal*, 10 (June 1967) 285–98.

Chandler, Albert R., *Rosenberg's Nazi Myth* (Ithaca, New York: Cornell University Press, 1945).

de Chardin, Pierre Teilhard, *The Phenomenon of Man* (London: Collins, 1959).

Chiaromonte, Nicola, *The Paradox of History* (London: Weidenfeld and Nicolson, 1970).

Clayton, John J., *Saul Bellow: In Defense of Man* (London: Indiana University Press, 1968, revised 1979).

Cohen, Sarah Blacher, *Saul Bellow's Enigmatic Laughter* (London: University of Illinois Press, 1974).

Crozier, Robert D., 'Theme in Augie March', *Critique: Studies in Modern Fiction*, 7, No. 3 (Spring 1965) 18–32.

Detweiler, Robert, *Saul Bellow: A Critical Essay* (Grand Rapids, Michigan: Eerdmans, 1967).

Dutton, Robert R., *Saul Bellow* (Boston: Twayne, 1971).

Eisinger, Chester E., 'Saul Bellow: Love and Identity', *Accent*, 18 (Summer 1958) 179–203.

Eliot, T.S., *Four Quartets* (London: Faber, 1959).

Eliot, T.S., *Selected Poems* (London: Faber, 1961).

Emerson, Ralph Waldo, *The Complete Works of Ralph Waldo Emerson* (Cambridge, Mass.: Harvard University Press, 1971).

Fischer, David H., *Historians' Fallacies* (London: Routledge and Kegan Paul, 1971).

Fossum, Robert H., 'The Devil and Saul Bellow', *Comparative Literature Studies*, 3, No. 2 (1966) 197–206.

Frazer, Sir James George, *The Golden Bough* (London: Macmillan, 1911–1915).

Freud, Sigmund, *The Standard Edition of the Complete Psychological Works of Sigmund Freud*, ed. James Strachey (London: The Hogarth Press, 1954–1966).

Galloway, David D., *The Absurd Hero in American Fiction: Updike, Styron, Bellow, Salinger* (Austin, Texas: University of Texas Press, 1966).

Galloway, David D., '*Mr Sammler's Planet*: Bellow's Failure of Nerve', *Modern Fiction Studies*, 19, No. 1 (Spring 1973) 17–28.

Geismar, Maxwell, *American Moderns: From Rebellion to Conformity* (New York: Hill and Wang, 1958).

Gelfant, Blanche, 'In "Terror of the Sublime": Mr Sammler and Odin', *Notes on Modern American Literature*, 2, No. 4 (Fall 1978) Item 25, unpaginated.

Gerso, Steven M., 'Paradise Sought: The Modern American Adam in Bellow's *Herzog*', *McNeese Review*, 24 (1977–1978) 50–7.

Gerson, Steven M., 'Paradise Sought: The Modern American Adam in Bellow's *Herzog*', *McNeese Review*, 24 (1977–1978) 50–7.

Gerson, Steven M., 'The New American Adam in *The Adventures of Augie March*', *Modern Fiction Studies*, 25, No. 1 (Spring 1979) 117–28.

Gold, Herbert, 'Fiction of the Fifties', *Hudson Review*, 12 (Summer 1959) 192–201.

Guerard, Albert J., 'Saul Bellow and the Activists: On *The Adventures of Augie March*', *Southern Review*, 3 (Summer 1967) 582–96.

Harper, Gordon Lloyd, 'Saul Bellow – The Art of Fiction. An Interview', *Paris Review*, 9, No. 37 (Winter 1966) 49–73.

Harper, Howard M., *Desperate Faith: A Study of Bellow, Salinger, Mailer, Baldwin and Updike* (Chapel Hill: University of North Carolina Press, 1967).

Harris, James, 'One Critical Approach to *Mr Sammler's Planet*' *Twentieth Century Literature*, 18, No. 4 (October 1972) 235–50.

Hassan, Ihab H., 'Five Faces of a Hero', *Critique: Studies in Modern Fiction*, 3 (Summer 1960) 28–36.

Hassan, Ihab H., *Radical Innocence: Studies in the Contemporary American Novel* (Princeton. Princeton University Press, 1961).

Hawthorne, Nathaniel, *Selected Tales and Sketches*, ed. Hyatt H. Waggoner (New York: Rinehart, 1964).

Hegel, G.W.F., *The Phenomenology of Mind*, trans. J.B. Baillie (London: Allen and Unwin, 1910).

Hegel, G.W.F., *The Philosophy of Fine Art* (London: G. Bell and Sons, 1920).

Hoge, Alice Albright, 'Saul Bellow Revisited, At Home and At Work', *Chicago Daily News*, 18 February 1967, 5.

Jaspers, Karl, *The Origin and Goal of History*, trans. Michael Bullock (London: Routledge and Kegan Paul, 1953).

Josipovici, Gabriel, *The World and the Book* (London: Macmillan, 1971).

Jung, Carl Gustav, *The Collected Works of Carl Gustav Jung*, ed. Herbert Read, Michael Fordham and Gerhard Adler (London: Routledge and Kegan Paul, 1953–1967).

Kaplan, Harold, 'The Second Fall of Man', *Salmagundi*, 30 (Summer 1975) 66–89.

Kierkegaard, Søren, *Fear and Trembling*, trans. W. Laurie (Princeton: Princeton University Press, 1941).

Kulshrestha, Chirantan, 'A Conversation with Saul Bellow', *Chicago Review*, 23–24 (Spring–Summer 1972) 7–15.

Loewe, Frederick, *My Fair Lady: a musical play in two acts; based on Pygmalion by Bernard Shaw; adaptation and lyrics by A.J. Lerner: music by F. Loewe* (London: Chappell, 1956).

Malin, Irving, *Jews and Americans* (Carbondale: Southern Illinois University Press, 1965).

Malin, Irving, *Saul Bellow's Fiction* (Carbondale: Southern Illinois University Press, 1969).

Maloney, Stephen R., 'Half-way to Byzantium: *Mr Sammler's Planet* and the Modern Tradition', *South Carolina Review*, 6, No. 1 (November 1973) 31–40.

Mannix, Dan, 'Hunting Dragons with an Eagle', *Saturday Evening Post*, 18 January 1941, 20–21, 38, 40–41, 43.

Mannix, Jule, *Married To Adventure* (London: Hamish Hamilton, 1954).

Markos, Donald W., 'Life Against Death in *Henderson the Rain King*' *Modern Fiction Studies*, 17, No. 2 (Summer 1971) 193–205.

Marx, Karl and Friedrich Engels, *Selected Works* (London: Lawrence and Wishart, 1968).

Maurocordato, Alexandre, *Les quatre dimensions du Herzog de Saul Bellow*, Archives des Lettres Modernes No. 102 (Paris: Lettres Modernes, 1969).

Mellard, James M., 'Consciousness Fills the Void: Herzog, History and the Hero in the Modern World', *Modern Fiction Studies*, 25, No. 1 (Spring 1979) 75–92.

Mosher, Harold J., 'The Synthesis of Past and Present in Saul Bellow's *Herzog*', *Wascana Review*, 6, No. 1 (1971) 28–38.

Newman, Judie, 'Saul Bellow: *Humboldt's Gift*– The Comedy of History', *Durham University Journal*, 72, No. 1 (December 1979) 79–87.

Newman, Judie, 'Bellow's Indian Givers: *Humboldt's Gift*', *Journal of American Studies*, 15, No. 2 (August 1981) 231–8.

Newman, Judie, 'Saul Bellow and Trotsky: "The Mexican General"', *Saul Bellow Newsletter*, 1, No. 1 (Fall, 1981) 26–31.

Nietzsche, Friedrich Wilhelm, *The Complete Works of Friedrich Nietzsche*, ed. Oscar Levy (London: Foulis, Allen and Unwin, 1909–1913).

Noble, David W., *The Eternal Adam and the New World Garden: The Central Myth in the American Novel since 1830* (New York: Braziller, 1968).

Opdahl, Keith M., *The Novels of Saul Bellow: An Introduction* (London: Pennsylvania State University Press, 1967).

Ortega Y Gasset, José, *The Revolt of the Masses* (New York: W.W. Norton, 1932).

Ortega Y Gasset, José, *Towards A Philosophy of History* (New York: W.W. Norton, 1941).

Ortega Y Gasset, José, *The Dehumanisation of Art and Other Writings on Art and Culture*, trans. Willard R. Trask (Garden City, New York: Doubleday, 1956).

Orwell, George, *Collected Essays* (London: Secker & Warburg, 1961).

Orwell, George, *Nineteen Eighty-Four* (London: Penguin, 1976).

Pinsker, Sanford, 'Saul Bellow in The Classroom', *College English*, 34 (April 1973) 975–82.

Pinsker, Sanford, 'Moses Herzog's Fall into the Quotidian', *Studies in the Twentieth Century*, 14 (Fall 1974) 105–16.

Pinsker, Sanford, 'Saul Bellow's Cranky Historians', *Historical Reflections*, 3, No. 2 (1976) 35–47.

Popper, Karl, *The Poverty of Historicism* (London: Routledge and Kegan Paul, 1961).

Porter, M. Gilbert, *Whence the Power? The Artistry and Humanity of Saul Bellow* (Columbia, Missouri: University of Missouri Press, 1974).

Quinton, Anthony, 'The Adventures of Saul Bellow', *London Magazine*, 6 (December 1959) 55–9.

Rahv, Philip, *Literature and the Sixth Sense* (Boston: Houghton Mifflin, 1969).

Rickman, H.P. (ed.), *Meaning in History: Wilhelm Dilthey's Thoughts on History and Society* (London: George Allen and Unwin, 1961).

Rieff, Philip, 'The Meaning of History and Religion in Freud's Thought', *The Journal of Religion*, 31 (1951) 114–31.

Rieff, Philip, 'The World of Wilhelm Reich', *Commentary*, 38, No. 3 (September 1964) 50–8.

Rodrigues, Eusebio L., 'Bellow's Africa'. *American Literature*, 43, No. 2 (May 1971) 242–56.

Rodrigues, Eusebio L., 'Reichianism in *Henderson the Rain King*', *Criticism*, 15, No. 3 (Summer 1973) 212–34.

Rodrigues, Eusebio L., 'Augie March's Mexican Adventure', *Indian Journal of American Studies*, 8, No. 2 (July 1978) 39–43.

Rosenberg, Alfred, *Der Mythus des 20. Jahrhunderts* (Munich: Hoheneichen Verlag, 1930).

Rosenberg, Harold, 'Form and Despair', *Location*, 1 (Summer 1964) 7–9.

Ross, Theodore J., 'Notes on Saul Bellow', *Chicago Jewish Forum*, 28 (Fall 1959) 21–7.

Scheer-Schäzler, Brigitte, *Saul Bellow* (New York: Ungar, 1972).

Scheik, William J., 'Circle Sailing in Bellow's *Mr Sammler's Planet*', *Essays in Literature*, 5 (Spring 1979) 95–101.

Edmond Schraepen (ed.), *Saul Bellow and His Work* (Brussels: Centrum voor taal – en literatuurwetenschap, Vrije Universiteit, 1978) (Contents: Edmond Schraepen 'Introduction', pp. 7–10; Malcolm Bradbury, '"The Nightmare in which I'm Trying to get a Good Night's Rest": Saul Bellow and Changing History', pp. 11–30; John J. Clayton, 'Transcendence and the Flight From Death', pp. 31–48; David Galloway, 'Culture-Making: The Recent Works of Saul Bellow', pp. 49–60; Keith Opdahl, '"True Impressions": Saul Bellow's Realistic Style', pp. 61–72; M. Gilbert Porter, 'Hitch Your Agony to a Star: Bellow's Transcendental Vision', pp. 73–88; Earl Rovit, 'Saul Bellow and the Concept of the Survivor', pp. 89–102; Brigitte Scheer-Schäzler, 'Epistemology as Narrative Device in the Work of Saul Bellow', pp. 103–18; Edmond Schraepen, '*Herzog*: Disconnection and Connection', pp. 119–30; Tony Tanner, 'Afterword', pp. 131–8.).

Schulz, Max F., *Radical Sophistication: Studies in Contemporary Jewish American Novelists* (Athens, Ohio: Ohio University Press, 1970).

Schwartz, Delmore, *What Is To Be Given* (Manchester: Carcanet New Press, 1976).

Scott, Nathan A., *Adversity and Grace: Studies in Recent American Literature* (Chicago: University of Chicago Press, 1968).

Scott, Nathan A., *Three American Moralists: Mailer, Bellow, Trilling* (Notre Dame: University of Notre Dame Press, 1973).

Smith, Herbert J., '*Humboldt's Gift* and Ruldolf Steiner', *Centennial Review*, 22 (1978) 478–89.

Staley, Thomas F. and Lester F. Zimmerman (ed.), *Literature and Theology* (Tulsa: University of Tulsa, 1969).

Starkie, Enid, *Arthur Rimbaud in Abyssinia* (Oxford: Oxford University Press, 1937).

Steers, Nina A., "'Successor" to Faulkner?: An Interview with Saul Bellow', *Show*, 4 (September 1964) 36–8.

Stock, Irwin, 'The Novels of Saul Bellow', *Southern Review*, 3, No. 1 (Winter 1967) 13–42.

Tanner, Tony, 'Saul Bellow: The Flight from Monologue', *Encounter*, 24, No. 2 (February 1965) 58–70.

Tanner, Tony, *Saul Bellow* (Edinburgh: Oliver and Boyd, 1965).

Tanner, Tony, *City of Words: American Fiction, 1950–1970* (London: Cape, 1971).

Tobin, Patricia Drechsel, *Time and the Novel* (Princeton: Princeton University Press, 1978).

Toulmin, Stephen and June Goodfield, *The Discovery of Time* (London: Hutchinson, 1965).

Trachtenberg, Stanley (ed.), *Critical Essays on Saul Bellow* (Boston: G.K. Hall, 1979).

Updike, John, 'Draping Radiance with a Worn Veil', *The New Yorker*, 51, No. 30 (15 September 1975) 122 and 125–30.

Valéry, Paul, *Reflections on the World Today*, trans. Francis Scarfe (London: Thames and Hudson, 1951).

Villaseñor, José Sanchez, *Ortega Y Gasset Existentialist* (Chicago: Regnery, 1949).

Vogel, Dan, 'Saul Bellow's Vision Beyond Absurdity: Jewishness in *Herzog*', *Tradition*, 9 (Spring 1968) 65–79.

Wahl, Jean, *Les philosophes de l'existence* (Paris: Librairie Armand Colin, 1959).

Way, Brian, 'Character and Society in *The Adventures of Augie March*', *British Association for American Studies Bulletin*, No. 8 (June 1964) 36–44.

Weinberg, Helen, *The New Novel in America. The Kafkan Mode in Contemporary Fiction* (Ithaca, New York: Cornell University Press, 1970).

Widmer, Kingsley, 'Poetic Naturalism in the Contemporary Novel', *Partisan Review*, 26 No. 3 (Summer 1959) 467–72.

Zavarzadeh, Mas'ud, 'The Apocalyptic Fact and the Eclipse of Fiction in Recent Prose Narratives', *Journal of American Studies*, 9 (April 1975) 69–83.

Index